Are Traditional Media Dead?

Are Traditional Media Dead?
Can Journalism Survive in the Digital World?

Ingrid Sturgis, editor

International Debate Education Association
New York, London & Amsterdam

Published by
The International Debate Education Association
400 West 59th Street
New York, NY 10019

Library of Congress Cataloging-in-Publication Data
Are traditional media dead?: can journalism survive in the digital world?
Ingrid Sturgis, editor.
  p. cm.
  ISBN 978-1-61770-025-5
  1. Journalism—History—21st century. 2. Journalism—Technological
innovations. 3. Online journalism. 4. Digital media. I. Sturgis, Ingrid.
  PN4815.2A84 2012
  070.9'051—dc23   2012001583

Composition by Brad Walrod/Kenoza Type, Inc.
Printed in the USA

 IDEBATE Press

IDEA SOURCEBOOKS ON
CONTEMPORARY CONTROVERSIES

The International Debate Education Association (IDEA) has dedicated itself to building open and democratic societies through teaching students how to debate. The IDEA Sourcebooks on Contemporary Controversies series is a natural outgrowth of that mission. By providing students with books that show opposing sides of hot button issues of the day as well as detailed background and source materials, the IDEA Sourcebooks on Contemporary Controversies give students the opportunity to research issues that concern our society and encourage them to debate these issues with others. IDEA coordinates the activities of local nongovernmental organizations that promote the free exchange of ideas, tolerance, and international cooperation.

Contents

Introduction   1

Part 1: Does Journalism Have One Foot in the Grave?   13

The U.S. Newspaper Industry in Transition *by Suzanne M. Kirchhoff*   15

Troubles for Traditional Media—Both Print and Television *by Harris Interactive*   28

Newspapers Face a Challenging Calculus *by Pew Research Center for the People & the Press*   41

Anatomy of a Death Spiral: Newspapers and Their Credibility *by Philip Meyer and Yuan Zhang*   48

The Wolf in Reporter's Clothing: The Rise of Pseudo-Journalism in America *by John S. Carroll*   61

Part 2: How New Media Have Impacted Traditional Media   71

Social Media as a First Draft of Journalism and a Rallying Cry for Democracy *by Endy M. Bayuni*   73

How Technology Turned News into a Conversation *by Turi Munthe*   77

New Media, Old Media: How Blogs and Social Media Agendas Relate and Differ from the Traditional Press *by Pew Research Center, Project for Excellence in Journalism*   80

How to Save the News *by James Fallows*   104

Part 3: How Traditional Media Can and Are Fighting Back   125

The Associated Press v. All Headline News: How Hot News Misappropriation Will Shape the Unsettled Customary Practices of Online Journalism *by Daniel S. Park*   127

Clues in the Rubble: A User-First Framework for Sustaining Local News *by Bill Mitchell*   152

Bad Public Relations or Is This a Real Crisis?: YES *by Lauren Rich Fine*   169

Getting Media Right: A Call to Action *by Michael J. Copps*   183

Saving the News: Toward a National Journalism Strategy *by Victor Pickard, Josh Stearns, and Craig Aaron*   192

The Carnegie-Knight Initiative on the Future of Journalism Education: Improving How Journalists Are Educated & How Their Audiences Are Informed *by Susan King*   208

Introduction

When *New York Times* publisher Arthur Sulzberger Jr. declared in 1999 that he was unconcerned about what form the *Times* would take in the future, journalists everywhere took notice.[1] His comments came when newspapers were still powerful, and no one was concerned about the effect of the electronic revolution. Journalists viewed the Internet more as a curiosity than a threat. Today, newspapers, along with other traditional news media—radio, television, cable TV, and news magazines—have been shaken to the core by a host of changes that have transformed the landscape in which they operate. The rise of the Internet, smart phones, and social media has changed the way news is gathered and disseminated, while the growth of blogs and online services has also undermined the financial model of traditional newspapers. A wave of consolidation has limited competition, while the decision to turn many news organizations into publically traded corporations has made robust profits rather than public accountability the primary goal of many news companies. The growth of pseudo-journalism has blurred the distinction between news and entertainment, while ethical and professional lapses have heaped scorn on journalism as a profession, thus sapping its credibility.

In light of these developments, many fear that traditional news media have entered a death spiral. A 2010 Harris Poll revealed that a majority of Americans think that traditional media will disappear within a decade.[2] But traditional media are fighting back and adapting, changing the way they cover and report news, experimenting with new business models, and refashioning the profession of journalism. Set against these developments, this book seeks to examine the question: Are traditional media really dead?

BACKGROUND

Newspapers, the oldest of the traditional mass media, have had a long and productive life in the United States. They first developed during the eighteenth century, when they were aimed primarily at the political and business elite, who financed them through subscriptions or donations to like-minded publishers. Papers were printed using handpresses that cranked out a few hundred copies an hour. Consequently, circulation was small (in cities such as Boston or New York, no more than 3,500 at the time of the American Revolution). Nevertheless, the audience for papers was large and copies were passed among people, read aloud, or left in public gathering places such as taverns.

Newspapers exercised considerable influence during the Revolution; in the early days of the Republic, they were a forum for public debates about the direction of the new nation. The *Federalist Papers,* the classic treatise on government that advocated the ratification of the Constitution, were first published as a series of newspaper essays. By the end of the century, newspapers were closely aligned to emerging political parties, promoting party agendas while benefiting from party patronage.

During the nineteenth century, technological advances set the stage for transformational change that propelled newspapers into a modern mass medium. The development of high-capacity, high-speed presses and Linotype helped to speed typesetting and printing, while photoengraving allowed newspapers to easily incorporate visuals, which spurred the growth of advertising. In addition, the telegraph helped to increase the speed of publication and was one of the factors that led to the development of the Associated Press, a cooperative of newspapers that shares reporting resources.

An outgrowth of these developments was the penny press—cheap newspapers filled with human interest (sometimes sensationalist) fare designed to entice a large, enthusiastic working-class audience. Demand for these papers was so great that some newspapers grew to a million circulation.

The media business model also changed as advertising became a major source of revenue. This shift made newspapers more independent. Advertising dollars replaced political patronage as a major source of funds, and newspapers moved from being voices of the mainstream parties in the early part of the century to more independent advocates of reform impulses in the Gilded Age.

The role of the press also evolved over the course of the century. Journalists became more professional, and journalism became increasingly powerful. Editors were influential figures in politics and business—*New York Tribune* editor Horace Greeley ran for president in 1872—and what their newspapers wrote about helped to set policy. Newspapers and magazines often led crusades against government corruption or to address social ills, while the nationalist thinking reflected in papers such as those owned by William Randolph Hearst helped push the country into war in 1898.

The twentieth century witnessed a media revolution as newspapers faced competition first from radio in the 1920s and then from television in the 1950s.

These technological developments changed the way people experienced media. They shortened the time needed for news to reach audiences and democratized access to the news. At the same time, newsgathering and dissemination became increasingly centralized in large radio and television networks.

As television became the most popular medium for news and information, newspapers steadily declined. Circulation began dropping in the 1970s, as did the advertising dollars on which newspapers depended. Economic decisions made in the last decades of the twentieth century accelerated the trend. The industry underwent a wave of consolidations as family-owned newspapers sold out to large chains, like Gannett Newspapers, McClatchy, or Times Mirror. Consequently, some cities became newspaper monopolies with diminished coverage. Other papers became publically traded companies increasingly driven by Wall Street's demand for higher profits. Responding to the pressure, publishers eliminated staff, cut resources, and limited news coverage. By the 1980s and 1990s, this short-sighted business model left newspapers financially fat and flush, but circulation continued to decline.

Media pundits lamented. The late Texas newspaper columnist Molly Ivins called the trend the kiss of death for journalism: "Our product isn't selling as well as it used to, so they think we need to cut the number of reporters, cut the space devoted to the news and cut the amount of money used to gather the news, and this will solve the problem," she said. "For some reason, they assume people will want to buy more newspapers if they have less news in them and are less useful to people.... What cutting costs does, of course, is increase the profits, thus making Wall Street happy. It also kills newspapers."[3]

In 2008, the worst economic recession since the Depression delivered another blow to the industry. Newspaper advertising fell by nearly 44 percent between 2005 and 2009. The business was further decimated by the number of media companies that took on burdensome debt, some the victim of the worst timing when they purchased news properties just before their value plunged and just as the economy was sinking into recession. This move pushed The Philadelphia Newspapers and Times Mirror into bankruptcy, both of which have since emerged much diminished.

The media response to the recession was more cost cutting, including layoffs, newspaper closings, and mergers. The size of publications was trimmed and the number of news stories covered cut. Eight major U.S. newspaper companies filed for bankruptcy between 2008 and early 2010.[4] Overall, the Bureau of Labor Statistics reported that nearly 90,000 non-Internet publishing jobs (including newspapers, magazines, and books) were lost between 2008 and 2009.[5] Since

2009, longstanding publications like the *Christian Science Monitor, Seattle Post-Intelligencer, Minneapolis Star Tribune, Rocky Mountain News,* and *Tucson Citizen* closed, declared bankruptcy, or moved to web-only production. In 2009, more than 140 newspapers and 350 U.S. magazines went out of business.[6] Among them was the venerable newsmagazine *Newsweek,* which was sold for a dollar. Ultimately it merged with The Daily Beast blog.

CHALLENGES FROM TECHNOLOGY

Some experts say traditional media are at the tough end of a natural business cycle: Customers become less enthusiastic about the product, the company fails to sufficiently innovate, quality declines, and customers leave for another comparable product. Amid the natural business cycle, however, other factors have roiled the industry, principally the electronic revolution and the growth of social media, which have not only changed the way news is collected and disseminated but also challenged the traditional role of the journalist.

Technology has created a fundamental shift in the balance of power between traditional media and their audience; traditional media are no longer the gatekeepers of news. Those who say they are looking for more accessible—and reliable—sources of news and information are free to roam the Internet, often using tools created to help citizen journalists. For example, Ushahidi, an open-source project, allows international users to crowdsource crisis information to be sent via mobile, and the Ujima Project ("collaboration" in Swahili) scours websites of governments and international organizations for data, then collects, cleans, and categorizes it for use worldwide.

The electronic revolution has done far more than open up sources of information, however. Now citizens are free to do their own reporting and writing on blogs or using smart phones. Bloggers wear their badge of "new media" proudly, disdaining the title "mainstream media"—a term they use as a pejorative.

Blogging, first introduced in the late 1990s, initially was a tool for personal journaling. Now, the availability of easy-to-use blogging software has allowed bloggers to evolve from navel gazing to covering their communities and "fact checking" professional journalists. These tools have made it possible for anyone to publish and have their words read across the world. Bloggers have asserted themselves by covering everything from child rearing to presidential politics. In 2008, Democrats and Republicans made a place for bloggers—even those lacking professional experience—at their national conventions. In addition, Flip video cameras, smart phones, and digital recorders put powerful tools in the hands of anyone who wants to report. Some of those reports show up—often unvetted or verified—in social media sites like Facebook, Twitter, or YouTube.

The new media world initially had less access to one of the most important assets of traditional media—a team of content creators. As small-scale operations, most blogs lacked experienced journalists who can research, report, and write news stories. RSS technology has helped to level the playing field, however. News aggregation became an essential component for sites such as Drudge and Huffington Post, Google News and Yahoo! News. For example, Google News aggregates news from nearly fifty thousand sources—including articles from established traditional media such as the *New York Times* or *Washington Post*—and then links the reader to the original story.

The adoption of social media challenges professional journalists with citizen journalists who can report, break, and disseminate news more quickly, even if the first draft is often unverified or incorrect. In this wireless world, journalists and editors are no longer able to hold stories until the facts are verified. For example, in May 2011 @ReallyVirtual in Pakistan tweeted the attack of U.S. forces on the compound housing terrorist leader Osama bin Laden, as journalists worldwide scrambled to verify the facts.

The move to online has had a dramatic effect on the business of news as well. As readers migrated to the Internet, advertising followed, with local classified ads (typically 30 percent of a newspaper's revenue) going to Craigslist and job listings moving to Monster.com. In addition, readers have lost the habit of handling a physical product. By making content available for free, newspapers gave customers the expectation that they should not have to pay for news. The audience has been empowered by the options given to them by technology.

ACCOUNTABILITY AND TRUST

At the same time that traditional media were being buffeted by economic and technological change, they also faced issues of accountability and trust. Critics claim that traditional media have abdicated their role as public watchdogs, catering instead to advertisers, corporate interests, and powerful political figures. Authors Philip Meyer and Yuan Zhang have warned, in "Anatomy of a Death Spiral: Newspapers and Their Credibility," that "cutbacks in content quality will erode public trust, weaken societal influence, and eventually lead to losses in circulation and advertising dollars."[7]

Public accountability was at its weakest after the 9/11 terrorist attacks and during the run-up to the Iraq war. Instead of digging hard for the truth about who was responsible for the attacks and about the threat posed by the regime of Iraqi president Saddam Hussein, journalists seemed cowed by the White House. They failed to question administration assertions about the danger posed by Iraq and underplayed opposition to the invasion. Many thought that the press had rolled over and played dead for fear of being called soft on terrorism if they challenged Bush administration statements and policies.

Concerns about reporting lapses increased in the wake of the financial crisis of 2008. Critics maintained that the mainstream press had failed to adequately alert the public to the housing bubble that precipitated the economic meltdown or to investigate and analyze the factors behind the crash. They asserted that reporting was more anecdotal than analytical, with little investigative reporting done.

In the opening decade of the twenty-first century, a public spate of fraudulent reporting by reporter Jayson Blair at the *New York Times* and writer Stephen Glass at the *New Republic* gave readers further reason to believe that they could not trust what was being reported in the mainstream media. This belief was reinforced in 2011 when Rupert Murdoch's global media titan News Corp. became embroiled in a telephone hacking scandal that turned the core principles of journalism on their head as members of the British-based *News of the World* magazine preyed on the vulnerable.

Never have more people been more skeptical about what is being reported in the news. In fact, a 2010 study by Pew Research Center for the People & the Press found that only about one-third of those polled say they believe what is reported by the fourteen largest news organizations.[8] The perception does not bode well for traditional media.

Today, the traditional role of the journalist has become further marginalized by the proliferation of "pseudo-journalism" programming such as *The Daily Show with Jon Stewart* and *Saturday Night Live*'s "Weekend Update." Some would include shows on Fox News and MSNBC in this category. In a 2004 speech, John S. Carroll, former editor of the *Los Angeles Times,* called the spread of faux journalism a troubling development. "Across America, there are offices that resemble newsrooms, and in those offices there are people who resemble journalists, but they are not engaged in journalism. It is not journalism because it does not regard the reader—or, in the case of broadcasting, the listener, or the viewer—as a master to be served," Carroll said. "To the contrary, it regards its audience with a cold cynicism. In this realm of pseudo-journalism, the audience is something to be manipulated."[9]

IMPACT OF CHANGE

The effect of these transformational changes is already being felt in American political life. Even the closing of a small newspaper can have a major impact on a community. For example, according to an unpublished case study titled "Do Newspapers Matter" by Sam Schulhofer-Wohl and Miguel Garrido, a decrease in press scrutiny has had an impact on elections in Kentucky. The study found that fewer candidates ran for municipal office in 2008 and incumbents were more likely to win reelection because of lower voter turnout and decreased campaign spending. The authors attribute this development to the closing of the small *Cincinnati* (Ohio) *Post* (circulation 27,000) in 2007, which previously had covered nearby suburban communities in Kentucky and had competed in Ohio with the *Cincinnati Inquirer.*[10]

Press coverage is just as important on the national level as on the local level. Declining news coverage has resulted in 25 states having no full-time reporter to cover Capitol Hill. Christopher Dodd, who served as senator from Connecticut from 1981 to 2011, has said that at one point in his Senate career, more than ten reporters covered him. By the time he left Congress, Dodd had none. If the trend continues, the public will become vastly uninformed because no one is monitoring those in power.

TRADITIONAL MEDIA FIGHTING BACK AND ADAPTING

Pundits and bloggers are sounding the death knell for traditional media, but they may be premature. The plight of traditional media has elicited concern from all quarters—from government agencies such as the Federal Communications Commission to NGOs such as the Poynter Institute, the Aspen Institute, and the Pew Center—all of which believe that the functions of the traditional press as conveyers of accurate information and watchdogs are essential to a thriving democracy. These groups have convened panels and issued reports devoted to ideas about and strategies for the survival of traditional journalism. Suggestions range from adopting new business models to changing government policy. Some emphasize creating new value for readers, others stress finding new sources of revenue—including donations. Still others say that journalism is so important to a democracy that the government must offer help by adjusting the tax code, relaxing antitrust policy, tweaking copyright law, or helping newspapers reorganize as nonprofit organizations.

Still others have focused on the evolving role of reporters. The Poynter Institute offers journalists workshops in multimedia storytelling and video productions as well as courses in developing mobile apps. Reporters are learning to employ cutting-edge investigative techniques using technology to mine data and connect the obscure dots to tell powerful interactive multimedia stories that incorporate video, audio, and photos. The Knight News Challenge holds an annual media innovation contest that awards as much as $5 million for ideas that develop tools, platforms, and services to inform and transform community news. Winners have included Storify, an online platform that allows reporters and editors to act as a new type of wire editor who "curates" a topic, incorporating elements taken from social websites to enhance traditional reporting, and DocumentCloud, which journalists can use to analyze, annotate, and publish original source documents to help in traditional investigative reporting. An American Press Institute initiative, Newspaper Next, helps news organizations identify technological tools that help to create innovative products for audience development across multiple platforms and devices.

Many journalists and news organizations have been proactive in addressing the challenges. For example:

- The *New York Times* has adopted more interactive features and competes head-to-head with bloggers with its own blogs. It also has created a team of developer/journalists to staff its Interactive Newsroom Technologies, which creates interactive graphics.

- The *Washington Post* now has a national innovations editor whose job is to develop cutting-edge interactive news features and tools that keep readers coming back.

- Some newsrooms have implemented a Twitter stream in place of a police scanner. Other news organizations have developed Facebook pages and encourage their reporters to use an array of social networking tools to research and develop stories, find sources, and connect with readers. The Associated Press turned to Facebook to locate sources during the campus shooting at Virginia Tech in 2007; it turned to Twitter, Facebook, Flickr, and YouTube to find photos of the US Airways flight that landed in the Hudson River in 2009.

- Journalists now use crowdsourcing techniques that rely on user participation to report stories, as CNN did in reporting the 2010 earthquake in Haiti.

- The Associated Press, the oldest news organization in the United States, has been particularly aggressive in fighting what it considers to be copyright infringement. In one example, AP sued and settled a copyright infringement lawsuit against Shepard Fairey, an artist whose iconic Obama Hope poster became a collector's item during the 2008 presidential election. The poster was adapted from a copyrighted photo taken by an AP photographer.

ABOUT THE BOOK

Are Traditional Media Dead? presents an overview of the challenges facing traditional media and their response in a series of 15 articles written by longtime observers of the industry. Part 1 asks: Does journalism have one foot in the grave? The readings in this section provide an overview of the enormous changes that have taken place in the world of traditional journalism and describe some of the challenges the industry faces. The section begins with an excerpt from *The U.S. Newspaper Industry in Transition* by Suzanne M. Kirchhoff of the Congressional Research Service. The report was developed at the request of Congress to provide legislators with information to determine whether a federal response is needed to help the news industry. Next, "Troubles for Traditional Media—Both Print and Television," an overview of a 24/7 Wall St./Harris Poll and "Newspapers Face a Challenging Calculus," by Pew Research Center for the People & the Press, offer data on changing patterns of media consumption that are having a devastating impact on newspapers. Research by Phillip Meyer and Yuan Zhang in "Anatomy of a Death Spiral: Newspapers and Their Credibility" makes a case that a newspaper's profitability is tied to its credibility. Finally, in a speech titled "The Wolf in Reporter's Clothing: The Rise of Pseudo-Journalism in America," John S. Carroll describes how manipulating and misleading the audience is creating a level of mistrust for news organizations.

The articles in Part 2 present an overview of how new media have impacted traditional media. Each of the essays acknowledges the dramatic effect that new media and the electronic revolution have had on the news industry, but none view these changes as leading to the death of the industry. The first two articles examine how new media have changed the role of the professional journalist. In "Social Media as a First Draft of Journalism and a Rallying Cry for Democracy," Endy M. Bayuni describes how social media have changed journalism in Indonesia, with professionals forced to share the field with amateurs. Then Turi Munthe, in "How Technology Turned News into a Conversation," discusses how real-time interaction between reporters and citizen journalists has created a journalistic form of "live-blog reporting." Both Bayuni and Munthe see separate roles for citizen and professional journalists, with professionals working to evaluate and edit raw data supplied by citizen journalists, turning information into meaningful stories.

The next two articles in this section look at the impact of new media on the industry. In "New Media, Old Media: How Blogs and Social Media Agendas Relate and Differ from the Traditional Press," the Pew Research Center's Project for Excellence in Journalism found that news increasingly is a shared social experience. Most original reporting still comes from traditional journalists, but technology had made it possible for citizens to influence a story's total impact. Finally, while "How to Save the News" by *Atlantic* correspondent James Fallows is at first an article on Google's role in helping to save the news, it also is one of the best explanations of how the search giant's Google News aggregator and highly profitable classified advertising business have had a devastating impact on the newspaper industry.

Part 3: How Traditional Media Can and Are Fighting Back includes articles on the ways traditional media have and could address their challenges. In *"The Associated Press v. All Headline News,"* Daniel S. Park describes how the Associated Press resurrected a 90-year-old legal doctrine to protect its information. The following two articles suggest ways to put journalism on solid economic footing. "Clues in the Rubble: A User-First Framework for Sustaining Local News" by Bill Mitchell maintains that journalism will survive if news organizations shift the debate from what publishers might charge to what users actually want and are willing to pay for. Next, in "Bad Public Relations, or Is This a Real Crisis?: YES," Lauren Fine offers a number of prescriptive measures newspapers can take to change their business model and improve their finances.

The section continues with two articles that see the changes in the news industry as threats to democracy and recommend that government play a role in helping media return to an emphasis on public stewardship. In "Getting Media Right: A Call to Action," FCC chairman Michael J. Copps recommends that the FCC impose a public value test for broadcast stations to renew their license. "Saving the News: Toward a National Journalism Strategy," by Victor Pickard, Josh Stearns, and Craig Aaron, views the current state of journalism as a crisis that calls for a national journalism strategy in which the government supports efforts at reform and innovation and experiments in finding new models for the news industry.

Finally, among the solutions being considered to help save traditional media is better training for journalists. In "Improving How Journalists Are Educated & How Their Audiences Are Informed," Susan King recommends that journalism schools emphasize not just technical and practical skills but also subject expertise and critical thinking skills to produce well-rounded journalists who could become future industry leaders.

THE FUTURE

Are traditional media dead? The most influential minds say there will always be a market for traditional media. Few believe that the largest of traditional media will succumb to the devastating market forces and technology innovations that have rocked the industry. One version of the future of traditional media seems to look a lot like its past. The newspaper of the future may be a small publication, supported by a wealthy, literate elite willing to pay for expensive subscriptions to support like-minded publishers. There will be a world wide web of information available but users will have to learn to discern the truth from the bits of information garnered from bloggers, Twitter feeds, Facebook friends, and Google+ circles. Many news companies have adopted the mantra "adapt or die." So do traditional media have a fighting chance? Most say yes.

NOTES

1. Candace Carpenter, "Future Forum 2," *Advertising Age*, September 20, 1999, http://adage.com/article/news/future-forum-2/61026/.

2. The Harris Poll, "Troubles for Traditional Media—Both Print and Television," no. 130, October 28, 2010, http://www.harrisinteractive.com/NewsRoom/HarrisPolls/tabid/447/mid/1508/articleId/604/ctl/ReadCustom%20Default/Default.aspx.

3. Molly Ivins, Creators.com, March 23, 2006, http://www.creators.com/opinion/molly-ivins/molly-ivins-march-23.html.

4. Suzanne M. Kirchhoff, "Summary," *The U.S. Newspaper Industry in Transition*, Congressional Research Service report for Congress, September 9, 2010, http://www.fas.org/sgp/crs/misc/R40700.pdf.

5. Bureau of Labor Statistics, "The Employment Situation—November 2009," news release, December 4, 2009, at http://www.bls.gov/news.release/archives/empsit_12042009.pdf.

6. Reflections of a Newsosaur, "Presses Stopped Forever at 140+ Papers in 2009," http://newsosaur.blogspot.com/2009/12/presses-stopped-forever-at-140-papers.html; Crain's New York Business.com, "367 magazines Shuttered in 2009," December 11, 2009, http://www.crainsnewyork.com/article/20091211/FREE/912119988.

7. Philip Meyer, and Yuan Zhang, *Anatomy of a Death Spiral: Newspapers and Their Credibility* (paper delivered at the Media Management and Economics Division, Association for Education in Journalism and Mass Communication, Miami Beach, Fla., August 10, 2002), 4.

8. "American Spending More Time Following the News: Ideological News Sources: Who Watches and Why," Section 5, News Media Credibility, Pew Research Center for the People & the Press (September 12, 2010). http://www.people-press.org/2010/09/12/section-5-news-media-credibility.

9. John S. Carroll, "The Wolf in Reporter's Clothing: The Rise of Pseudo-Journalism in America" (Ruhl Lecture delivered at the University of Oregon School of Journalism and Communication, May 6, 2004).

10. Sam Schulhofer-Wohl, and Miguel Garrido, "Do Newspapers Matter? Short-Run and Long-Run Evidence from the Closure of The Cincinnati Post," Working Paper 14817, National Bureau of Economic Research, March 2009, http://www.Nber.org/Papers/W14817.

RESOURCES

Collier's Encyclopedia. "History of Newspapers" by Mitchell Stephens, http://www.nyu.edu/classes/stephens/Collier's%20page.htm.

Fancher, Michael R. "Of the Press: Models for Transforming American Journalism." Aspen Institute, May 2, 2010, http://www.aspeninstitute.org/publications/press-models-transforming-american-journalism.

Ivins, Molly. "Newspaper Suicide." Creators Syndicate, March 23, 2006, http://www.creators.com/opinion/molly-ivins/molly-ivins-march-23.html.

Wohl, Sam Schulhofer, and Miguel Garrido. "Do Newspapers Matter? Short-Run And Long-Run Evidence from the Closure of the Cincinnati Post." Working paper 14817, National Bureau of Economic Research, March 2009, http://www.Nber.Org/Papers/W14817.

Part 1:

Does Journalism Have One Foot in the Grave?

This section offers a series of studies, polls, and speeches that provide an overview of the problems currently facing traditional media. These include outdated economic models, challenges from new media, failures in government policy, and lack of creditability and trust.

Congress was so concerned that the financial state of the industry might pose a public policy issue warranting federal action that it commissioned the Congressional Research Service (CRS) to investigate the extent of industry woes. The report *The U.S. Newspaper Industry in Transition* by CRS analyst Suzanne Kirchhof, an excerpt of which is included in this section, paints a picture of an industry in decline. By all measures—income, sales, circulation, and money spent on research and development, the industry is in trouble.

Next, two polls detail the migration of readers to new media. "Troubles for Traditional Media—Both Print and Television," analyzes a 24/7 Wall St./Harris Poll that indicates that traditional media are in trouble. The amount of time Americans spend reading print media is declining, while the amount of time spent on online information sites has increased. A majority of Americans believe that traditional media will cease to exist in 10 years. The poll asserts that print publications will have to reinvent themselves if they want to retain readers under 45. Similarly, "Newspapers Face a Challenging Calculus," by the Pew Research Center for the People & the Press, reports that fewer people are reading traditional newspapers as young people turn to the Internet, where readership is growing. This development has created a vicious cycle. As a result of declining income from lower readership and ads, traditional news organizations are slashing budgets, shrinking the news hole (the amount of space given to news content), and cutting staff and coverage as they retrench to survive. But these cuts mean fewer reporters covering local, regional, and national issues, and, consequently, less news to entice a reader to buy a newspaper.

In "Anatomy of a Death Spiral: Newspapers and Their Credibility," Philip Meyer and Yuan Zhang report that there is a link between credibility and robust circulation. The more people believe what they read in a paper, the stronger circulation penetration.

Finally, in "The Wolf in Reporter's Clothing: The Rise of Pseudo-Journalism in America," John Carroll, former editor of the *Los Angeles Times*, contends that pseudo-news has broken the bonds of trust that traditional media once had with readers and may ultimately contribute to the undoing of American journalism.

The U.S. Newspaper Industry in Transition

by Suzanne M. Kirchhoff*

SUMMARY

The U.S. newspaper industry is suffering through what could be its worst financial crisis since the Great Depression. Advertising revenues have plummeted due in part to the severe economic downturn, while readership habits have changed as consumers turn to the Internet for free news and information. Some major newspaper chains are burdened by heavy debt loads. Between 2008 and early 2010, eight major newspaper chains declared bankruptcy, several big city papers shut down, and many laid off reporters and editors, imposed pay reductions, cut the size of the physical newspaper, or turned to Web-only publication.

Newspaper publishers in 2010 have seen some improvement in financial conditions, with many reporting higher profits, but the industry has not yet turned the corner. Advertising dollars are still declining and newspapers have not found a stable revenue source to replace them. As the problems continue, there are growing concerns that the decline of the newspaper industry will impact civic and social life. Already there are fewer newspaper reporters covering state capitols and city halls, while the number of states with newspapers covering Congress full-time dwindled to 23 in 2008 from the most recent peak of 35 in 1985.

As old-style, print newspapers decline, new journalism startups are developing around the country, aided by low entry costs on the Internet. The emerging ventures hold promise but do not yet have the experience, resources, and reach of shrinking mainstream newspapers.

Congress has begun debating whether the financial problems in the newspaper industry pose a public policy issue that warrants federal action. Whether a congressional response to the current turmoil is justified may depend on the current causes of the crisis. If the causes are related to significant technological shifts (the Internet, smart phones and electronic readers) or societal changes that are disruptive to established business models and means of news dissemination, the policy options may be quite limited, especially if new models of reporting (and, equally important, advertising) are beginning to emerge. Governmental policy actions to bolster existing businesses could stall or retard such a shift. In this case, policymakers might stand back and allow the market to realign news gathering and delivery, as it has many times in the past. If, on the other hand, the current crisis is related to the struggle of some major newspapers to survive the current recession, possible policy options to ensure the continuing availability of in-depth local and national news coverage by newspapers might include providing tax breaks, relaxing antitrust policy, tightening copyright law, providing general support for the practice of journalism by increasing funding for the Corporation for Public Broadcasting (CPB) or similar public programs, or helping newspapers reorganize as nonprofit organizations. Policymakers may also determine that some set of measures could ease the combination of social and technological transition and the recession-related financial distress of the industry.

INTRODUCTION

The U.S. newspaper industry is in the midst of a historic restructuring, buffeted by a deep recession that has battered crucial advertising revenues, long-term structural challenges as readers turn to free news and entertainment on the Internet, and heavy debt burdens weighing down some major media companies. Eight major U.S. newspaper companies filed for bankruptcy between 2008 and early 2010 (though nearly all have since emerged as reorganized companies), while hundreds of smaller papers went out of business or moved to Web-only publications. Concerned about the potential loss of independent news outlets, lawmakers have debated legislation to assist the industry. Additionally, the Federal Trade Commission (FTC) held a series of three workshops beginning in December 2009 to look at challenges facing newspapers, television, and radio in the Internet age.[1]

Publishers are experimenting with new business approaches, but there is no widely agreed-upon model to restore the link between newspaper content and earnings, which has been partially severed on the Internet. Newspapers historically have depended on advertising for about 80% of revenues. Even after investing major sums in technology, and attracting millions of online readers, only about 10% of overall newspaper ad dollars was Internet-driven in 2009.[2] At the same time, print readership is falling, further cutting into subscription and advertising revenues (see Table 1). Vin Crosbie, a noted Syracuse University professor and consultant, has predicted that more than half of the approximately 1,400 daily newspapers in the country could be out of business by the end of the next decade.[3]

Concerns extend beyond the tens of thousands of reporters and editors losing their jobs. A robust, free press has been viewed by many as an essential check on government and business since the early days of the Republic. "The only security of all is in a free press," Thomas Jefferson wrote in 1823.[4] House Speaker Nancy

Table 1. Daily Print Newspaper Readership
Percentage of Total Adults Who Read a Print Newspaper on a Weekday

Year	Percentage of Total Adults	Percentage of Men	Percentage of Women
1998	58.6	62.2	55.2
1999	56.9	60.6	53.4
2000	55.1	58.8	51.7
2001	54.3	57.5	51.3
2002	55.4	58.2	52.8
2003	54.1	56.8	51.5
2004	52.8	55.5	50.2
2005	51.6	54.1	49.2
2006	49.9	52.3	47.6
2007	48.4	51.0	45.9

Source: Scarborough Research, Top 50 Market Report 1998–2007, prepared by Newspaper Association of America.

Pelosi, in a March letter to the Justice Department, argued that current problems in the newspaper sector pose a significant challenge to democracy.[5]

Despite First Amendment sensitivities, Congress has intervened in the past to assist newspapers and other media, building a broad record of regulation and support. Federal actions include the 1970 Newspaper Preservation Act, providing limited exemption from antitrust law; laws allocating the public airwaves;[6] copyright and fair content regulation;[7] postal subsidies,[8] and financial aid through the Corporation for Public Broadcasting (CPB) and indirectly through the National Endowment for the Humanities (NEH).[9] According to one study, the federal, state, and local governments provided more than $1 billion to the news media in 2009 via tax policy, postal subsidies, and legal requirements to disseminate public notices in print, though the level of support has declined in recent years.[10] Congress has ratified treaties governing fair use of intellectual property on the Internet,[11] and, in the 111th Congress, the House has considered and passed the Free Flow of Information Act of 2009 (H.R. 985) to give journalists a right to withhold information in grand jury proceedings.[12] The bill was referred to the Senate Judiciary Committee.

Congress is now debating whether current financial problems, which have been most acute at large, general-interest daily papers, pose a public policy issue that requires federal action. If the answer is "yes," options might include aiding existing newspapers as they grapple with the transition to a digital news world;

supporting the practice of journalism writ large; or taking a hands-off approach to allow what might arguably be a major social, political, and technological realignment in the way Americans choose to inform themselves about local, state, and national news. Lawmakers have so far expressed little interest in a broad bailout of the industry, similar to aid for the automobile or financial sectors. Senator Benjamin Cardin, who has introduced S. 673 to make it easier for newspapers to reorganize as nonprofit organizations, has said he does not support a financial rescue for newspapers.[13] The bill was referred to the Senate Finance Committee.

There are critics of government action. Ken McIntyre, of the Heritage Foundation, has argued that nonprofit status could "de-fang" the press, by preventing newspapers from endorsing candidates or taking positions against whatever political party was in power.[14] McIntyre endorses the concept of a technology shift of Gutenberg proportions, citing media expert Clay Shirky: "... We're collectively living through 1500, when it's easier to see what's broken than what will replace it ... Society doesn't need newspapers. What we need is journalism."[15]

INDUSTRY HISTORY

The newspaper industry has gone through prior periods of boom and bust. The popular press took off in the 1830s with the creation of the so-called penny press: inexpensive papers that were sold by street vendors, instead of the previous up-front subscription model.[16] The industry grew in importance, profitability, and influence, including the rise of sensationalistic "yellow journalism" in the late 1800s.

During the Great Depression, plunging revenues and competition from the emerging technology of radio hurt newspapers. Newspaper advertising revenue fell 45% from 1929 to 1933, and was still down 20% in 1941. Hundreds of newspapers went out of business or suspended operations, while a third of newspaper salaried workers lost their jobs. Radio increased in importance and was the only media segment that realized gains in advertising during the Depression.[17]

With the rise of television, the newspaper business faced another major transformation. In the 1960s, television surpassed newspapers as a source of information, and TV networks became more adept at capturing national advertising.[18] Thereafter, the newspaper sector consolidated as family-owned papers were bought by growing chains. Between 1960 and 1980, 57 newspaper owners sold their properties to Gannett Co. By 1977, 170 newspaper groups owned two-thirds of the country's 1,700 daily papers. From 1969 to 1973, 10 newspaper companies went public, including the Washington Post Co., New York Times Co., and Times Mirror Co.[19]

As chain ownership grew an increasing number of cities became one-paper towns, leading to concerns about lack of competition and a diminished watchdog role for the media—similar to worries voiced today. In 1910, nearly 60% of cities had competing daily papers. By 1930, that figure had fallen to 21%, and by 1971 to 2%.[20]

Some local papers around the country tried to combat the economic stresses by pooling advertising and circulation operations. The U.S. Supreme Court in the 1969 decision *United States v. Citizen Publishing Co.* ruled against such arrangements. In response, Congress passed the Newspaper Preservation Act of 1970 (P.L. 91-353; 15 U.S.C. 43).[21] The law provided a limited antitrust exemption for certain newspapers that combined financial functions but maintained separate newsrooms. While there were 25 to 30 such agreements in force at any one time in recent decades, just a handful remain today, and they have not been sufficient to save some weakening newspapers.[22] The *Seattle Post-Intelligencer, Minneapolis Star Tribune, Rocky Mountain News,* and *Tucson Citizen*—papers that were part of joint operating agreements—recently closed, declared bankruptcy, or moved to Web-only production.

The increasing importance of cable television in the 1980s had a far-reaching impact on newspapers, as consumers turned to 24-hour cable news stations for information. Still, many newspapers continued to enjoy extremely profitable, quasi-monopoly status in their communities. Major newspaper companies posted double-digit returns on equity (profit compared to average shareholder equity) through most of the current decade. Profits peaked at 22.7% in 2000 and declined to just over 10% in 2008, as newspaper companies instituted severe budget cuts and layoffs.[23] Cash flow margins for big, public newspaper companies reached their high in the late 1990s at 29%, an average that declined to 13% in 2008 with large differences from paper to paper.[24]

INDUSTRY CONDITIONS

There are now about 1,400 daily newspapers in the United States and thousands of community papers, which generally publish weekly or biweekly. A handful of papers, including the *Wall Street Journal, USA TODAY,* and the *New York Times,* have a national print readership topping a million or more.[25] The top 50 papers account for about a third of circulation, among them the big city papers that have had some of the largest circulation declines.[26] Overall, the newspaper industry, including printers, reporters, advertising salespeople and other personnel, was a roughly $50 billion business in 2002, according to Census Bureau data, employing about 400,000 people.[27]

Industry Cost Cutting: Key to Survival?

For the traditional, general-interest print newspapers analyzed in this report, labor has made up about 50% of costs, with production and distribution accounting for 30% and other expenses for the rest.[28] Newspapers have taken dramatic steps to cut costs as their financial picture has worsened, including trimming the size of the print newspaper, eliminating staff, or reducing the number of days the print newspaper is delivered to subscribers.

Daily papers cut their newsrooms by 11%, or 6,000 full-time workers, in 2008, the biggest one year drop since 1978. Newspaper publishers reduced newsroom staff by another 5,200 jobs in 2009, for a total reduction in daily newsroom staffing of more than 25% from the recent 2001 peak of 56,400.[29] According to Erica Smith, a reporter with the *St. Louis Post-Dispatch*, more than 2,200 workers at U.S. newspapers were laid off or took buyouts in the first eight months of 2010.[30] The number of reporters covering state legislatures in 2009 was down more than 30% from 2003.[31]

The Regional Reporters Association, an organization of newspaper journalists assigned to cover Washington, DC, has seen its membership decline from more than 200 a decade ago to about 55 today.[32] For example, roughly 10 years ago, 15 regional reporters covered Congress and other federal agencies for Connecticut-based newspapers. In 2009 there were none, according to the U.S. Senate Daily Press Gallery. (The Gallery in 2010 approved press credentials for a reporter for a startup online news organization, the *Connecticut Mirror*.) The *Dallas Morning News* Bureau has shrunk from 11 reporters in Washington, DC, to three, according to the *American Journalism Review*,[33] which in a recent study of the Washington press corps also noted that the Newhouse, Cox, and Media General newspaper chains closed their capital bureaus in recent years.[34]

Declining Advertising Revenues, Recession, and the Internet

Retail, classified, and national ads have traditionally accounted for 80% of newspaper revenues, with subscriptions and newsstand sales making up most of the rest. Sunday newspapers, with their bulky ad inserts and extra sections, along with papers published later in the week, have brought in more than half of newspaper print dollars at some publications.[35]

The traditional advertising model for years generated healthy profits, subsidized expensive foreign, investigative, and other reporting and helped keep subscription and newsstand prices low. But the model is breaking down. Newspapers have seen a dramatic drop in advertising during the recession. While other media have also been hurt, newspapers have had some of the sharpest declines

Figure 1. Percent Change in 2009 Media Ad Revenues, by Publication
January–September 2009, compared to January–September 2008

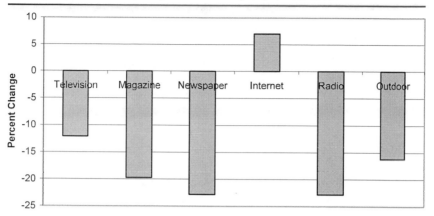

Source: TNS Media Intelligence.

Notes: Overall U.S. media ad spending declined by 14.7% in the first nine months of 2009. More recent TNS data indicate that media spending increased in the first quarter of 2010, compared to the same period in 2009.

(see Figure 1). Total advertising revenue at daily newspapers plunged from $49.4 billion in 2005 to $27.6 billion in 2009—a 44% decrease.[36]

The Pew Center's Project for Excellence in Journalism in 2009 estimated that about half of the recent drop in advertising was due to the poor economy, as auto dealers went out of business and other retailers cut back. But it is not clear that most of those ad dollars will come back as business activity revives.[37]

Newspapers are also in the throes of long-term, structural changes as readers and advertisers move to the Internet. While newspapers' online presence is surging, Internet revenues lag far behind Internet readership. Online ad revenues made up about 10% of newspaper advertising in 2009, a figure that rose to about 12% during the second quarter of 2010.[38]

In one example, classified advertising, which accounted for about 50% of ad revenues for many papers at its peak in 2008,[39] has gravitated from print to specialized websites like Craigslist and auto, real estate, and help wanted sites.[40] Media companies have tried various strategies to hold on to the classified market, with big chains like McClatchy, the Tribune Co., the Washington Post Co., A.H. Belo, and Gannett Co. jointly owning Classified Ventures, which runs sites like cars.com and homegain.com.[41] A coalition of media firms created CareerBuilder. com, a job placement site.[42] The sour economy has, at least temporarily, undercut those efforts, with the volume of classified ads plunging online and in print.

Nationally, classified advertising in daily papers declined 38% in 2009, with some categories falling even faster. Help-wanted ads fell 64% in 2009 compared to the previous year.[43]

More broadly, the traditional formula—80% of newspaper revenues from advertising—is no longer holding steady as newspapers try new strategies to raise revenue, such as sharply increasing the price of the print newspaper, starting affiliated websites, and other strategies. At some newspapers, advertising now makes up only about one-half to two-thirds of revenues.[44]

Other Factors

Another reason the newspaper industry is in trouble: red ink. Some large newspaper companies took on significant debt shortly before the economic downturn hit. Real estate developer Sam Zell, for instance, took the Tribune Co.—one of the nation's most prominent newspaper chains—private in 2007 in a leveraged $8.2 billion deal he later called a mistake.[45] The Tribune Co., now in bankruptcy, has imposed large staff reductions, consolidated operations, and taken other steps to reorganize. In 2006, McClatchy Co. bought newspaper chain Knight Ridder for more than $4 billion. In May 2009, the company offered to buy back more than $1 billion of its debt at a discount.[46]

Investors have soured on newspapers. Some large newspaper companies saw their stock prices drop by more than 80% in 2008—far beyond the overall decline in the publishing industry and various stock indices.[47] Stock prices regained some ground in 2009 and 2010, but were still well under previous peaks. For example, the New York Times Co. stock price rose from less than $4 in early 2009 to $14 a share early in 2010, before declining to about $8 a share in September. Still, even the recent peak was well below the $32 level of 2005.

With revenues declining and their ability to raise new capital impaired, some newspaper companies have been in danger of breaching financing agreements with their lenders. If that happens, lenders could terminate lines of credit and call in existing loans. Lee Enterprises, a newspaper publishing company based in Davenport, Iowa, in its first quarter 2009 report, noted that to secure new lines of credit, it had agreed, among other things, to limit capital spending.[48] In 2010, Lee said it had been able to meet all its financial covenants, and expected to keep repaying debt mainly with cash flow.[49]

In a last-ditch bid to remain viable, a number of major newspaper companies declared bankruptcy between 2008 and 2010. Most have emerged from the bankruptcy process, several after being purchased by hedge funds with little prior experience in the news business. Some companies that bought the reorganized newspaper companies do not plan to assume their pension obligations. That is forcing the federal Pension Benefit Guaranty Corp. (PBGC) take over underfunded plans, and leaving retirees with the prospect of smaller pension payments.[50] Among the companies:

- The Tribune Co., which publishes the *Chicago Tribune, Los Angeles Times, Baltimore Sun,* and five other large metro daily papers. The Tribune Co. is enmeshed in a legal battle that has hampered its ability to emerge from bankruptcy.

- Philadelphia Newspapers LLC, which publishes the *Philadelphia Inquirer* and the *Philadelphia Daily News,* filed for bankruptcy in February 2009. It was sold to a group of financial firms in April 2010 after a competitive auction,[51] though the deadline for the sale was delayed until mid-September due to protracted negotiations with affected labor unions. Pension payments have been an issue in the dispute.[52]

- Sun-Times Media Group, which owns the *Chicago Sun Times* and suburban papers, filed for bankruptcy in March 2009. The company was acquired by Sun-Times Media Holdings, led by financier James Tyree, in October 2009.[53] The PBGC in August 2010 assumed seven Sun-Times pension plans, covering nearly 2,360 workers. According to the PBGC, the plans were 53% funded, with $55.8 million in assets to cover $106.5 million in benefit liabilities.[54]

- Star Tribune Holdings Co., which owns the *Star Tribune* of Minneapolis, filed for bankruptcy in January 2009. It emerged as a reorganized entity in September 2009.[55]

- Journal-Register Co., which owns the *New Haven Register, Trentonian* and *Daily Local News* of West Chester, Pa., among other papers, filed for bankruptcy in February 2009. It emerged from bankruptcy, reorganized, in August 2009.[56]

- American Community Newspapers, which publishes the *Stillwater (MN) Gazette* and the *Plano Star Courier,* in addition to non-daily papers in four states, filed for bankruptcy in April 2009. The company emerged, reorganized, in June 2009.[57]

- Creative Loafing, which publishes alternative newspapers including the *Chicago Reader, Washington City Paper,* and others, filed for bankruptcy in September 2008. The company was purchased by hedge fund Atalaya Capital Management at a bankruptcy auction in August 2009.[58]

- MediaNews Group Inc., the publisher of dozens of newspapers, including the *Denver Post* and *San Jose Mercury News*, filed for bankruptcy protection in January 2010. It emerged from bankruptcy in March 2010.[59]

In recent months, newspaper companies have reported improved, but mixed, earnings. Many major newspaper groups were profitable in the second quarter of 2010.[60] However, a number of newspaper companies reported that print advertising revenues continued to decline during the period, even when compared to the low figures realized in the second quarter of 2009. The rate of decline slowed, however. While ad revenues at some major newspaper firms dropped by about 30% in the second quarter of 2009 compared to the previous year, they fell by less than 10% in the second quarter of 2010.[61] Companies eked out earnings by cutting staff, raising the price of the newspaper, reducing circulation costs, and other strategies.

Smaller community papers generally have not experienced as severe a falloff in staff and revenues as big metro dailies, though they have taken large hits during the downturn. Ad revenue at community papers was down about 18.7% in the first quarter of 2009, compared to an average decline of 28.8% at bigger papers.[62] Newspaper analyst John Morton has estimated that about 1,000 smaller daily papers, with circulations under 50,000, remain profitable. Smaller papers are in a better financial position than large dailies for several reasons. Smaller papers are less dependent on classified ads, operate in less complex markets, and tend to be closer to their readers and advertisers than large dailies.[63]

The University of Missouri-Columbia, in an annual survey for community papers, found high brand loyalty, a preference for the print product, and less Internet competition than at big city papers. The most recent study looked at weekly community papers located in markets of 25,000 or less.[64]

[...]

NOTES

1. Federal Trade Commission, "From Town Criers to Bloggers: How Will Journalism Survive the Internet Age?" Workshop Transcript, June 15, 2010, http://www.ftc.gov/opp/workshops/news/jun15/100615transcript.pdf.

2. Newspaper Association of America, "Trends and Numbers, Advertising Expenditures," http://www.naa.org/TrendsandNumbers/Advertising-Expenditures.aspx. The percentage of newspaper advertising derived from Web operations rose to 12% in the second quarter of 2010.

3. Crosbie, Vin, "Transforming American Newspapers," Corante, August 20, 2008. http://rebuildingmedia.corante.com/archives/2008/08/20/transforming_american_newspapers_part_1.php.

4. Thomas Jefferson to Lafayette, 1823. *The Writings of Thomas Jefferson*, Memorial Edition (Lipscomb and Bergh, editors) 20 Vols., Washington, D.C., 1903–04, Vol. 15, p. 491. See

University of Virginia Library, Thomas Jefferson Digital Archive, Freedom of the Press. http://etext.virginia.edu/jefferson/quotations/jeff1600.htm#Top.

5. Letter from Nancy Pelosi, Speaker of the House, to the Honorable Eric Holder, Attorney General, March 16, 2009.

6. CRS Report R40009, *Fairness Doctrine: History and Constitutional Issues*, by Kathleen Ann Ruane.

7. CRS Report R40194, *The Google Library Project: Is Digitization for Purposes of Online Indexing Fair Use Under Copyright Law?*, by Kate M. Manuel.

8. CRS Report R40162, *Postage Subsidies for Periodicals: History and Recent Developments*, by Kevin R. Kosar.

9. CRS Report RS22168, *The Corporation for Public Broadcasting: Federal Funding and Issues*, by Mark Gurevitz and Glenn J. McLoughlin.

10. Geoffrey Cowan and David Westphal, USC Annenberg School for Communication & Journalism, *Public Policy and Funding the News*, January, 2010, p. 2, http://communicationleadership.usc.edu/pubs/Funding%20the%20News.pdf; David Westphal, "American government: It's always subsidized commercial media," *OJR: The Online Journalism Review*, November 30, 2009, http://www.ojr.org/ojr/people/davidwestphal/200911/1801/.

11. CRS Report RL34292, *Intellectual Property Rights and International Trade*, by Shayerah Ilias and Ian F. Fergusson.

12. CRS Report RL34193, *Journalists' Privilege: Overview of the Law and Legislation in the 110th and 111th Congresses*, by Kathleen Ann Ruane.

13. Cardin, Benjamin, "A Plan to Save Our Free Press," *Washington Post*, April 3, 2009, p. A19.

14. McIntyre, Ken, "Death of Newspapers Does Not Mean the End of Journalism," *U.S. News and World Report*, May 8, 2009.

15. Ibid.

16. Emery, Edwin and Michael Emery, *The Press and America: An Interpretive History of the Mass Media, Fourth Edition*. Englewood Cliffs, NJ: Prentice-Hall, 1978, pp. 119–123.

17. Ibid., pp. 399–400, p. 428, p. 436.

18. Matthei, Harry, "Inventing the Commercial: The Imperium of Modern Television Advertising was Born in Desperate Improvisation," *American Heritage*, May/June 1997, Volume 48, Issue 3.

19. Neiva, Elizabeth M., "Chain Building: The Consolidation of the American Newspaper Industry, 1955–1980," *Business and Economic History*, Volume 24, No. 1, Fall 1995.

20. Report of the Assistant Attorney General in Charge of the Antitrust Division, In the Matter of: Application by the E.W. Scripps Co. and MediaNews Group Inc. For Approval of a Joint Operating Agreement Pursuant to the Newspaper Preservation Act, File No. 44-03-24-15 (September 8, 2000), p. 16–17.

21. Ibid.

22. Jones, Fredrick, "The Newspaper Preservation Act: Is it a Necessary Loophole in Antitrust Laws?," paper presented at the Annual Meeting of the Association for Education in Journalism, August 8–11, 1981. Farhi, Paul, "The Death of the JOA," *American Journalism Review*, September 1999.

23. Morton, John, "Not Dead Yet," *American Journalism Review*, June/July 2009 issue.

24. Fine, Lauren Rich, "Bad Public Relations or Is This a Real Crisis?: YES," Duke Conference on Nonprofit Media, May 4–5, 2009. http://www.pubpol.duke.edu/nonprofitmedia/documents/dwcrichfinefinal.pdf.

25. Audit Bureau of Circulations, "Circulation Averages for the Six Months Ended," March 31, 2010, http://abcas3.accessabc.com/ecirc/newstitlesearchus.asp.

26. Pew Research Center's Project for Excellence in Journalism, *The State of the News Media 2009: An Annual Report on American Journalism*. http://www.stateofthemedia.org/2009/index.htm.

27. U.S. Census Bureau, Industry Statistics Sampler, NAICS 511110, Newspaper Publishers.

28. Fine, Lauren Rich, "Bad Public Relations or Is This a Real Crisis?: YES," Duke Conference on Nonprofit Media, May 4–5, 2009.

29. "Decline in newsroom jobs slows," *American Society of News Editors*, April 11, 2010. http://asne.org/article_view/articleid/763/decline-in-newsroom-jobs-slows.aspx.

30. Johnston, David Cay, "Welcome to the Jungle: Journalists, meet the all-or-nothing job market," *Columbia Journalism Review*, May 22, 2009; Smith, Erica, "Layoffs and buyouts at U.S. newspapers in 2009," *Paper Cuts*. http://graphicdesignr.net/papercuts.

31. Dorroh, Jennifer, "Statehouse Exodus," *American Journalism Review*, April/May 2009. http://www.ajr.org/Article.asp?id=4721.

32. Interview with Thomas Burr of the *Salt Lake Tribune*, president of the Regional Reporters Association, June 3, 2010. Journalists pay a $20 fee to join the RRA. All reporters who cover Washington for out-of-town publications may not necessarily be members of the group. For example, *Associated Press* reporters who cover state congressional delegations, in addition to other subjects, may not choose to join.

33. Jodi Enda, "Capital Flight," *American Journalism Review*, June/July 2010, http://ajr.org/Article.asp?id=4877.

34. Ibid.

35. Pew Research Center's Project for Excellence in Journalism, *The State of the News Media 2009: An Annual Report on American Journalism*, http://www.stateofthemedia.org/2009/index.htm.

36. Newspaper Association of America, "Trends and Numbers, Advertising Expenditures," http://www.naa.org/TrendsandNumbers/Advertising-Expenditures.aspx.

37. Pew Research Center's Project for Excellence in Journalism, *The State of the News Media 2009: An Annual Report on American Journalism*.

38. Newspaper Association of America, "Trends and Numbers, Advertising Expenditures," http://www.naa.org/TrendsandNumbers/Advertising-Expenditures.aspx.

39. Fine, Lauren Rich, "Bad Public Relations or Is This a Real Crisis?: YES," Duke Conference on Nonprofit Media, May 4–5, 2009, p. 11.

40. Vogel, Harold L., *Entertainment Industry Economics: A Guide for Financial Analysis*, Sixth Edition, Cambridge: University Press, 2004, p. 318.

41. Learmonth, Michael, "Newspapers Build Digital Portfolios," *Advertising Age*, May 5, 2009.

42. Gannett, the Tribune Co., McClatchy, and Microsoft own Careerbuilder.com. http://www.careerbuilder.com/share/aboutus/profile_main.aspx.

43. National Newspaper Association, "Trends and Numbers, Advertising Expenditures," http://www.naa.org/TrendsandNumbers/Advertising-Expenditures.aspx.

44. Ken Doctor, "The Newsonomics of the Fading 80/20 Rule," Nieman Journalism Lab, August 5, 2010, http://www.niemanlab.org/2010/08/the-newsonomics-of-the-fading-8020-rule/.

45. Miles, Greg and Brian Louis, "Billionaire Zell Says 'I Made a Mistake' in Purchasing Tribune," *Bloomberg.com*, April 15, 2009.

46. McClatchy Co., "McClatchy announces private debt exchange offer for $1.150 billion of debt securities," Press Release, May 21, 2009.

47. Pew Research Center's Project for Excellence in Journalism, *The State of the News Media 2009: An Annual Report on American Journalism*. http://www.stateofthemedia.org/2009/index.htm.

48. Securities and Exchange Commission. Form 10-Q filed by Lee Enterprises for the period ended March 29, 2009.

49. Lee Enterprises, "Lee Enterprises reports Q3 earnings growth," Press Release, July 20, 2010.

50. Pension Benefit Guaranty Corporation, "PBGC Assumes Responsibility for Chicago Sun-Times Pension Plans," News Release, August 12, 2010.

51. Christopher K. Hepp and Harold Brubaker, "Phila. Newspapers Sold to Lenders," *Philadelphia Inquirer,* April 28, 2010.

52. Christopher K. Hepp, "Newspapers' sale deadline extended for 2 weeks," *Philadelphia Inquirer,* August 31, 2010.

53. Sun-Times Media Holdings, LLC, "Sun-Times Media Holdings LLC Announces Completion of Asset Transaction," Press Release, October 26, 2009, http://suntimesnewsgroup.com/releasedetail.cfm?ReleaseID=418749.

54. Pension Benefit Guaranty Corporation, "PBGC Assumes Responsibility for Chicago Sun-Times Pension Plans," News Release, August 12, 2010.

55. Star Tribune, "Star Tribune Emerges from Bankruptcy," September 28, 2009, http://startribune reorg.com/pressrelease.pdf.

56. Mark Fitzgerald, "CEO Paton: Journal Register Co. Q2 EBITDA Exceeds Goal, Profit-Sharing Could Kick In," *Editor & Publisher,* August 16, 2010.

57. Editor & Publisher, "ACN Emerges from Bankruptcy," June 29, 2009.

58. Jacqueline Palank, "Hedge Fund Taps Media Vets to Lead Creative Loafing," *Wall Street Journal,* September 2, 2009.

59. Denver Business Journal, "MediaNews Group Parent Emerges From Chapter 11," http://denver.bizjournals.com/denver/stories/2010/03/15/daily69.html.

60. The *New York Times* reported that its operating profit in the second quarter of 2010 doubled from the same period in 2009. Gannett Co. and the Washington Post Co. also reported improved earnings.

61. Alan Mutter, "Q2 newspaper sales: less bad, but not good," Reflections of a Newsosaur, August 2, 2010, http://newsosaur.blogspot.com.

62. Lane, Nancy, "Community Papers Report First Quarter 2009 Results," Suburban Newspapers of America, June 2, 2009. http://www.suburban-news.org/News/SNANewsDetail.aspx?ID=100335.

63. Morton, John, "Not Dead Yet," *American Journalism Review,* June/July 2009 issue.

64. Donald W. Reynolds Journalism Institute's Center for Advanced Social Research at the Missouri School of Journalism at the University of Missouri, "2008 Community Newspaper Study," with the National Newspaper Association.

[. . .]

*Suzanne M. Kirchhoff is an analyst in industrial organization and business at the Congressional Research Service.

Suzanne M. Kirchhoff, excerpt from *The U.S. Newspaper Industry in Transition,* Congressional Research Service report for Congress, September 9, 2010, 1–10, http://www.fas.org/sgp/crs/misc/R40700.pdf.

Used by permission.

Troubles for Traditional Media— Both Print and Television

by Harris Interactive*

Traditional media is in trouble. Newspapers are struggling with circulation and magazines like *Newsweek* are being sold for $1. And, while two-thirds of Americans (67%) still agree that they prefer to get their news in more traditional ways such as network television and/or reading newspapers or magazines in print, over half of Americans (55%) say traditional media as we currently know it will no longer exist in ten years. Additionally, half of U.S. adults (50%) say they tend to get almost all their news online.

These are some of the findings of a new 24/7, Wall Street/*Harris Poll* survey of 2,095 U.S. adults surveyed online between October 8 and 12, 2010 by Harris Interactive.

Focusing on specific media sources, when Americans are looking for news, almost half (46%) say they go to local television news all the time while about one-third say they go to local newspapers (35%) and network television news (31%). Two in five adults, however, say they never go to national newspapers like the *New York Times* or weekly news magazines (42% each) when they are looking for news.

Additionally, in looking at the amount of time people are spending with print media, one-quarter of adults say over the past year, the time they have spent reading newspapers in print and reading magazines in print has declined (25% and 23% respectively). Conversely, three in ten adults (28%) say the time they have spent visiting online news and information sites has increased over the past year.

AGE MATTERS FOR MEDIA CONSUMPTION

One reason traditional media should be worried is that media consumption and attitudes towards media are very different by age. Only one-third (33%) of those 55 and older say they tend to get almost all their news online compared to almost two-thirds (65%) of those 18–34 years old. And, while four in five of those 55 and older (81%) prefer to get their news in more traditional ways, just over half of 18–34 year olds (57%) feel the same way.

Where people go for news also changes by age. Adults 55 and older are much more likely than 18–34 year olds to go to local television news all the time or occasionally (88% vs. 63%) and to local newspapers (81% vs. 56%) when they are looking for news. However over half of 18–34 year olds go to websites that aggregate news (52%) compared to two in five adults 55 and older (39%).

Network TV versus Cable TV versus Watching Online

Besides traditional print media, network television also has to face many battles—both against people watching more television online and watching more cable television shows. Currently, two-thirds of Americans (67%) say they watch television shows primarily on television, while 5% watch them primarily or mostly on their computer. If this is examined by age, again, there is a large difference with over four in five adults 55 and older watching primarily on television (84%) compared to less than half of those 18–34 (48%).

When it comes to cable versus network television, there is an even split. Three in ten Americans (30%) say they watch shows primarily or mostly on network TV while three in ten say they watch shows primarily or mostly on cable (29%); one-third (36%) watch cable and network shows equally. While four in five U.S. adults (82%) believe that network television shows will always be a large part of Americans' viewing habits, two-thirds (65%) believe people will watch more television on cable than on the networks in the near future. One reason may be quality. Over half of Americans (51%) say cable television shows are much higher quality than network television shows.

So What?

While they might not have abandoned print media or network television completely, Americans are welcoming and embracing other media in leaps and bounds. And, as one might expect, younger Americans are setting the pace as they are getting their news online and not through local newspapers. In fact, for local newspapers, readership is clearly being driven by those who are 45 and older. Traditional media may need to reinvent themselves to give younger Americans a reason to buy local papers or turn on their local news. Network television may not be in as much trouble as print, but they also have to watch their backs as cable television is clearly winning eyes and the counter-programming they did that was once mocked by the networks is now being copied.

Table 1. Opinions about News

"Thinking about news and information in general, please indicate how strongly you agree or disagree with each of the following statements."

	Agree (NET) %	Strongly agree %	Somewhat agree %	Disagree (NET) %	Somewhat disagree %	Strongly disagree %	Not applicable %
While printed news will continue to decline, there will always be a need for newspapers in print.	81	37	44	17	14	3	3
I prefer to get my news in more traditional ways such as network television and/or reading newspapers or magazines in print.	67	33	34	29	21	8	3
Traditional media as we currently know it will no longer exist in 10 years.	55	15	40	42	33	10	3
I tend to get almost all my news online.	50	22	28	47	27	20	3
The day of the printed newspaper is gone.	43	10	33	54	36	18	2

Base: All U.S. adults online

Note: Percentages may not add up to 100% due to rounding

Table 2. Opinions about News

"Thinking about news and information in general, please indicate how strongly you agree or disagree with each of the following statements."

Summary of those saying "strongly agree" or "somewhat agree"

	Total %	Age				Education		
		18–34 %	35–44 %	45–54 %	55+ %	H.S. or less %	Some college %	College grad + %
While printed news will continue to decline, there will always be a need for newspapers in print.	81	76	76	85	87	85	76	80
I prefer to get my news in more traditional ways such as network television and/or reading newspapers or magazines in print.	67	57	65	69	81	71	66	64
Traditional media as we currently know it will no longer exist in 10 years.	55	51	55	56	58	56	53	55
I tend to get almost all my news online.	50	65	54	41	33	43	54	53
The day of the printed newspaper is gone.	43	47	44	42	39	39	46	46

Base: All U.S. adults online

Note: Percentages may not add up to 100% due to rounding

Table 3. TV Watching on Television vs. Computers

"Thinking about how you currently watch television shows, which of the following best describes you?"

	Total %	Age					Education		
		18–34 %	35–44 %	45–54 %	55+ %		H.S. or less %	Some college %	College grad + %
Watch TV shows (NET)	96	94	97	96	96		96	95	96
Watch TV shows primarily/mostly on TV (NET)	85	72	90	90	96		90	82	83
I watch television shows primarily on television.	67	48	69	74	84		75	65	59
I watch television shows mostly on television, but sometimes on my computer.	18	24	20	16	11		15	17	24
I watch television shows equally on television and my computer.	5	10	5	4	*		4	8	5
Watch TV shows primarily/mostly on computer (NET)	5	12	3	3	1		3	6	8
I watch television shows mostly on my computer.	2	5	1	1	—		1	3	3
I watch television shows primarily on my computer.	3	7	2	2	1		1	3	5
I don't watch television shows.	4	6	3	4	4		4	5	4

Base: All U.S. adults online

Note: Percentages may not add up to 100% due to rounding

Table 4. News Sources

"Thinking now of when you are looking for news, how often do you go to each of these news sources?"

	Ever (NET) %	All the time/ occasionally (NET) %	All the time %	Occasionally %	Rarely %	Never %	Not applicable %
Local television news	91	76	46	30	15	8	2
Cable TV news stations like CNN, MSNBC or FOX	82	60	25	34	22	16	3
Local newspapers	89	69	35	34	20	10	2
Network television news	84	66	31	35	19	13	2
Websites that aggregate different news sources	71	49	16	33	22	26	3
Websites for cable TV news stations	66	36	9	27	30	31	3
Websites for national newspapers	64	36	9	27	28	33	3
National newspapers like the NY Times or USA Today	55	25	6	18	31	42	3
Weekly news magazines, such as Newsweek or Time	55	25	6	19	30	42	3

Base: All U.S. adults online

Note: Percentages may not add up to 100% due to rounding

Table 5. News Sources

"Thinking now of when you are looking for news, how often do you go to each of these news sources?"

Summary of those who say "all the time" or "occasionally"

	Total %	Age				Education		
		18–34 %	35–44 %	45–54 %	55+ %	H.S. or less %	Some college %	College grad + %
Local television news	76	63	74	85	88	82	73	72
Local newspapers	69	56	69	76	81	71	64	71
Network television news	66	52	61	72	81	72	62	61
Cable TV news stations like CNN, MSNBC or FOX	60	51	62	62	67	60	60	60
Websites that aggregate different news sources	49	52	59	45	39	38	49	61
Websites for cable TV news stations	36	36	40	41	29	31	37	41
Websites for national newspapers	36	40	38	36	30	29	35	45
National newspapers like the NY Times or USA Today	25	28	24	21	24	18	23	36
Weekly news magazines, such as Newsweek or Time	25	27	23	23	25	20	21	34

Base: All U.S. adults online

Note: Percentages may not add up to 100% due to rounding

Table 6. Time Spent with Various News Sources

"Over the past year, how, if at all, has the amount of time you spend doing each of the following things changed?"

	Increased (NET) %	Increased significantly %	Increased somewhat %	Has not changed %	Decreased (NET) %	Decreased somewhat %	Decreased significantly %	Not applicable %
Visiting online news and information sites	28	6	23	56	8	5	2	8
Listening to the radio	19	4	15	58	19	13	6	4
Reading newspapers online	17	4	14	53	12	8	4	17
Watching cable TV news	17	4	13	58	15	11	4	10
Watching TV network news	14	3	11	62	18	13	6	5
Reading magazines in print	13	3	10	58	23	16	7	6
Reading newspapers in print	11	3	8	60	25	15	9	5

Base: All U.S. adults online

Note: Percentages may not add up to 100% due to rounding

Table 7. Time Spent with Various News Sources

"Over the past year, how, if at all, has the amount of time you spend doing each of the following things changed?"

Summary of those saying "increased significantly" or "increased somewhat" over the past year

	Total %	Age				Education		
		18–34 %	35–44 %	45–54 %	55+ %	H.S. or less %	Some college %	College grad + %
Visiting online news and information sites	28	29	34	29	22	25	28	32
Listening to the radio	19	24	21	15	13	18	20	20
Reading newspapers online	17	18	19	17	15	13	18	22
Watching cable TV news	17	13	17	17	22	15	18	19
Watching TV network news	14	12	14	12	17	14	14	14
Reading magazines in print	13	18	11	9	10	11	13	15
Reading newspapers in print	11	13	9	10	11	11	11	10

Base: All U.S. adults online

Note: Percentages may not add up to 100% due to rounding

Table 8. Television Shows

"Thinking now of the television shows you watch for entertainment, which statement best describes you?"

	Total %	Income				Gender	
		Less than $35K %	$35K–$49.9K %	$50K–$74.9K %	$75K+ %	Male %	Female %
Watch shows on network TV (NET)	30	37	25	33	26	26	33
I primarily watch shows on network television	18	27	15	20	13	16	20
I mostly watch shows on network television, sometimes on cable.	12	10	8	12	13	11	13
I watch cable and network shows equally.	36	29	36	36	39	36	36
Watch shows on cable TV (NET)	29	24	32	26	32	33	25
I mostly watch shows on cable, sometimes on network television.	16	12	17	14	19	20	13
I primarily watch shows on cable.	12	12	15	11	14	13	11
Not sure	5	9	7	6	2	4	6

Base: All U.S. adults
Note: Percentages may not add up to 100% due to rounding

Table 9. Network vs. Cable

"Please indicate how strongly you agree or disagree with the following statements."

	Agree (NET) %	Strongly agree %	Somewhat agree %	Disagree (NET) %	Somewhat disagree %	Strongly disagree %	Not applicable %
Network television shows will always be a large part of Americans' viewing habits.	82	32	50	15	13	2	3
People will watch more television on cable than on the networks in the near future.	65	20	46	29	26	3	6
Cable television shows are much higher quality than network television shows.	51	13	38	42	35	7	7
It doesn't matter if it's cable or the networks, television shows today are just horrible.	48	13	35	48	30	18	5

Base: All U.S. adults

Note: Percentages may not add up to 100% due to rounding

Table 10. Network vs. Cable

"Please indicate how strongly you agree or disagree with the following statements."

Summary of those saying "strongly agree" or "somewhat agree"

	Total %	Age 18–34 %	35–44 %	45–54 %	55+ %
Network television shows will always be a large part of Americans' viewing habits.	81	81	85	80	80
People will watch more television on cable than on the networks in the near future.	67	63	66	69	72
Cable television shows are much higher quality than network television shows.	53	57	57	46	51
It doesn't matter if it's cable or the networks, television shows today are just horrible.	48	42	47	46	56

Base: All U.S. adults

Note: Percentages may not add up to 100% due to rounding

METHODOLOGY

This 24/7 Wall St./Harris Poll was conducted online within the United States between October 8 and 12, 2010 among 2,095 adults (aged 18 and over). Figures for age, sex, race/ethnicity, education, region and household income were weighted where necessary to bring them into line with their actual proportions in the population. Where appropriate, this data were also weighted to reflect the composition of the adult online population. Propensity score weighting was also used to adjust for respondents' propensity to be online.

All sample surveys and polls, whether or not they use probability sampling, are subject to multiple sources of error which are most often not possible to quantify or estimate, including sampling error, coverage error, error associated with nonresponse, error associated with question wording and response options, and post-survey weighting and adjustments. Therefore, Harris Interactive avoids the words "margin of error" as they are misleading. All that can be calculated are different possible sampling errors with different probabilities for pure, unweighted, random samples with 100% response rates. These are only theoretical because no published polls come close to this ideal.

Respondents for this survey were selected from among those who have agreed to participate in Harris Interactive surveys. The data have been weighted to reflect the composition of the adult population. Because the sample is based on those who agreed to participate in the Harris Interactive panel, no estimates of theoretical sampling error can be calculated.

*Harris Interactive is a leading custom market research firm. 24/7 Wall St. is a leading independent financial news and opinion website focused on the U.S. and global equity markets. Regina Corso is senior vice president of Harris Poll, Public Relations and Youth Research.

The Harris Poll, "Troubles for Traditional Media—Both Print and Television," New York, October 28, 2010, http://www.harrisinteractive.com/NewsRoom/HarrisPolls/tabid/447/mid/1508/articleId/604/ctl/ReadCustom%20Default/Default.aspx.

Used by permission.

Newspapers Face a Challenging Calculus

by Pew Research Center for the People & the Press

The trend is unmistakable: Fewer Americans are reading print newspapers as more turn to the internet for their news. And while the percentage of people who read newspapers online is growing rapidly, especially among younger generations, that growth has not offset the decline in print readership.

In the Pew Research Center's 2008 news media consumption survey, 39% said they read a newspaper yesterday—either print or online—down from 43% in 2006. The proportion reporting that they read just the print version of a newspaper fell by roughly a quarter, from 34% to 25% over the two-year period.

Overall newspaper readership declined in spite of an increase in the number of people reading online newspapers. 14% of Americans said they read a newspaper online yesterday, up from 9% in 2006. This includes those who said they read only a newspaper online (9% in 2008), as well as those who said they read both print and Web versions of a newspaper (5%). These numbers may not include the number of people who read content produced by newspapers, but accessed through aggregation sites or portals such as Google or Yahoo.

The balance between online and print readership changed substantially between 2006 and 2008. In 2008, online readers comprised more than a third

Newspaper Readership: Print and Online

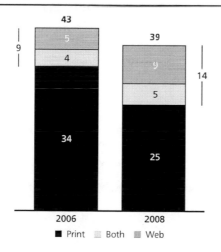

Print ■ Both Web

2006   2008

of all newspaper readers; two years earlier, fewer than a quarter of newspaper readers viewed them on the Web. This is being driven by a substantial shift in how younger generations read newspapers.

In 2008, nearly equal percentages in Generation Y (born 1977 or later) read a newspaper online and in print; 16% said they read only a print newspaper, or both the Web and print versions, while 14% said they read a newspaper only on the internet, or both online and in print. In 2006, more than twice as many in Gen Y said they read a printed newspaper than the online version (22% vs. 9%).

There is a similar pattern in newspaper readership for Generation X (born between 1965 and 1976). In 2008, 21% read only a print newspaper, or both an online and a print newspaper; 18% read a newspaper only on the Web, or both online and in print. In 2006, 30% of Gen X read a newspaper in print, while just 13% read a web version.

Baby Boomers (born between 1946 and 1964) and the Silent/Greatest Generations (born before 1946) continue to read newspapers at higher rates than do those in younger age cohorts.

However, the proportion of Baby Boomers who said they read a newspaper yesterday slipped between 2006 and 2008, from 47% to 42%. The decline among Baby Boomers has come entirely in print readership (from 42% to 34%).

AGE COHORTS OVER TIME

The Pew Research Center's measures of where people got news "yesterday" date to the early 1990s. Since then, the proportions of Americans saying they got news yesterday from television, radio or newspapers have declined. Over the last decade, however, the percentage saying they watched TV news yesterday has remained relatively stable, while the audiences for radio and newspapers have fallen steadily. The percentage saying they got news online yesterday has increased over the last two years. (For more details on long-term changes in news consumption, see "Key News Audiences Now Blend Online and Traditional Sources," Aug. 17 2008).[1]

There has long been a sizable "generation gap" in newspaper readership. In 1998, those in the oldest age cohort—the Greatest/Silent Generations (born before 1946)—were more than twice as likely as those in the youngest generation at that time (Generation X) to read a newspaper yesterday (65% vs. 31%). Older age cohorts continue to read newspapers at much higher rates than do younger cohorts [...].

For Younger Age Cohorts, Web Newspapers Rival Print

	Total %	Gen Y 1977– %	Gen X 1965–76 %	Silent/ Boomer 1946–64 %	Greatest Pre-1946 %
2008					
Newspaper yesterday	39	27	33	42	55
Print only	25	13	15	28	48
Web only	9	11	12	8	3
Both	5	3	6	6	4
NET: Web version	14	14	18	14	7
Net: Print version	30	16	21	34	52
2006					
Newspaper yesterday	43	29	38	47	56
Print only	34	20	25	36	52
Web only	5	7	8	5	1
Both	4	2	5	6	3
NET: Web version	9	9	13	11	4
Net: Print version	38	22	30	42	55

Figures for web newspaper readership and overall readership include people who said they got news online yesterday and, when prompted, said they visited the websites of one or more newspapers when online yesterday. Nets for both web and print versions include people who said they read a newspaper online and in print.

Yet the decline in newspaper readership is not solely attributable to the fact that the youngest cohorts are increasingly less likely to read newspapers; newspapers also are suffering from a loss of readership within older age cohorts. Over the past decade, there has been a sizable decline in newspaper readership among the cohort that has been the most faithful readers of newspapers—the Silent/Greatest Generations.

In the 2008 survey, slightly more than half (53%) of those in this age cohort said they read a newspaper yesterday. A decade earlier, 65% of those in the Silent/Greatest Generations did so. There also has been a large decline in the percentage of Baby Boomers who reported reading a newspaper yesterday, from 48% in 1998 to 38% a decade later.

By contrast, newspaper readership has been more stable among younger age cohorts. In 2008, 26% of those in Generation X said the read a newspaper yesterday, compared with 31% in 1998. Last year, 21% of those in Generation Y

Media Source by Generation

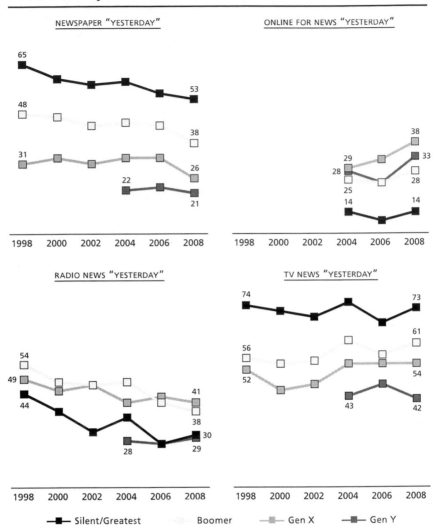

NEWSPAPER "YESTERDAY"

ONLINE FOR NEWS "YESTERDAY"

RADIO NEWS "YESTERDAY"

TV NEWS "YESTERDAY"

—■— Silent/Greatest   Boomer   —■— Gen X   —■— Gen Y

said they read a newspaper on the previous day, which was little changed from 2004 (22%).

The generational pattern in television news viewership is somewhat different: Within each age cohort, the percentages saying they watched television news yesterday have remained stable in recent years. As with newspapers, a far lower proportion of Gen Y than older age cohorts reports watching TV news on a typical day. Unlike newspapers, however, there is even a sizable gap in television news viewership between Gen Y and Gen X. In 2008, just 42% of Gen Y said they watched television news yesterday, compared with 54% of Gen X and even higher percentages of Boomers (61%) and the Silent/Greatest Generations (73%).

Like newspapers, radio news has seen a gradual overall decline over the past decade. In 2008, as in previous news consumption surveys, those in their prime working years were more likely than others to report listening to radio news yesterday. Radio news listenership was higher among Gen X (41%) and Boomers (38%) than among either the Silent/Greatest Generations (30%) or Gen Y (29%).

Most Frequented Online News Sites

Websites used most often	%
Yahoo	28
MSN/Microsoft	19
CNN	17
NEWSPAPER SITES (NET)	13
Local newspapers	7
New York Times	4
Wall Street Journal	2
USA Today	2
Washington Post	2
Google	11
MSNBC/MSN	10
AOL	8
FOX	7
Local TV news websites	4
BBC	2
ESPN/Other sports site	2
ABC	2
Drudge Report	2
CNBC	2
Internet service provider	2
CBS	1
Other websites	18

Open-ended questions based on those who go online for news. Figures add to more than 100% because multiple responses permitted.

In contrast to traditional media sources, use of online news on a typical day has increased in recent years. Nearly all of this growth has come in Gen X (from 32% in 2006 to 38% in 2008) and Gen Y (from 24% to 33%).

ONLINE NEWS SOURCE

The 2008 news consumption survey found that the familiar distinctions among news sources are breaking down. Online news consumers have access to a vast array of news sources—from traditional news organizations to web portals and internet-only news sites.

Notably, more online news consumers (50%) said they access news sites indirectly—by following links to specific stories— than by going directly to the home pages of news organizations (41%). Among online news consumers younger than 25, 64% said they more often follow links to stories, rather than going directly to the sites of news organizations.

When online news consumers were asked what websites they used most often for news and information, Web portals and familiar names dominated. However, while sizable minorities mentioned well-known sites—28% cited Yahoo while 19% cited MSN/Microsoft—numerous sites were mentioned by 2% of respondents or less.

Newspapers, taken collectively, were mentioned by 13%, placing them behind the most popular news sites. In fact, fewer online news users cited any newspaper site than mentioned the most frequented television news site (CNN.com at 17%).

At the same time, several individual newspapers were included among the "long tail" of less frequently cited news websites: 4% cited the *New York Times*,

Online Newspapers Attract the Highly Educated

Websites used most often	Total %	Education Post-grad %	BA/BS %	Some coll. %	HS or less %
(NET) Newspapers	13	28	16	10	7
Local Newspapers	7	12	7	7	5
New York Times	4	12	6	3	0
Wall Street Journal	2	4	2	1	1
USA Today	2	4	1	1	1
Washington Post	2	4	3	1	*
N	1005	226	332	253	240

while 2% each mentioned the *Wall Street Journal, Washington Post* and USA *Today* websites. Another 7% mentioned local newspaper websites.

Newspaper websites are especially popular with highly educated online news consumers. More than a quarter of those who have attended graduate school (28%) cite a newspaper website as where they go most often for news and information. That compares with 16% of those with no more than a college degree and much smaller percentages of those with less education.

NOTE

1. For comparability, long-term generational trends in newspaper readership include only those who said they read a newspaper yesterday (34% of the public). Previous figures also include those who said they did not read a newspaper yesterday, but said they got news online yesterday and while online visited a newspaper website, for a total of 39%.

*Pew Research Center for the People & the Press is an independent public opinion survey research project that studies attitudes toward the press, politics, and public policy issues. It is best known for regular national surveys that measure public attentiveness to major news stories and for polling that charts trends in values and fundamental political and social attitudes.

Pew Research Center for the People & the Press, "Newspapers Face a Challenging Calculus," Washington, DC., February 26, 2009, http://pewresearch.org/pubs/1133/decline-print-newspapers-increased-online-news.

Used by permission.

Anatomy of a Death Spiral: Newspapers and Their Credibility

by Philip Meyer and Yuan Zhang*

Editors have long believed in their hearts that the economic success of newspapers depends on their credibility. We find evidence to support this belief by examining 21 counties where newspaper credibility has been measured. The more people believe what they read in the papers, the greater the robustness of circulation penetration over a recent 5-year period. Unfortunately, both credibility and readership are falling in what appears to be a classic reinforcing process.

INTRODUCTION

While newspaper editors have fretted about their credibility for decades, they have been unable to do much about it. Given limited resources by their publishers and owners, they remain mostly frozen at the wheel while both readership and confidence in the press decline steeply and consistently.

The surface evidence suggests a classic death spiral or reinforcing process.[1] Waning confidence in the press causes lower readership, which reduces profits which limits the availability of resources for the editorial product, causing confidence to fall still more. The trend lines in Figure 1 and Figure 2 provide the evidence. According to the General Social Survey, expressions of "a great deal" or "some" confidence in the press have declined at 0.8 points per year. The proportion who read a newspaper every day has fallen a percentage point per year since the first measurement by the National Opinion Research Center in 1967.[2]

However, it is imprudent to draw causal inferences from parallel changes across time. Both readership and confidence could be the result of some secular trend that affects everything in society. Textbooks abound with illustrations of spurious correlation over time, e.g., between liquor consumption and church attendance. (Both increase due to the growing population.)

To see if there is really a causal link between low confidence and low readership, we need an experimental design that holds time constant. Because the problem is too large for the laboratory, we need a natural experiment that can tell us whether confidence and readership covary within a limited time frame. This report describes such a natural experiment. It builds on work that others

Figure 1. Percent with "a great deal" or "some" confidence in the press

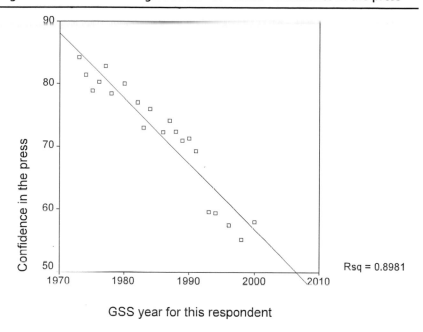

Rsq = 0.8981

Figure 2. Percent who read a newspaper "every day" by year

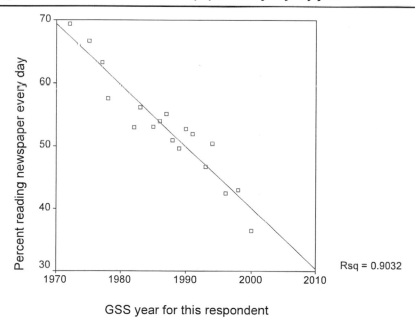

Rsq = 0.9032

began as far back as 1985 when two major studies produced contrasting interpretations of the problem.

PREVIOUS CREDIBILITY RESEARCH

The most alarming report came from Kristin McGrath of MORI Research, hired by the American Society of Newspaper Editors to do a national survey. "Threefourths of all adults have some problem with the credibility of the media," she wrote, "and they question newspapers just as much as they question television."[3]

A contrasting report was issued early the following year by the Times Mirror newspaper after it hired The Gallup Organization to cover the same territory.

"If credibility means believability, there is no credibility crisis," said this report, written by Andrew Kohut and Michael Robinson. "The vast majority of the citizenry thinks the major news organizations are believable."[4]

Oddly, the data collected by the two organizations were not very different. Their varying question forms obscured close comparison, but 84% in the Times Mirror study gave a positive rating to their local daily newspaper on a scale where "4 means you can believe all or almost all of what they say, and 1 means you can believe almost nothing of what they say."[5] The ASNE study used a 5-point scale, and 85% gave either a positive or neutral rating on accuracy of the newspaper with which they were the most familiar.

Another contribution to the conversation came in 1998 when Christine Urban, also working for ASNE, produced another report. Hers made no reference to the earlier work, but it did propose six major sources of low trust. Number one on the list: "The public sees too many factual errors and spelling or grammatical mistakes in newspapers."

Two purely descriptive studies were published in 2001. News credibility was one of a very broad array of social indicators asked about in 1999 by the Knight Foundation which found that 67 percent believe "almost all or most" of what their local daily newspaper tells them.[6] A similar result was published at the same time by American Journalism Review, based on fieldwork in 2000 funded by the Ford Foundation. This study reported that 65 percent believe all or most of what they read in the local paper.

Designers of none of these studies made any effort to attain compatibility with previous work so that comparisons could be made over time. Still, American Journalism Review's author declared, "newspapers seem to be rising in readers' esteem."[7]

Nor were any of the studies informed by any kind of theory that might help us understand how much credibility a newspaper needs, how much it costs to get it, and whether the cost is worth it. As careful and detailed as they were, they generated little but description "waiting for a theory or a fire."[8]

A PROPOSED MODEL

Much of the variation in historical concern with the credibility problem may be based more on emotion than reality. The purpose of this inquiry is to find a more solid theoretical basis for assessing the problem. One untested theoretical assumption is that credibility has something to do with business success. It was expressed eloquently by a Knight Ridder executive a quarter century ago:

> A newspaper's product is neither news nor information. We are in the influence business. We create two kinds of influence: societal influence (not for sale) and influence on the decision to buy (for sale). But they are related, because the former enhances the value of the latter.[9]

The appeal of the influence model is that it provides a business rationale for social responsibility. The way to achieve societal influence is to obtain public trust by becoming a reliable and high-quality information provider, which frequently involves investments of resources in news production and editorial output. The resulting higher quality justifies more public trust attributed to the newspaper and, not only larger readership and circulation, but influence with which advertisers will want their names associated.

Because trust is a scarce good, it could be a natural monopoly, as argued by Meyer.[10] Once a consumer finds a trusted supplier, there is an incentive to stay with that supplier rather than pay the cost in time and effort of evaluating a substitute.

It follows then that societal influence of a newspaper achieved from practicing quality journalism could be a prerequisite for financial success. Social responsibility in the democratic system supports, rather than impedes, the fulfillment of a newspaper's business objectives, through the channels of obtaining public trust and achieving societal influence, which then feeds back into further fulfillment of the public mission, thereby creating a virtuous cycle (see Figure 3).

Reversing the argument, cutbacks in content quality will erode public trust, weaken societal influence, and eventually lead to losses in circulation and advertising dollars. But managers, under pressure from owners and investors, will do this anyway because reducing quality has a quick effect on revenue that is instantly visible while the costs of lost quality are distant and uncertain.

Figure 3. Societal Influence Model for the Newspaper Industry

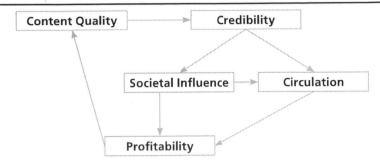

If those distant costs could be made more concrete and predictable, managers and investors might make different decisions. The purpose of this study is to reduce the uncertainty about the long-term cost of low credibility using individual communities as the level of analysis. Previous studies using communities have focused on editorial quality in general rather than specifically targeting credibility.

COMMUNITY BASED STUDIES

The Washington Post's coverage of the Pentagon Papers and the Watergate affair provided anecdotal evidence that good journalism could be profitable.[11] The success of *USA Today* proved that innovations in format and content could pay off in the form of circulation and advertising success.[12] Becker et al. studied 109 New England newspapers and found that circulation penetration (circulation divided by households) was related to news quality.[13] Stone et al. also reported positive correlation between newspaper quality and circulation in a sample of 124 papers.[14] Using content analysis to judge quality, Lacey and Fico found that the level of newspaper quality in 1984 was positively related to circulation (with market size controlled) in 1985 for 106 daily newspapers.[15] Blankenburg examined quality-related variables such as staff size, number of news pages, and news-editorial budget in 149 newspapers, and found that these variables were highly correlated with circulation.[16] More recently, Lacey and Martin's case study of the Thompson papers found that they lost revenue and circulation during the 1980s when high profits goals were set.[17] Overall, most studies have found a positive relationship between quality and circulation. However, they are mostly dated and have not used direct measures of credibility as an indicator of quality. Today's pressing media environment calls for new empirical evidence, particularly in regard to the priorities the newspaper industry has to take.

Our test of the model will be a very basic one: a search for a correlation between credibility and profitability. We need to be able to measure these two variables at the level of individual newspapers. Fortunately, a convenience sample is available.

THE NATURAL EXPERIMENT

The Knight Foundation keeps track of the 26 communities where John S. and James L. Knight operated newspapers in their lifetimes.[18] They range from large (Philadelphia and Detroit) to very small (Milledgeville, Ga., and Boca Raton, Fla.). This common history will make our findings less generalizable to the universe of all daily newspapers, but it carries an offsetting advantage. By removing some of the differences in corporate culture and history from the causal model, the choice of these communities reduces some possible sources of spuriousness. Like a laboratory experiment conducted at constant temperature, this inquiry holds aspects of corporate history and culture constant.

Our independent variable is credibility as measured in a social indicators study fielded in 1999 by the Knight Foundation.[19] The dependent variable is a little more complicated. We call it circulation robustness, and we measure it by comparing changes in newspaper household penetration as measured by the 1995 and 2000 county penetration reports of the Audit Bureau of Circulations (ABC). Penetration declined almost everywhere. We define penetration as robust when the 2000 figure is a high proportion of the penetration in the 1995 report.[20] We eliminated two Knight communities where the survey geography was not defined by counties.[21]

This made it possible to match data from other sources, including the Audit Bureau of Circulations, in a clear and minimally ambiguous way.

We are left with a sample of 24 markets. In two of them, Columbia, S.C., and south Florida, the Knight Foundation's historic relationship with the communities led it to define them by two counties rather than single counties. We have combined the data from other sources to match that design in the case of Richland and Lexington counties in South Carolina. In more heavily populated south Florida, we separated Dade and Broward counties and treated them as separate communities. Now we have 25.

Most of them have newspapers that are now, or have been, owned by Knight Ridder. Several have more than one strong newspaper. No attempt was made to isolate the effects of individual newspapers. These effects are selfweighting because circulation robustness is measured by the circulation of all ABC newspapers in each county, while the credibility question measures the paper with which respondent is "most familiar."

The percent who say they believe all or almost all of what they read in the paper ranges from 13 in Tallahassee to 30 in Grand Forks (mean = 21, S.D. = 3.9). Previous research has suggested that credibility, defined straightforwardly as believability, is a stable attribute.[22]

The same cannot be said for our dependent variable. It is based on circulation which can be subject to intense short-term fluctuations depending on local conditions.

Robustness, expressed by taking 2000 penetration as a proportion of 1995 penetration, ranged from .59 (Baldwin Co., Georgia) to 1.02 (Miami). The range was so vast in fact that a probe of the outliers was called for. Tukey's box plot makes the outliers visible. The box represents the interquartile range or middle 50%, and the outliers are cases more than 1.5 box lengths from the edge of the box (Figure 4).

Figure 4. Tukey box plot showing outliers

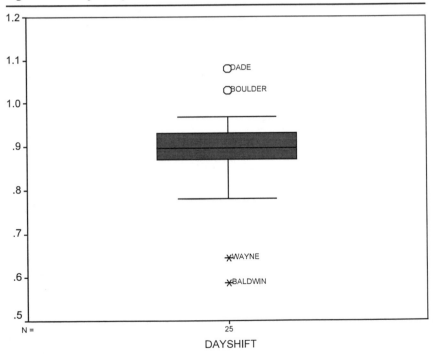

Investigating each of the outliers in turn, we found:

Dade County, Fla.—*The Miami Herald's* explosive circulation boom was the result of an artifact, the unbundling of *El Nuevo Herald* from its mother ship. After the separation, ABC counted circulation of the Spanish language edition separately for the first time. We could think of no way to correct for this for a before-after comparison, and Dade County was dropped from the sample.[23]

Boulder County, Colo.—In the months before the creation of the joint agency by the owners of the *Denver Post* and the *Rocky Mountain News* in 2000, the two Denver newspapers were engaged in a bitter circulation war that saw the price of a newspaper drop to a penny per copy. This battle extended into neighboring Boulder County. While it cost the local paper circulation, total newspaper circulation in the county—the variable we are using to define penetration robustness—soared. Because of this extraneous cause, we dropped Boulder County.[24]

Wayne County, Mich.—Detroit, always a strong labor town, underwent a bitter newspaper strike that began in 1995 and led to many union members losing their jobs. In a display of sympathy and solidarity, enough working people in the home county stopped buying the paper to cause a catastrophic circulation decline. We took Wayne County out of the sample.

Baldwin County, Ga.—The leading newspaper, the *Milledgeville Union-Recorder,* is not an ABC member. The precipitous loss of ABC circulation can be ascribed to the decision of the *Macon Telegraph* to close its Baldwin County bureau. Since our sample is defined by audited circulation, Baldwin County was removed from the sample.

That leaves 21 communities without obvious exogenous variables to mask the effect of credibility on circulation. Here's how we operationalized credibility.

The question in the Knight Foundation surveys was, "Please rate how much you think you can believe each of the following news organizations I describe. First, the local daily newspaper you are most familiar with. Would you say you believe almost all of what it says, most of what it says, only some, or almost nothing of what it says?"

We know from the previous reports of McGrath, Urban, and Stepp that two demographics, age and race, have a substantial impact on newspaper credibility. Blacks and older citizens are more suspicious of what they read in newspapers.

This difference is also found in the 1999 Knight data. In the total the sample, ($N = 15,481$), belief in the newspaper was negatively correlated with age ($r = -.129$, $p < .01$) and positively, although less importantly, with race treated as a binary variable where black = $1 (r = -.065, p < .01)$.

Because our counties differ in the proportions of blacks and older citizens, we chose to account for those effects before looking for the effect of credibility on penetration retention.

We leveled the playing field by running multiple regression with trust as the dependent variable and percent black and mean age—both from the survey data—as the independent variables. The unstandardized regression residuals represent each county's trust score with the effects of race and age filtered out (observed minus expected). For example, Grand Forks County's score of 7.8 means that the newspaper's credibility score was 7.8 percentage points above what the age and racial makeup of its citizens would have led us to predict.

Here are the counties with their credibility scores and 1995–2000 penetration robustness listed in order of their credibility.

The correlation coefficient is .609, meaning that the credibility of a county's newspapers explains 37 percent of the robustness in their combined daily

County	Credibility Adj.	Robustness
Grand Forks, ND	7.89	.96
Muscogee, GA	4.83	.97
Broward, FL	4.64	.87
Harrison, MS	3.65	.90
Brown, SD	2.17	.96
Lexington, SC*	0.91	.84
St. Louis, MN	0.58	.87
Centre, PA	0.54	.84
Mecklenburg, NC	0.44	.89
Manatee, FL	0.23	.90
Philadelphia, PA	0.06	.93
Bibb, GA	−0.10	.91
Fayette, KY	0.68	.94
Allen, IN	−1.04	.90
Horry, SC	−1.13	.92
Ramsey, MN	−1.72	.88
Palm Beach, FL	−1.73	.88
Santa Clara, CA	−1.84	.87
Summit, OH	−4.71	.91
Sedgwick, KS	−4.89	.84
Leon, FL	−8.09	.78

*Includes Richland County

Figure 5. Circulation robustness by credibility

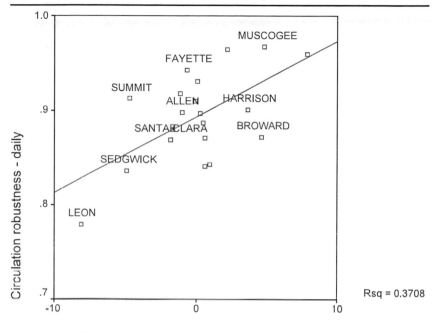

Credibility adjusted for age and race

penetration. The probability that this relationship is due to chance is less than one half of 1 percent (p = .003).

When the robustness of Sunday circulation is used as the dependent variable, 38 percent of the variance is explained (r = .613, p = .003). The first link in the model in Figure 3 is established. Credibility is related to circulation. The relationship is clearer if we look at the scatter plot (Figure 5).

We now have the first quantitative measure of the benefit of credibility. The slope of the regression line is .008, meaning that circulation robustness—the ability of a county's newspapers to hold their collective circulation in the face of all of the pressures degrading it—increases by .8 of a percentage point for each 1 percent increase in credibility. And the finding is robust. When credibility is left unadjusted for age and race, the correlation is diminished only slightly and remains statistically significant.[25]

Correlation, of course, neither proves causation, nor establishes its direction. While it can be taken as evidence in support of the model in Figure 3, it does not tell us whether it is a picture of a virtuous cycle or a vicious cycle.

Stepp, who has the advantage of holding the most recent credibility data, argues that the news is good, that the public's faith in newspapers is improving. He bases this on weak evidence: one question in one survey in which respondents are asked to compare their present attitude with their remembered attitudes from the past. He is supported by an uptick in the NORC 2000 data—from 58 percent who have a great deal or some confidence in the press, compared to 55 percent two years earlier. But the difference is within the range of measurement error. More data points are needed to overcome the gloomier picture painted by NORC's 30-year trend line on readership and confidence in the press.

FURTHER RESEARCH

We need more thorough testing of the model. While the link between credibility and robustness of circulation may deserve the priority we gave it, there is also a strong need to test the link between content and credibility. The demonstrated value of credibility should motivate us to find how credibility can be created through content—or whether content makes a difference at all.

An obvious variable to investigate is accuracy in reporting. Urban's 1999 study provided cross-section evidence at the level of the individual reader. But it is almost a tautology that people who perceive errors in the paper are less likely to believe it. To make Urban's finding convincing, we need evidence at the community level. Is a newspaper that is objectively more accurate also more believed? A replication of Mitchell Charnley's pathbreaking accuracy study in each of the markets where trust is also measured could give us stronger evidence.[26]

Beyond content, the history of a newspaper's relationship with its community should be considered. David Loomis, looking at the same data we are using, noticed a striking difference in credibility between two similar southern newspaper markets, Columbus, Ga., and Tallahassee, Fla., and did some first-hand investigating in both communities.[27]

He found that the leading papers in the two towns had quite different histories from the civil rights movement. The paper in Tallahassee, before its acquisition by the Knights in 1965 was a die-hard supporter of segregation. The paper in Columbus took a mediating role in the community, and today Columbus is one of the few places where newspaper credibility is as high among blacks as whites. Perhaps no ordinary amount of content manipulation can overcome history.

Efforts are also needed to measure a newspaper's societal influence and its effect on both credibility and profitability. McGrath's study for ASNE led to some secondary analysis that suggested that credibility has a community affiliation dimension that interacts with simple believability.[28] Despite the intriguing opportunity this information offered for a theoretical basis for civic journalism, we know of no attempts to replicate or build upon that finding. However, an opportunity exists in both the Knight Foundation data and another recent set of community benchmark surveys organized by Robert Putnam for his Saguaro Seminar.[29] Both measure community involvement as well as trust in media. However, the Putnam survey asked about trust in media generally, rather than newspapers specifically as the Knight Foundation did.[30]

Because our model attempts to describe a string of causal relationships, time series studies are needed to clarify and validate it. Fortunately, the Knight Foundation has designed its community surveys for periodic measurement, and the second in the series entered the field in 2002.

We regret not starting this work years ago. The decline of newspapers is not likely to be halted or reversed until investors can see a measurable benefit from a newspaper's community influence, its social responsibility. Without such measurements, owners and managers will continue to regard quality as mere cost, and the self-reinforcing loop of the death spiral will continue.

NOTES

1. Reinforcing processes are examined from a systems theory perspective by Peter M. Senge in *The Fifth Discipline: The Art & Practice of the Learning Organization*, Currency Doubleday, 1990, p. 81.

2. NORC first asked the newspaper readership question in 1967 as part of Sidney Verba and Norman Nie's Participation in America study. It became part of the General Social Survey in 1972.

3. *Newspaper Credibility: Building Reader Trust, a National Study Commissioned by the American Society of Newspaper Editors*. MORI Research, Inc., Minneapolis, April 1985

4. *The People & the Press: A Times Mirror Investigation of Public Attitudes Toward the News Media Conducted by The Gallup Organization*. Times Mirror, January 1986.

5. *The People & the Press*, p. 20.

6. *Listening and Learning: Community Indicator Profiles of the Knight Foundation Communities and the Nation*, Miami: Knight Foundation, 2001.

7. Carl Sessions Stepp, "Positive Reviews," *American Journalism Review*, March 2001, p. 58.

8. This phenomenon is not confined to media businesses. Ronald Coase, in a critique of early institutional studies in business administration, said, "Without a theory they had nothing to pass on except a mass of descriptive material waiting for a theory or a fire." Quoted by Oliver E. Williamson in Giovanni Dosi, Davide J. Teece and Josef Chytryl, Eds., *Technology, Organization and Competitiveness: Perspectives on Industrial and Corporate Change*, Oxford University Press, 1998.

9. Hal Jurgensmeyer (1931–1995) in a conversation with the first author, Miami, Fla., 1978.

10. Philip Meyer, "Learning to Love Lower Profits," *American Journalism Review*, December, 1995.

11. Nancy H. Maynard, "Can Media Economics Match Its Aspirations?" *Nieman Reports*, 49 (2), 1995, p. 35–37.

12. John Morton, "Short Term Losses, Long Term Profits," *American Journalism Review*, 19 (7) 1997.

13. Lee B. Becker, Randy Beam, and John Russial, "Correlates of Daily Newspaper Performance in New England," *Journalism Quarterly*, Spring 1978, p. 100–108.

14. Gerald C. Stone, Donna B. Stone, and Edgar P. Trotter, "Newspaper Quality's Relation to Circulation," *Newspaper Research Journal*, Spring 1981, p. 16–24.

15. Stephen Lacey and Frederick Fico (1991), "The Link Between Newspaper Content Quality and Circulation," *Newspaper Research Journal*, Spring, p. 46–57.

16. William B. Blankenburg (1989), "Newspaper Scale and Newspaper Expenditures," *Newspaper Research Journal*, Winter, p. 97–103.

17. Stephen Lacey and Hugh J. Martin (1998), "Profits Up, Circulation Down for Thompson Papers in 80s," *Newspaper Research Journal*, Summer, p. 70–76.

18. The John S. and James L. Knight Foundation promotes excellence in journalism worldwide and invests in the vitality of 26 U.S. communities where the communications company founded by the Knight brothers published newspapers. The Foundation is wholly separate from and independent of those newspapers.

19. *Listening and Learning.*

20. Periods covered by these reports varied, but the audits generally fell in the year preceding the report.

21. Long Beach, California, and Gary, Indiana.

22. Philip Meyer, "Defining and Measuring Credibility of Newspapers: Developing an Index," *Journalism Quarterly*, 65:3 (Fall 1988), 567–575.

23. We appreciate the help of Armando Boniche, research manager of The Miami Herald, in sharing this history.

24. Barrie Hartman, former executive editor of the Boulder Daily Camera provided this background.

25. When credibility without the controls for age and race is the dependent variable, the variance explained is 35% and 30%, respectively, for daily and Sunday circulation robustness.

26. Mitchell Charnley, "Preliminary Notes on a Study of Newspaper Accuracy," *Journalism Quarterly*, 13:4 (December 1936), pp. 394–401.

27. David O. Loomis, *Tale of Two Cities: Connections Between Community, Corporate Culture, and Civic Journalism*, PhD dissertation, University of North Carolina at Chapel Hill, 2002.

28. Meyer, "Defining and Measuring Credibility of Newspapers." See also Mark Douglas West, "Validating a Scale for the Measurement of Credibility: A Covariance Structure Modeling Approach," *Journalism Quarterly* 71:1, Spring 1994, pp. 159–168.

29. Putnam's codebook was available in February 2002 at www.cfsv.org/communitysurvey/docs/survey_instrument.pdf.

30. We checked credibility as measured by Putnam against penetration robustness and found no correlation. When respondents are asked about "media," we suspect that they tend to answer in terms of television rather than newspapers.

***Philip Meyer** is professor emeritus and former Knight Chair of Journalism at the University of North Carolina at Chapel Hill.

Yuan Zhang is assistant professor in the School of Mass Communications at Virginia Commonwealth University.

Philip Meyer and Yuan Zhang, "Anatomy of a Death Spiral: Newspapers and Their Credibility" (paper delivered to the Media Management and Economics Division, Association for Education in Journalism and Mass Communication, Miami Beach, Fla., August 10, 2002).

Used by permission.

The Wolf in Reporter's Clothing: The Rise of Pseudo-Journalism in America

*by John S. Carroll**

It's a lovely spring afternoon here in Eugene, and today we gather to honor the memory of Robert W. Ruhl, the late editor and publisher of the *Medford Mail Tribune*, with a lecture on ethics. I confess that in my youth, the prospect of a lecture on ethics, particularly on a day like this one, did not exactly make my heart leap. So I thank you for being here.

One reason I was drawn to my chosen career is its informality, in contrast to the real professions. Unlike doctors, lawyers or even jockeys, journalists have no entrance exams, no licenses, no governing board to pass solemn judgment when they transgress. Indeed it is the Constitutional right of every citizen, no matter how ignorant or how depraved, to be a journalist. This wild liberty, this official laxity, is one of journalism's appeals.

I was always taken, too, by the kinds of people who practiced journalism. Like Robert Ruhl, my father, Wallace Carroll, was editor and publisher of a regional newspaper, in Winston-Salem, North Carolina. The people he worked with seemed more vital and engaged than your normal run of adults. They talked animatedly about things they were learning—things that were important, things that were absurd. They told hilarious jokes. I understood little about the work they did, except that it entailed typing, but I felt I'd like to hang around with such people when I grew up. Much later, after I'd been a journalist for years, I became aware of an utterance by Walter Lippmann that captured something I especially liked about life in the newsroom. "Journalism," he declared, "is the last refuge of the vaguely talented."

Here is something else I've come to realize: The looseness of the journalistic life, the seeming laxity of the newsroom, is an illusion. Yes, there's informality and humor, but beneath the surface lies something deadly serious. It is a code. Sometimes the code is not even written down, but it is deeply believed in. And, when violated, it is enforced with tribal ferocity.

Consider, for example, the recent events at the *New York Times*.

Before it was discovered that the young reporter Jayson Blair had fabricated several dozen stories, the news staff of the *Times* was already unhappy. Many members felt aggrieved at what they considered a high-handed style of editing. I know this because some were applying to me for jobs at the *Los Angeles Times*. But until Jayson Blair came along, the rumble of discontent remained just that, a low rumble.

When the staff learned that the paper had repeatedly misled its readers, the rumble became something more formidable: an insurrection. The aggrieved party was no longer merely the staff. It was the reader, and that meant the difference between a misdemeanor and a felony. Because the reader had been betrayed, the discontent acquired a moral force so great that it could only be answered by the dismissal of the ranking editors. The Blair scandal was a terrible event, but it also said something very positive about the *Times*, for it demonstrated beyond question the staff's commitment to the reader.

Several years ago, at the *Los Angeles Times*, we too had an insurrection. To outsiders the issue seemed arcane, but to the staff it was starkly obvious. The paper had published a fat edition of its Sunday magazine devoted to the opening of the city's new sports and entertainment arena, called the Staples Center. Unknown to its readers—and to the newsroom staff—the paper had formed a secret partnership with Staples. The agreement was as follows: The newspaper would publish a special edition of the Sunday magazine; the developer would help the newspaper sell ads in it; and the two would split the proceeds. Thus was the independence of the newspaper compromised—and the reader betrayed.

I was not working at the newspaper at the time, but I've heard many accounts of a confrontation in the cafeteria between the staff and the publisher. It was not a civil discussion among respectful colleagues. Several people who told me about it invoked the image of a lynch mob. The Staples episode, too, led to the departure of the newspaper's top brass.

What does all this say about newspaper ethics? It says that certain beliefs are very deeply held. It says that a newspaper's duty to the reader is at the core of those beliefs. And it says that those who transgress against the reader will pay dearly.

The commitment to the reader burns bright at papers large and small. Earlier today, we honored Virginia Gerst with the Payne Award. Working at the *Pioneer Press* in the suburbs of Chicago, she was ordered to publish a favorable review of a restaurant that didn't deserve it. Her publisher, eager to get the restaurant's advertising dollars, insisted. Unwilling to mislead her readers, Virginia Gerst lost her job after twenty-seven years at the paper.

It was never my privilege to know Robert Ruhl, who died in 1967 after years of service in Medford. I am certain, though, that at least part of the reason he is remembered with such respect is that he was, in the end, a servant of the reader.

I suspect, too, that he would look favorably on those who took a stand recently at the *New York Times,* the *Los Angeles Times,* the *Pioneer Press* and other newspapers where the reader had been treated cavalierly.

And he would be vexed, I suspect, by another aspect of today's journalistic landscape.

All across America, there are offices that resemble newsrooms, and in those offices there are people who resemble journalists, but they are not engaged in journalism. It is not journalism because it does not regard the reader—or, in the case of broadcasting, the listener, or the viewer—as a master to be served.

To the contrary, it regards its audience with a cold cynicism. In this realm of pseudo-journalism, the audience is something to be manipulated. And when the audience is misled, no one in the pseudo-newsroom ever offers a peep of protest.

If Mr. Ruhl were here, I feel certain he would not approve.

* * * * * *

Last Halloween, I was stuck in traffic on a freeway in Los Angeles, punching the buttons on the car radio to alleviate the boredom. That's pretty much the way we live in Los Angeles, but I'm not complaining because that night I came across a very interesting program. It was a rebroadcast, 65 years after the fact, of Orson Welles' famous dramatization of *War of the Worlds.*

For those who don't know the story, this radio drama portrayed a Martian invasion so realistically that it prompted hysteria. A study by a professor at Princeton calculated that the program had reached about six million people, of whom 1.2 million panicked, believing that creatures from Mars were actually invading the town of Grover's Mill, New Jersey. Listeners ran out into the streets, jammed police switchboards and gathered in churches to pray for deliverance.

As I listened to the broadcast, it became obvious why people believed the Martians were at hand. It didn't sound like fiction; it sounded like journalism. The actors who described the unfolding events at Grover's Mill had the same stylized cadences and pronunciations as broadcast journalists of the time. Their voices quavered with dread, a sound they had learned by listening to tapes of the Hindenburg airship disaster from the previous year.

This is how the 23-year-old genius Orson Welles learned that journalism can be faked, and that people will react to something that sounds like journalism but isn't.

Some of you may have guessed where I'm going with this anecdote. Yes, we'll [be] talking about Fox News. But not solely Fox News. Rather, I'd like to discuss a broader array of talk shows and web sites that have taken on the trappings of journalism but, when studied closely, are not journalism at all.

Superficial examination might place the modern talk show host within a great tradition of opinion journalists—that of Lippmann, Reston, Murrow, Sevareid and others whose are still held in high regard. They were, foremost, journalists, not entertainers or marketers. Their opinions were rigorously grounded in fact. It was the truthfulness of these commentators—their sheer intellectual honesty— that causes their names to endure.

Today, the credibility painstakingly earned by past journalists lends an unearned legitimacy to the new generation of talk show hosts. Cloaked deceptively in the mantle of journalism, today's opinion-brokers are playing a nasty Halloween prank on the public, and indeed on journalism itself.

* * * * * * *

Let's depart from the generalizations now to hear some eyewitness testimony— my own.

Last fall, my newspaper did something rash. Alone among the news media that covered the California recall election, the *Los Angeles Times* decided to investigate the character of a candidate for governor named Arnold Schwarzenegger. That caused consternation among the talk shows.

The recall campaign lasted only two months, so we had to hurry in determining whether, as rumored, Schwarzenegger had a habit of mistreating women. It turned out that he did. By the time we nailed the story down, the campaign was almost over, and we had a very tough decision to make: whether to publish the findings a mere five days before the election.

We decided to do it, figuring that choice was better than having to explain lamely to our readers after Election Day why we had withheld the story. We braced for an avalanche of criticism, and we got it. What we didn't expect was criticism for things that had never occurred.

Long before we published the story, rumors circulated that we were working on it, and the effort to discredit the newspaper began. On Fox News, the Bill O'Reilly program embarked on a campaign to convince its audience that the *Los Angeles Times* was an unethical outfit that attacked only Republicans and gave Democrats a free ride. As evidence, O'Reilly said that the paper had overlooked Bill Clinton's misbehavior in Arkansas. Where, he asked, was the *L.A. Times* on the so-called Troopergate story? Why hadn't it sent reporters to Arkansas? How could it justify an investigation of Schwarzenegger's misbehavior with women and not Clinton's?

I wasn't employed in Los Angeles at the time of Troopergate, but I do have a computer, so, unlike Fox News, I was able to learn that the *Los Angeles Times* actually was in Arkansas. It sent its best reporters there, and it sent them in force. At one point, it had nine reporters in Little Rock. And when two of them wrote the first Troopergate story to appear in any newspaper, they made the *L.A. Times* the leader on that subject. Not a leader, but the leader. Their story would be cited frequently by as other newspapers tried to catch up.

The bogus Troopergate accusation on Fox was only the beginning.

The worst of it originated with a freelance columnist in Los Angeles, who claimed to have the inside story on unethical behavior at the *Times*. Specifically, she wrote, the paper had completed its Schwarzenegger story long before election day but maliciously held it for two weeks in order to wreak maximum damage.

Now if this were true, I wouldn't be here at the University of Oregon delivering a lecture on ethics. The reporters and editors involved in the story would have given me the same treatment Jayson Blair's editors got in New York. In all likelihood I would no longer be employed.

But it wasn't true. The idea that the newspaper held the story for two weeks was a fabrication. Nothing resembling it ever occurred.

It is instructive to trace the path of this falsehood. Newspapers have always been magnets for crackpots. Hardly a day goes by that we don't get a report of a UFO visit, or a complaint from someone whose head has been rewired by the CIA, or a tortured theory as to why the newspaper did or didn't publish something. I tend to shrug such things off, figuring that nobody would believe them anyway and that it's unseemly for a large newspaper to quarrel with a reader.

But we live in changed times. Never has falsehood in America had such a large megaphone. Instead of being ignored, the author of the column was booked for repeated appearances on O'Reilly, on CNBC, and even on the generally trustworthy CNN. The accusation was echoed throughout the talk-show world. This is how the tale of the two-week delay—as false as any words ever penned by Jayson Blair—earned the columnist not infamy but fame. Millions of Americans heard it and no doubt believed it. And why not? It sounded just like journalism.

* * * * * * *

Let us turn now to a mundane subject: corrections. At the outset, I should state that there are corrections, and then there are corrections.

Recently, my newspaper, in an article about a rapper named Lil' Kim, characterized the MAC-11 as a machine gun. It is actually a submachine gun. This might not mean much here in Eugene, but it's meaningful to music lovers in Los Angeles, so we published a correction. It was an easy correction to make—factual, straightforward and not particularly humiliating to the paper.

Here's an example of a more difficult kind of correction:

In 1979, I became editor of the *Lexington Herald* in Kentucky, and I soon became aware of skeletons in the newspaper's closet. As I got to know the staff, we used to joke that someday, along with the routine corrections on page two, we should run the following item:

A CLARIFICATION

It has come to the editor's attention that the *Herald* neglected to cover the Civil Rights movement. We regret the omission.

We never published that one, though we probably should have made amends in some fashion, for corrections large and small are essential to our credibility.

Like a factory on a river, daily journalism is an industry that produces pollution. Our pollution comes in the form of errors. America's river of public discourse —if I may extend this figure of speech—is polluted by our mistakes. A good newspaper cleans up after itself.

Every fact a newspaper publishes goes into a database. So do the errors. A good newspaper corrects those errors and appends the corrections to the original stories, so that the errors are not repeated. Thus we keep the river clean.

Last year at the *Los Angeles Times*, we published 2,759 corrections. Some of you may be shocked that a newspaper could make so many mistakes. Others may be impressed that the paper is so assiduous in correcting itself.

It has now been six months since Fox and the other talk shows told their audiences that the *Los Angeles Times* did not cover the Troopergate scandal. It has been six months since they accused the newspaper of a journalistic felony by timing its story about Arnold Schwarzenegger. These are simple factual matters, easily provable. Nevertheless I'm getting the feeling that the corrections are not forthcoming.

As editor of the *Los Angeles Times*, I'm not happy about it, but at least I know the truth. The deeper offense is against those who don't—the listeners who credit the "facts" they hear on Fox and the talk shows.

In the larger scheme, these two falsehoods represent two relatively minor discharges of pollution into America's river of public discourse. I suspect there are many others, and on much more consequential subjects—the war in Iraq, for example.

You may be familiar with a study published last October on public misconceptions about the war in Iraq.† One of those misconceptions was that Saddam Hussein's weapons of mass destruction had been found.

Another was that links had been proven between Iraq and Al Qaeda.

A third was that world opinion favored the idea of the U.S. invading Iraq.

Among people who primarily watched Fox News, 80 percent believed one or more of those myths. That's 25 percentage points higher than the figure for viewers of CNN—and 57 percentage points higher than that for people who got their news from public broadcasting.

How could Fox have left its audience so deeply in the dark? I'm inspired to squeeze one last bit of mileage out of our river metaphor: If Fox News were a factory situated, say, in Minneapolis, it would be trailing a plume of rotting fish all the way to New Orleans.

* * * * * * *

If pseudo-journalism is not journalism, what is it? Where did it come from? Will it last?

Some view the difference between the talk shows and traditional journalism in political terms, as a simple quarrel between left and right, between liberal and conservative. Those differences exist, but they're not of great consequence.

What we're seeing is a difference between journalism and pseudo-journalism, between journalism and propaganda. The former seeks earnestly to serve the public. The latter seeks to manipulate it.

The propaganda technique that has invaded journalism is of a particular breed. It springs not from journalistic roots but from modern politics—specifically, that woeful subset known as attack politics.

In attack politics, the idea is to "define" one's rival in the eyes of the public. This means repeating derogatory information so often that the rival's reputation is ruined. Sometimes the information is true; sometimes it is misleading; sometimes it is simply false. A citizen who enters politics these days must face the prospect of being "defined" by smear artists equipped with computers, polls and attack ads.

It is the netherworld of attack politics that gave us Roger Ailes, the architect of Fox News. Having spent much of his career smearing politicians, he now refers to himself as a journalist, but his bag of tricks remains the same.

* * * * * * *

It is consoling to note that demagogues on the airwaves have come and gone ever since commercial broadcasting began. Such figures as Father Coughlin and Senator McCarthy have made their sordid appeals to the angry and the gullible and have been duly swept into the dustbin. Over time, I believe, the public will become increasingly aware of the discrepancy between what they're told by pseudo-journalists and what turns out to be the truth. They may even grow weary of the talk show persona—the schoolyard bully we all know so well.

Recently our newspaper had the good fortune of winning five Pulitzer Prizes. Between us, I'm not sure we're worthy of all that, but we won't turn them down. I wonder how the news of the awards struck the talk-show fans who know the *Los Angeles Times* only for its ethical outrages.

Surely they must have been scratching their heads over that one.

But they probably they didn't worry about it long. My guess is that they sat back on their sofas and consoled themselves with more soothing thoughts, such as the way President Bush saved America from catastrophe by seizing those weapons of mass destruction in Iraq while the whole world cheered.

* * * * * *

Let us conclude by returning to the legacy of Robert Ruhl.

Surely Mr. Ruhl would be vexed by what journalism has become since his departure.

He would feel pained, I suspect, by the scandals in the traditional media. Yet I hope he would also take heart, as I do, from the spontaneous revulsion expressed in the newsrooms where they occurred.

He would be honored that his years in journalism at the *Medford Mail Tribune* are still being invoked on occasions such as this.

He would be pleased, I think, to see this crowd of young people headed forth into the world, equipped with good educations and high ideals.

And he would have hopes for you. He would hope—I feel certain—that you'll take up his calling, the calling of journalism, and find it deeply rewarding. And he would hope, I believe, that you will choose the path of real journalism, not pseudo-journalism, and that you will forever regard the reader—or the listener, or the viewer—as a worthy sovereign who must always be served in good faith.

NOTE

[†]"Misperceptions, the Media, and the Iraq War," published Oct. 2, 2003 by the Program on International Policy Attitudes; Knowledge Networks; the Center for International and Security Studies at Maryland; and the Center on Policy Attitudes.

*John S. Carroll has been editor of the *Los Angeles Times, Baltimore Sun* and *Lexington Herald-Leader.* He was a reporter in Vietnam, the Middle East, and Washington. He was a member of the Pulitzer Prize board for nine years and was its chair in 2003.

John S. Carroll, "The Wolf in Reporter's Clothing: The Rise of Pseudo-Journalism in America" (Ruhl Lecture at University of Oregon, School of Journalism and Communication, Eugene, May 6, 2004).

Used by permission.

DISCUSSION QUESTIONS

1. Will younger readers ever become strong news consumers?
2. Were traditional media adequately prepared to handle the transformative changes brought about by technology?
3. Can traditional media adapt to the changes they face? If so, how?
4. Do satirical programs like *The Daily Show with John Stewart Show* undermine the role of the traditional media?

Part 2:

How New Media Have Impacted Traditional Media

The articles in this section detail not only how new media have changed the news industry and but also how they have affected the traditional practice of journalism. In "Social Media as a First Draft of Journalism and a Rallying Cry for Democracy," Endy M. Bayuni acknowledges that professional journalists are no longer gatekeepers of the news—they now compete for breaking stories against bloggers and citizen journalists. But he sees an important role for professional journalists in evaluating and synthesizing information and presenting it—on a variety of platforms—in a way that is accessible to the public.

Similarly, Turi Munthe, in "How Technology Turned News into a Conversation," details how the professional journalist's role is evolving with the use of Twitter and Facebook. He acknowledges that social media have had a significant effect on journalism, moving news from the front page or television newscast to the Twitter stream or Facebook status update and creating a new and exciting news ecosystem in which even a small voice can break through the babble. In this new world, he sees a different role for amateurs and professionals. Citizen journalists can report breaking stories—essentially supply information. What they cannot do is provide context or tell a meaningful story. That is the role of the professional, who can use the data from the crowd and curate it to determine what is significant.

In "New Media, Old Media: How Blogs and Social Media Agendas Relate and Differ from the Traditional Press," the Pew Research Center's Project for Excellence in Journalism gathered data that demonstrate that traditional media continue to have a large footprint, even in the blogosphere. According to the study, four news organizations—the BBC, CNN, the *New York Times* and the *Washington Post*—are responsible for 80 percent of the stories appearing on blogs. Acknowledging this development, legacy outlets are forming partnerships and sharing content across a variety of platforms from tablets to smart phones and using technological advances to develop new products and services.

Finally, in "How to Save the News," *Atlantic* magazine correspondent James Fallows describes how Google, whose juggernaut search engine, Google News, and highly profitable classified advertising business have had a devastating impact on the newspaper industry, is working with the news industry to bring it back to life. The article details the company's efforts to help hundreds of major and small newspapers, magazines, and broadcast-news organizations, including The Associated Press, the Public Broadcasting System and the *New York Times* find new ways to engage the public and devise new distribution and monetization models. Google and news organizations share the same goal—to keep professional journalism robust, a goal Google considers crucial to its own prospects.

Social Media as a First Draft of Journalism and a Rallying Cry for Democracy

by Endy M. Bayuni*

The Twitter message flashing on the screen of my handset shortly after 7:30 a.m. one Friday in July 2009 was unequivocal: "RT @DanielTumiwa Bom @ marriot and ritz Carlton kuningan jakarta." Someone had re-tweeted a message posted by a man who was inside one of the two adjacent hotels that was bombed that morning. News of the simultaneous blast that killed 14 people was first broken by ordinary citizens with no training in journalism, but with a passion that matched the best.

The bad news for journalists is that in the increasingly wired world, they have lost the virtual monopoly they once enjoyed in disseminating news and information. The good news is that professional journalists have come to rely on the social media to help keep abreast of the very latest news. And even better news is that journalism can improve upon those raw, early reports of social media by scrutinizing them with such traditional journalistic values as accuracy and fairness.

For the next hours that day, Twitterland was buzzing with news of the blasts, courtesy of Daniel Tumiwa and others like him who were tweeting and re-tweeting information in packets of 140 characters or less. Thanks to them, news of the latest deadly terrorist attack in the Indonesian capital was known worldwide, not through the ordinary media like television and radio and not by journalists in the traditional sense of the word. Images and short video clips, admittedly poor quality but uncensored with gory bodies of victims, were soon posted on Twitter and Facebook, the two most popular social media among Indonesians.

Here are some more messages taken from @DanielTumiwa, who must have thumbed them in haste, but they were pretty accurate and descriptive.

- "2 boms go off inside Ritz Carlton and Marriott coffee shops! Not kidding. Am here."
- "Left location. Shocked. Lots of blood. Breakfast meetings at coffee shops while bombs went off."
- "Thanks for all the concern. Back home. Safe. Shocked. Blood...smoke ...glass...everywhere...prayers to the victims...."

It was more than half an hour later before local TV stations, whose crews struggled through the Jakarta morning rush-hour traffic to reach the two bombed hotels, began their live broadcasts from the scene. Prior to this, the stations had put out news flashes, with the protective line "unconfirmed reports" until they were able to verify the news themselves on the ground. Most likely they had picked up the story from the Internet.

There have been many other times since then that Twitter and Facebook became the first media to break important news in Indonesia As far as speed is concerned, and anyone in this business knows that speed is one of the most important elements after accuracy, citizen journalists are beating professional journalists at our own game.

And the public is responding.

With cell phones becoming affordable to most people, and with Internet connection costs coming down dramatically in the past year, more and more Indonesians have come to use social media like Twitter and Facebook as their prime sources of news and information.

Even journalists find them indispensable professional tools.

I learned of the death of Indonesia's former president Abdurrahman Wahid in December 2009 from Twitter only a few minutes after he drew his last breath. The speed was unbeatable. No TV or radio station—you can forget my own newspaper—could have matched the speed with which the news was disseminated, tweeted and re-tweeted, with constant updates by the minute if not by the second.

There are some downsides to this, however. The nation learned about the death of its most famous composer, Gesang, one week before it happened, and also the passing of former first lady Ainun Habibie a few days too early.

Some overzealous Twitterers, wanting to be first to break the news, couldn't resist the temptation and tweeted the news before Gesang and Habibie were dead. Foolishly, some TV stations, caught in the competition of reporting the news first, picked up both false stories and broadcast them.

Credibility should distinguish the work of professionals, who are trained to put accuracy ahead of speed. Mistakes can be fatal to their integrity and to the credibility of the media they work for. The market will punish an organization devalued by its own behavior. For citizen journalists, and some of the people who follow them, speed may come before accuracy.

In this increasingly more wired world, professional journalists have to share the field (and the audience) with amateurs and their values. Each group has its place and its role in keeping the public informed. Anyone with mobile and Internet access can be a journalist, or do the work that journalists do any time they update their Twitter or Facebook accounts, for these are disseminated to a large audience online. Everybody is a journalist.

Citizen journalists in Indonesia have shown that they can be just as effective, if not more so, at influencing public opinion. The wide space that the Internet is providing has been widely used for an open public debate on just about anything in Indonesia as people take advantage of the guarantees of free speech. Sometimes out of these debates, a movement emerges and people rally behind certain causes.

For example, there was a petition that garnered more than one million signatures on Facebook demanding President Susilo Bambang Yudhoyono release two deputies of the anti-corruption commission who were detained by the police as they were investigating high-profile cases. The president responded by setting up an independent team of inquiry, which sure enough, recommended the release of the two deputies two weeks later.

Another Facebook petition demanded the release of a young mother who was arrested by the police after an email she had written to a friend, complaining about the services of a private hospital near Jakarta, was posted in various discussion groups. The Omni International hospital filed libel charges against Prita Mulyasari, who had written the email, and since the crime carries a maximum jail penalty of six years under Indonesia's new cybercrime law, the police were obliged to put her under arrest pending the investigation and trial.

Under strong public pressure from Facebook petitioners, the police released her, but when the civil law trial proceeded, she was found guilty and the court ordered her to pay 300 million rupiah ($30,000) in damages. Facebookers were quick off the mark, and organized a collection nationwide, called Coin for Prita, to help her pay that sum. The response was massive and the organizers raised more than 800 million rupiah. They were about to dump the coins, which had been loaded in trucks, outside the Omni International gate when the hospital decided to waive its claim. The money has since been given to a foundation named after Prita to help poor people seek justice.

There have been many other Face book movements since then, albeit on smaller scales. But in the social media, anyone, poor and rich, powerful and strong, can find their voice. They also find that Facebook, and other platforms like it, can be more effective in airing grievances than taking it to the streets. The next people power movement in Indonesia, if and when the need arises, will be conducted through the 'Net.

In this Internet age, there continues to be a need for the kind of services that professional journalists provide: Gather, collect and sort information, verify, and package it in a way that is easily understandable to the public, using text, sound and still or moving images.

The medium may be different, from print, broadcasting to the digital, but the rules of the game and the ethics that govern the profession are essentially the same. Journalism is one of the oldest professions in the world, and for now at least, it is irreplaceable. With so many more players competing, however, the only way to survive is to improve skills and professionalism, and to practice good journalism.

Democracy is well served to include many more players besides professional journalists. But it is served even better if professional journalists strengthen their role in keeping everyone else in check. The survival of journalism depends on it.

*Endy M. Bayuni is the former editor in chief of the *Jakarta Post*. He also writes columns commenting on Indonesian national politics, political Islam, international affa‰oirs, and the media scene.

Endy M. Bayuni, "Social Media as a First Draft of Journalism and a Rallying Cry for Democracy," in *IPI Report: Brave News Worlds: Navigating the New Media Landscape* (Vienna: International Press Institute, 2010): 68–70, http://www.freemedia.at/fileadmin/media/Images/World_Congress_2010/Brave_News_World_IPI_Poynter.pdf.

How Technology Turned News into a Conversation

by Turi Munthe*

Not even 15 years ago, the only way for a non-professional journalist to join the news debate (apart from being its subject, of course) was to write in to the papers. And in the UK at least, the likelihood of being published in the left-wing press if you weren't a trade-union leader was as slim as being published in the right-wing press if you weren't a Lord. A rare Oxbridge academic might merit a mention, but as an exception rather than the rule. The news was a lecture; op-eds were sermons: journalism was a job for pulpiteers.

Today, news is a conversation:

- Some of the first pictures of the Hudson River plane crash in January 2009 were published via Twitpic by non-journalist Janis Krums.

- With professional journalists jailed or deported during the Iran election in June 2009, the world subsisted for a fortnight on local Twitter updates hash-tagged #iranelection that were circulated over one billion times, as well as through YouTube, opposition leader Mir Hossein Mousavi's Facebook group, and Demotix, which I run.

- Twitter—by which I mean thousands of people's Twitter feeds—broke the Trafigura story. Flickr, back in 2005, was the resource of record for the Kifaya demonstrations In Egypt; Blogger for news of the Israel-Lebanon war in the same year.

Non-journalists, through a combination of the Web and social networks, are breaking, annotating and distributing global news stories in ever increasing ways. Technology has made journalism a conversation between the reporter and the reader (and often the participant). Today, the newspapers' online "letters" pages (also known as the comments stream) on any political article on any major news site on the Web can run into the hundreds, with rarely a Lord or trade-union chief's missive among them.

The role of the non-professional journalist in the news space has changed every aspect of the business. For sourcing, I don't know a single professional reporter who doesn't use social media as a feed, and I know of many who use it as an encyclopedia. When the MPs expenses scandal broke in the UK, the Guardian dropped the nearly half-million documents into a public widget that about 23,000 citizens across the country downloaded and helped dissect.

In story-telling, the advantages of immediate reporter/reader interaction have created a whole new journalistic form in the liveblog which reports, corrects and verifies as it publishes in direct communication with its readers, all in real-time.

But it is in distribution that 'people power' really flexes its muscles. It is no longer exclusively editors who choose what goes on the front page anymore—it is you. The unbundling of news on the Web—whereby you can get your cricket news from Pakistan's Dawn.com, your business news from London's Financial Times and your general info from CNN.com—essentially means that whatever is most popular amongst your friends on Facebook, or most tweeted amongst those you follow on Twitter, or most Digged, StumbledUpon or Reddited will be your front page of the day.

It's no surprise then, given the wash of information available (and its endless repetition, distortion and misattribution), that the top-hit news sources on the Web continue to be the mainstream news outlets. Trust is a major factor, but so is that critical journalistic function: editing. Not just in the packaging of what is told, but in choosing what counts as news.

We read the news not just to keep informed, but to be part of a conversation—regional, national, communitarian—about it. The news around us helps us define our relationship to the world, and to those also engaged in defining themselves. Newspapers and broadcasters create communities: just ask CNN viewers what they think about Fox News viewers.

But more than building communities of interest, old-fashioned journalism also speaks to an understanding of what news is that 'citizen journalism' cannot, because most news of real interest is built painstakingly and over time. Most news is, in fact, a story.

The kind of news that can be crowdsourced is bitty, image-led, or data-driven: Vide the examples above—pictures of surprise events like 9/11 or the tsunami, accidental reporting of the Mayhill Flower variety (who caught Obama referring to disenfranchised Pennsylvanians who "cling to guns or religion"), or the kind of (fantastic) work being done by a host of opendata outfits like Ushahidi, WIkiLeaks or the Open Knowledge Network. What it can't do is tell meaningful, full-length stories about that information, nor, critically, can it do possibly the most important form of news reporting on its own—that is, investigative journalism.

The trouble is, increasingly, neither can mainstream news. Although a handful of US news organizations still maintain robust foreign news operations, the once mighty foreign staff of the Baltimore Sun has been eliminated and the consolidation of Tribune Co. staffing overseas has trimmed those ranks as well.

The latest State of the News Media report found that US newsrooms lost 25 percent of their staffers over the last three years. Professional journalism has suffered not just in foreign reporting, but in domestic reporting and investigative journalism (which is increasingly the bailiwick of the nonprofit sector, see ProPublica and, in the UK, the Bureau for Investigative Journalism).

If old-fashioned news reporting has been brutally attacked by the Web's free-content-for-all business-model dictat, it has to look to the Web (and to its highly-informed, entrepreneurial reader-cum-activist-cum-contributors) for some of its salvation. Yesterday's sub-editor is today's commenter (get a fact wrong in an article online and you're a global laughing stock). Yesterday's roving foreign correspondent is today an army of local bloggers and local stringers.

Citizen journalists, amateur photographers and others willing to join the news conversation, or supply their content for free are often blamed for the ever-more harried (and underfunded) lot of the professional journalist. They shouldn't be. If anything is to blame for that, it is the wholesale departure of the classifieds market to independent sites like Craigslist, Facebook, et al, and the massively smaller ad revenues of the Web that no newspaper site has been able to marshal into a functioning business model. Citizen journalists, which today broadly means anyone with an Internet connection and an interest in the news, are part of the solution, not the problem. And while, of course, only a tiny fraction of Web surfers engage with real news, their engagement with the news has incomparably augmented the conversation, and expanded its reach.

As news organizations, professional journalists and geeks figure out new and more efficient ways to harness the power of millions of engaged voices and opinions on the Web, the quality of global news and reporting and information will explode. And that will only accelerate once the media moghuls figure out how to fix their business models.

Spare a thought for them, not for journalism as we know it.

*__Turi Munthe__ is the founder of Demotix, the multiple-award winning open newswire, with more than 3,000 reporters in 190 countries around the world.

Turi Munthe, "How Technology Turned News into a Conversation," in *IPI Report: Brave News Worlds: Navigating the New Media Landscape* (Vienna: International Press Institute): 15–17, http://www.freemedia.at/fileadmin/media/Images/World_Congress_2010/Brave_News_World_IPI_Poynter.pdf.

Used by permission.

New Media, Old Media: How Blogs and Social Media Agendas Relate and Differ from the Traditional Press

by Pew Research Center, Project for Excellence in Journalism*

News today is increasingly a shared, social experience. Half of Americans say they rely on the people around them to find out at least some of the news they need to know.[1] Some 44% of online news users get news at least a few times a week through emails, automatic updates or posts from social networking sites. In 2009, Twitter's monthly audience increased by 200%.[2]

While most original reporting still comes from traditional journalists, technology makes it increasingly possible for the actions of citizens to influence a story's total impact.

What types of news stories do consumers share and discuss the most? What issues do they have less interest in? What is the interplay of the various new media platforms? And how do their agendas compare with that of the mainstream press?

To answer these questions, the Pew Research Center's Project for Excellence in Journalism has gathered a year of data on the top news stories discussed and linked to on blogs and social media pages and seven months' worth on Twitter. We also have analyzed a year of the most viewed news-related videos on YouTube. Several clear trends emerge.

Most broadly, the stories and issues that gain traction in social media differ substantially from those that lead in the mainstream press. But they also differ greatly from each other. Of the 29 weeks that we tracked all three social platforms, blogs, Twitter and YouTube shared the same top story just once. That was the week of June 15–19, when the protests that followed the Iranian elections led on all three.

Each social media platform also seems to have its own personality and function. In the year studied, bloggers gravitated toward stories that elicited emotion, concerned individual or group rights or triggered ideological passion. Often these were stories that people could personalize and then share in the social forum—at times in highly partisan language. And unlike in some other types of media, the partisanship here does not lean strongly to one side or the other. Even on stories like the Tea Party protests, Sarah Palin and public support for Obama both conservative and liberal voices come through strongly.

News Topics Across Media Platforms
January 19, 2009–January 15, 2010*

	Blogs (% of stories)	Twitter (% of stories)	YouTube (% of videos)	Traditional Press (% of newshole)
Politics/Government	17	6	21	15
Foreign Events (non-U.S.)	12	13	26	9
Economy	7	1	1	10
Technology	8	43	1	1
Health and Medicine	7	4	6	11

*Twitter was tracked from June 15, 2009–January 15, 2010

On Twitter, by contrast, technology is a major focus—with a heavy prominence on Twitter itself—while politics plays a much smaller role. The mission is primarily about passing along important—often breaking—information in a way that unifies or assumes shared values within the Twitter community. And the breaking news that trumped all else across Twitter in 2009 focused on the protests following the Iranian election. It led as the top news story on Twitter for seven weeks in a row—a feat not reached by any other news story on any of the platforms studied.

YouTube has still other characteristics that set it apart. Here, users don't often add comments or additional insights but instead take part by selecting from millions of videos and sharing. Partly as a result, the most watched videos have a strong sense of serendipity. They pique interest and curiosity with a strong visual appeal. The "Hey you've got to see this," mentality rings strong. Users also gravitate toward a much broader international mix here as videos transcend language barriers in a way that written text cannot.

Across all three social platforms, though, attention spans are brief. Just as news consumers don't stay long on any website, social media doesn't stay long on any one story. On blogs, 53% of the lead stories in a given week stay on the list no more than three days. On Twitter that is true of 72% of lead stories, and more than half (52%) are on the list for just 24 hours.

And most of those top weekly stories differ dramatically from what is receiving attention in the traditional press. Blogs overlap more than Twitter, but even there only about a quarter of the top stories in any given week were the same as in the "MSM."

Instead, social media tend to hone in on stories that get much less attention in the mainstream press. And there is little evidence, at least at this point, of the traditional press then picking up on those stories in response. Across the entire year studied, just one particular story or event—the controversy over emails relating to global research that came to be known as "Climate-gate"—became a major item in the blogosphere and then, a week later, gaining more traction in traditional media.

These are some conclusions drawn from one of the first comprehensive empirical assessments of the relationships between social media and the more traditional press.

The study examined the blogosphere and social media by tracking the news linked to on millions of blogs and social media pages tracked by Icerocket and Technorati from January 19, 2009, through January 15, 2010.[3] It also tracked the videos on YouTube's news channel for the same period. It measured Twitter by tracking news stories linked to within tweets as monitored by Tweetmeme from June 15, 2009, through January 15, 2010.[4]

AMONG THE SPECIFIC FINDINGS:

- Social media and the mainstream press clearly embrace different agendas. Blogs shared the same lead story with traditional media in just 13 of the 49 weeks studied. Twitter was even less likely to share the traditional media agenda—the lead story matched that of the mainstream press in just four weeks of the 29 weeks studied. On YouTube, the top stories overlapped with traditional media eight out of 49 weeks.

- The stories that gain traction in social media do so quickly, often within hours of initial reports, and leave quickly as well. Just 5% of the top five stories on Twitter remained among the top stories the following week. This was true of 13% of the top stories on blogs and 9% on YouTube. In the mainstream press, on the other hand, fully 50% of the top five stories one week remained a top story a week later.

- Politics, so much a focus of cable and radio talk programming, has found a place in blogs and on YouTube. On blogs, 17% of the top five linked-to stories in a given week were about U.S. government or politics, often accompanied by emphatic personal analysis or evaluations. These topics were even more prevalent among news videos on YouTube, where they accounted for 21% of all top stories. On Twitter, however, technology stories were linked to far more than anything else, accounting for 43% of the top five stories in a given week and 41% of the lead items. By contrast, technology filled 1% of the newshole in the mainstream press during the same period.

- While social media players espouse a different agenda than the mainstream media, blogs still heavily rely on the traditional press—and primarily just a few outlets within that—for their information. More than 99% of the stories linked to in blogs came from legacy outlets such as newspapers and broadcast networks. And just four—the BBC, CNN, the New York Times and the Washington Post accounted for fully 80% of all links.

- Twitter, by contrast, was less tied to traditional media. Here half (50%) of the links were to legacy outlets; 40% went to web-only news sources such as Mashable and CNET. The remaining 10% went to wire stories or non-news sources on the Web such as a blog known as "Green Briefs," which summarized daily developments during the June protests in Iran.

- The most popular news videos on YouTube, meanwhile, stood out for having a broader international mix. A quarter, 26%, of the top watched news videos were of non-U.S. events, primarily those with a strong visual appeal such as raw footage of Pope Benedict XVI getting knocked over during Mass on Christmas Eve or a clip of a veteran Brazilian news anchor getting caught insulting some janitors without realizing his microphone was still live. Celebrity and media-focused videos were also given significant prominence.

In producing PEJ's New Media Index, the basis for this study, there are some challenges posed by the breath of potential outlets. There are literally millions of blogs and tweets produced each day. To make that prospect manageable, the study observes the "news" interests of those people utilizing social media, as classified by the tracking websites. PEJ did not make a determination as to what constitutes a news story as opposed to some other topic, but generally, areas outside the traditional notion of news such as gardening, sports or other hobbies are not in the purview of content.

By focusing on this type of subject matter, the study creates a close comparison between the news agenda of users of social media and of the more traditional news media. This approach could tend to make the agendas of the mainstream and new media platforms appear even more similar than they would be if a wider array of subject matter were practicable to capture. Thus the divergent agendas found here, if anything, are even more striking.

THE BLOGOSPHERE

Of the three social media platforms studied, news-oriented blogs share the most similarities with the mainstream press. Bloggers almost always link to legacy outlets for their information, and politics, government and foreign events garnered the greatest traction.

There are, however, also some clear differences. While the biggest topic areas overlap, there was considerable divergence in the specific news events that garnered attention. In less than one third of the weeks did the blogosphere and traditional press share the same top story. Bloggers tend to gravitate toward events that affect personal rights and cultural norms—issues like same-sex marriage, the rationing of health care or privacy settings on Facebook, while traditional media news agendas are more event-driven and institutional.

And a strong sense of purpose often accompanies the links in blogs and social networking media. In many cases, it is voicing strongly held and often divisive opinions. After the botched terror attack on Northwest Airlines Flight 253 on Christmas Day, for instance, a number of conservative bloggers immediately blamed Obama, while others claimed that the fear of terrorism had become larger and more irrational than it should be.

In others, the function was more to share personal connections to events or to take action.

"I'm not one to buy into mass hysteria, but I am AFRAID of this swine flu," admitted blogger mooneyshine the week that the H1N1 virus threatened to become a global pandemic. "I ain't landing in the hospital with no pig virus. Suddenly Piglet is not so cute anymore."

Alongside these more heated discussions, bloggers also enjoy sharing and commenting on unusual or off-beat findings and events buried deep in other media coverage.

Topics

In the broadest sense, the top news agenda in the blogosphere coincides with that of the traditional press; politics and foreign events are the topic areas linked to most often. The next most popular subject areas, however, tend to differ; science stories—often off-beat findings—were the No. 3 subject area in blogs and social media pages, followed by technology related news. (Those topics are much less popular in the traditional press).

In 2009, bloggers, like the mainstream media, were caught up in assessing the first year of the Obama administration. Fully 17% of the top five stories each week related to **U.S. politics and government affairs**, particularly the new president. This is similar to the level of attention in the mainstream press

Topics of News Coverage: Blogs vs. the Traditional Press
January 19, 2009–January 15, 2010

	Blogs (% of stories)	Traditional Press (% of newshole)
Politics/Government	17	15
Foreign Events (non-U.S.)	12	9
Science	10	1
Technology	8	1
Health and Medicine	7	11
Celebrity	7	2
Economy	7	10
Terrorism	6	4
Crime	6	6
Environment (including Global Warming)	4	2
Pop Culture	3	1
Oddball	3	<1
Gay issues	2	<1
Consumer News	2	<1
Education	2	1
Media	2	2
Religion	1	<1
Immigration	<1	<1
Race/Gender Relations	<1	1
Disasters/Accidents	<1	2

(15% of the newshole during that same period, according to PEJ's News Coverage Index).

The discussion accompanying the links in the blogosphere is quite different, however. Partisanship is strong, but unlike talk radio, the conversation here tends to draw a fairly even mix of conservative and liberal voices. The Tea Party protests, Sarah Palin and Obama's poll numbers, for example, all drew a wide mix of conservative and liberal commentary.

In February, as Congress debated the economic stimulus package, for instance, bloggers clashed over the list of programs included in the bill.

Conservative bloggers scorched the bill as being full of wasteful programs that lacked any economic benefits. "Take a look at some of the absolute garbage the Democrats are filling this bill with," the conservative blog East Coast Mark charged.

"Everything on the Republican list of 'wasteful projects' is stimulative," countered Gregg Carlstrom on Fedline. "$88 million for a new Coast Guard icebreaker? Someone is getting paid to build the ship."

Often bloggers make the issues and events highly personal. Linking to an interactive feature on the New York Times website that compared every presidential inaugural address since 1789, Elisha Blaha shared, "This is what I will tell my kids . . . I will tell them that I clapped my hands and stood on the couch as President Obama walked out on to the stage to cheers. I will tell them that I was gitty with excitement and so proud of the confident man who now represents my country."[5]

The second-biggest subject on blogs in the year was **foreign events**. Fully 12% of the top stories in blogs dealt with international events ranging from the protests in Iran to a vote on the number one song on the Christmas British pop charts. Access on the Web to overseas news outlets like to the BBC and the Guardian as well as prominent British bloggers buoys this tendency.

As with much of the domestic news agenda, many of the foreign event stories that inspired blogger interest received far less attention in the traditional American press, even if the stories linked to were originally found there.

A comment by a judge in Saudi Arabia that it was acceptable for husbands to slap wives who spend too lavishly, for example, was the second-biggest story one week in May, drawing large amounts of criticism in the blogosphere. It received almost no attention in the mainstream press.

"Isn't it ironic that a woman can be punished for spending too much money on a garment that they are forced to wear to authenticate their status as secondary citizens in a patriarchal society," remarked Womanist Musings.

Other popular topics often took on a less serious, or at least less divisive, tenor.

Science (at 10% of the top stories) was the third-largest topic on blogs and social media pages. That compares with just 1% of the newshole in the mainstream press, the No. 23 subject. Much of the interest here was in off-beat scientific findings, such as the research at the University of Sussex that showed cats have learned to manipulate their owners' emotions by emitting a specific kind of purr, the discovery of a new kind of large rat in Papa New Guinea, news that a chemical found in blue M&Ms might have therapeutic qualities, and the discovery of a meat-eating plant in the Philippines.

Technology (8%) was less of a draw in blogs and social media than on Twitter (where it accounted for 43% of all links), but it still outpaced the mainstream press (1%). The technology stories that attracted the most attention were often those about problems or dangers. News about an email phishing scam that compromised at least 30,000 email passwords around the world, for example, accounted for 45% of the links one week in October as bloggers spread warnings about how to prevent becoming a victim.

There was often a personal tone here, suggesting a sense of highly engaged citizens talking to each other. "It obviously bears repeating; NEVER give out your username and/or password to anyone. Ever. Not by phone, email, snail mail or in person," warned the Enertiahost Blog. "Legitimate companies will never solicit you for your personal information..."

Sprinkled in were stories of general technical interest: The unveiling of new gadgets such as a new version of the Kindle, an interview with the founders of Twitter, and the experiences of a 13-year-old British boy who used an old-fashioned Sony Walkman for a week to help mark the 30th anniversary of portable music technology, for instance, are examples of the kind of stories that attracted significant attention.

Bloggers also showed a propensity to want to pay respect to **celebrity figures** that passed away, and in many cases these were lesser-known celebrities such as TV pitchman Billy Mays and comedian Dom DeLuise. Most of the time, the attention to celebrity deaths was intense and fleeting.

Of the 17 times (7% of all stories) that a celebrity-focused story made the top five stories for blogs in a specific week, 12 of them (71%) involved a death. And that does not include the two additional weeks where new information following the death of pop icon Michael Jackson earned one of the top spots.

The environment (4%), and most specifically the issue of global warming, was also a topic of conversation more often in the blogosphere and in social media pages than in the mainstream press (2%). The passion here was strong enough that stories about global warming made the roster of top five stories in eight different weeks.

Much of this attention was on the so-called "climate-gate" scandal that took the blogosphere by storm in December after hacked emails from a British research unit raised the possibility of climate data manipulation. This discussion was led by voices like that of Teófilo de Jesús at Vivificat who call the science behind global warming "a fallacy."

Bloggers also demonstrated over the year a tendency to weigh in heavily on stories involving **changes in society**, ranging from the relatively trivial to hot-button cultural issues. These linked-to stories cut across topic areas with an emphasis on adding their voices to conversations that might otherwise be outside their purview.

Social media circles strongly rejected revised privacy settings on Facebook, for instance, campaigned against changes to the design of Tropicana's orange juice container and objected to content fees for streaming music online. On five separate occasions (2% of the top stories), bloggers repeatedly voiced strong support for the right to gay marriage. Those conversations were often spurred by state legislation or proposals that received minimum attention in the national press.

Sources

Despite the unconventional agenda of bloggers, traditional media still provides the vast majority of their information. More than 99% of the stories linked to came from legacy outlets like newspapers and broadcast networks. American legacy outlets made up 75% of all items.[6]

Web-only sites, on the other hand, made up less than 1% of the links in the blogosphere.

BBC News led the list of individual sources, constituting 23% of the links studied.

The next three largest sites were the traditional American media outlets of CNN.com (21%), the New York Times (20%), and the Washington Post (16%).

Just one other news site based outside of the U.S., The Guardian, received even 1% of the links.

Producers of Most Linked-to Stories from Blogs

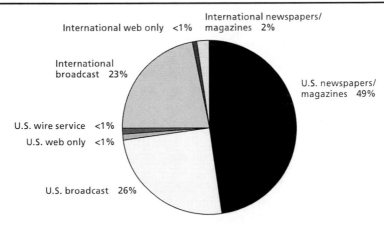

International web only <1%
International newspapers/ magazines 2%
International broadcast 23%
U.S. newspapers/ magazines 49%
U.S. wire service <1%
U.S. web only <1%
U.S. broadcast 26%

Topics of Linked-to Stories from BBC

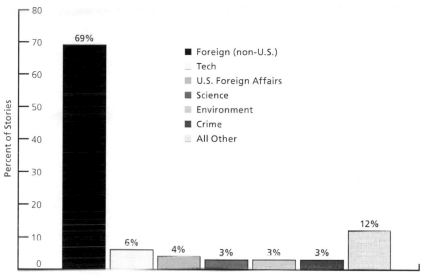

Topic of Linked-to Stories (n=373)

Topics of Linked-to Stories from CNN

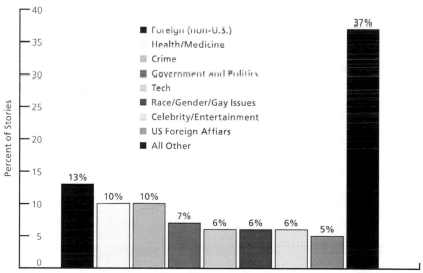

Topic of Linked-to Stories (n=349)

Topics of Linked-to Stories from the Washington Post

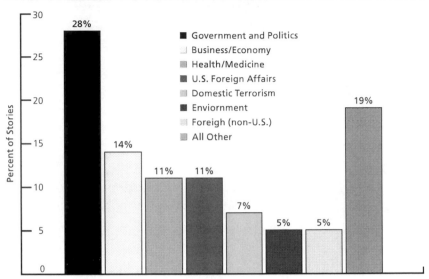

Topic of Linked-to Stories (n=263)

Topics of Linked-to Stories from the New York Post

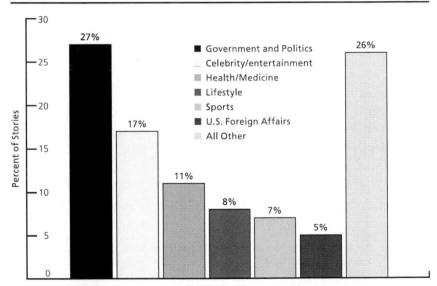

Topic of Linked-to Stories (n=93)

Topics of Linked-to Stories from Fox News

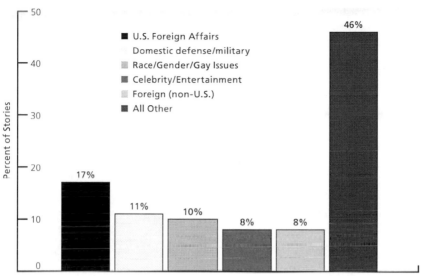

Topic of Linked-to Stories (n=72)

Legend:
- U.S. Foreign Affairs
- Domestic defense/military
- Race/Gender/Gay Issues
- Celebrity/Entertainment
- Foreign (non-U.S.)
- All Other

Values: 17%, 11%, 10%, 8%, 8%, 46%

Topics of Linked-to Stories from The New York Times

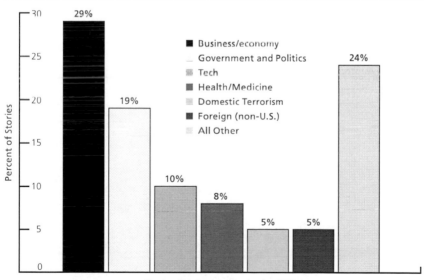

Topic of Linked-to Stories (n=319)

Legend:
- Business/economy
- Government and Politics
- Tech
- Health/Medicine
- Domestic Terrorism
- Foreign (non-U.S.)
- All Other

Values: 29%, 19%, 10%, 8%, 5%, 5%, 24%

Bloggers also tended to refer to different outlets for different topics. Newspapers were frequently the sources for stories about politics and government. Fully 44% of the stories linked to from USA Today were on those topics, 34% for the Los Angeles Times, 28% for the Washington Post and 19% for the New York Times.

The New York Times was more often linked to for business and economics news (28% of its links). Another 10% related to technology, while two other popular newspapers, the Washington Post and the Los Angeles Times, had no technology-focused stories in their mix.

CNN.com was a source for international news (13%), health news (10%) and crime news (10%), while only 7% of CNN's stories were focused on politics or government.

For celebrity news, the New York Post, the tabloid owned by Rupert Murdoch, was a major source, as 17% of the links directed toward its stories were on that subject—more than any other outlet.

And Fox News was the sole source for domestic defense and military news links, accounting 11% of all Fox News links and 100% of all U.S. defense stories.

For the most part, bloggers linked to news accounts rather than editorials or op-eds. Fully 87% of the stories linked to were straight news accounts, compared with only 13% that were opinion columns.

Most of the opinion columns came from the Washington Post (28% of all Washington Post linked to stories) and the New York Times (26%). Those two papers accounted for 73% of all of the opinion columns that bloggers linked to.

Format of Linked-to Stories from Blogs

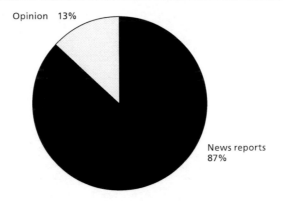

Opinion 13%

News reports 87%

For example, the No. 1 story the first week of September was a Washington Post op-ed where columnist George Will advocated for a pullout from Afghanistan. It was an opinion by a prominent conservative that sparked conversation in the blogosphere rather than reporting on new events or facts.

Other sites, however, were linked to primarily as sources for straight news accounts. Almost all (97%) of the stories linked to on CNN and the BBC (96%) were news reporting.

The majority of links bloggers examined were also text-based stories as opposed to interactive pages with multimedia components such as video, slide shows or interactive charts. Fully 83% of the links were to stories that were text-based stories compared with 17% of stories that were multimedia based.

TWITTER

The social networking site Twitter, which allows its users to share messages of up to 140 characters, has a very different feel and function than blogs, the study found. First, the subject matter was different. Consumers using Twitter focused far more on technology and Web issues than anything else. There were some instances of using the medium to promote activism and involvement, but they tended to be episodic and to some extent, special circumstances. Two cases involved the protests in Iran and the earthquake in Haiti, both instances where Web infrastructure was blocked or damaged. Far more often, tweets served a more immediate need: sharing breaking information. The traffic about news on Twitter also tended to stray more from traditional media for its content, relying more than blogs on online-only specialty sites.

The environment on Twitter was less overtly political than blogs. Instead, it tended to espouse a more inclusive tone of community, a sense of its users being advocates for one another other and for the Twitter platform itself. Twitters came down hard, for example, on a Scottish psychologist who suggested that the use of Twitter actually made people dumber, and they celebrated the posting of the five billionth tweet.

"Woo hoo! I account for 4.0×10^{-7} percent of all tweets in the world!" exclaimed user Giorgianni.

Topics

More so than any other subject area, Twitter users were consumed with stories about technology. Fully 43% of the stories that made the list of top five in a

Topics of News Coverage on Twitter
January 19, 2009–January 15, 2010

	Twitter (% of stories)
Technology	43
Foreign Events (non-U.S.)	13
Politics/Government	6
Crime	5
Celebrity	5
Science	5
Health and Medicine	4
Environment (including Global Warming)	4
Pop Culture	3
Oddball	3
Race/Gender Relations	2
Disasters/Accidents	2
Terrorism	1
Consumer News	1
Economy	1
Media	1
Sports	1
Weather	1
Other	1

given week were technology-based, more than three times as many as the next largest topic.

Most of the tech stories focused on web-related topics, with a heavy emphasis on Twitter, Apple and Facebook. On 13 occasions (making up 9% of the stories and 21% of the technology stories), Twitter made the list of top stories, more than any other specific subject matter.

Whether it was a new tool for tracking recent posts or the problems associated with Twitter's new "retweet" feature offered in November, Twitter users clearly saw a shared mission in advancing this social media platform.

Other technological developments to spark interest and sharing on Twitter were Apple products like the iPhone and the iPad, which made up 7% of all top stories. Stories about Facebook, such as the addition of new functions, accounted for another 7%; Developments involving Microsoft, such as the release of Windows 7, constituted another 4%; news about Google, including an outage of their email service, gmail, filled 4%.

Some areas earned less attention on Twitter than on blogs, such as politics (6% on Twitter versus 17% on blogs) and science (5% versus 10%). The two platforms devoted about the same degree of interest to environment (4% for both Twitter and blogs).

Whatever the topic, the vast majority of tweets that linked to news stories were not using Twitter to report or opine as much as to alert people to other content. Most tweets simply repeated the headline of the story (perhaps with a few words describing its contents) and provided a link. For example, following a two-hour outage of the site in August due to a denial-of-service attack, many Twitterers repeated the tweet first provided by actress Alyssa Milano, who linked to a CNN story explaining the cause. The message used by hundreds was simply, "CNN full story of DDoS attack and what DDoS means: http://bit.ly/StWZB."

In short, most of the time, Twitter was about sharing information rather than providing opinion or advocacy.

There was one major storyline, though, where the role of Twitter went much farther.

The Election and Protest in Iran

The role Twitter played in the post-election political protests in Iran in June amounted to something of a milestone in new technology in 2009 — so much so that some dubbed the event the "Twitter Revolution."

While Twitter was used widely within Iran to get out information about unfolding events, it also was used heavily by people outside the country to build support for the protestors and to highlight events. Much of what was captured in this index came from this second category and alone accounted for nearly half of all foreign event storylines. Overall, foreign events were the second-biggest topic on Twitter, with 13% of the links.

Iran proved to be the top story seven weeks in a row, raising the profile and repu-tation of Twitter. As the Iranian government tried to crack down on the popular uprising, Twitter posts served as a critical information source for people directly involved, enabling participation and activism in much the way satellite dishes and video tapes once did in the former satellite countries of the Soviet Union.

Among the most popular links in Iranian-related posts was a page entitled "cyberwar guide for beginners." It explained how users could help, or accidentally harm, the protest efforts online by spreading the word about those tweeting from within the country without revealing too much information about their identities. Others posted links to a Flickr page that scrolled through images of the protests and encouraged people to change their avatars to the color green as a show of solidarity with the protestors.

Twitter's own research also spoke to the dominance of Iran on the social networking site in 2009. According to Twitter's own blog, a review of all keywords, hashtags and phrases that proliferated on the site (not just those associated with news stories) showed that Iran was the "most engaging topic of the year." Three related terms, "#iranelection," "Iran" and "Tehran" were all in the top 21 trending topics.

In early 2010, Twitter emerged as a vehicle for online activism in another major foreign event—the earthquake in Haiti. Thousands of Twitterers used their 140 characters to promote the option to text the word "Haiti" to 90999 in order to donate $10 to the Red Cross relief effort. With the added endorsements of the White House blog and Secretary of State Hillary Clinton, the Red Cross reported that the phone messaging campaign raised $8 million within three days.

Sources

Contrary to blogs, Twitter users linked much less to traditional news sources and were more likely to use web-only news sources. Half (50%) of stories linked to from Twitter were to legacy outlets (30% to American legacy media), while 40% went to web-only sites such as Mashable and CNET. Part of this had to do with the subject matter, as these web-only sites are often leading sources for news about social media and other Internet topics.[7]

Non-U.S. sites accounted for a similar degree of the content here as on blogs (22%), though less dominated by the BBC, which received only 12% of the overall links.

Instead, the news outlet that received the most links from Twitter (19%) was CNET, an online portal that focuses on technology news and product reviews. The majority of CNET stories (61%) were technology-focused, while 23% were about business issues.

The second most linked to site was CNN.com at 17%. That site was the source of a diverse range of issues, as 18% of CNN's articles were about foreign events, 12% were about crime, and 10% each were about health issues and U.S. foreign relations.

Producers of Most Linked-to Stories on Twitter

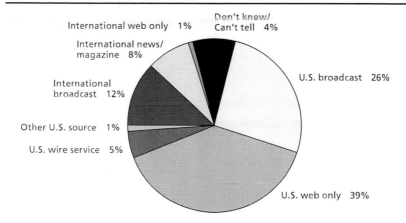

International web only 1%
Don't know/ Can't tell 4%
International news/ magazine 8%
International broadcast 12%
Other U.S. source 1%
U.S. wire service 5%
U.S. broadcast 26%
U.S. web only 39%

The next two most linked to sites were also legacy media sites. BBC News received 12% of the links from Tweets, and Fox News received 7%. Wired, a technology-focused magazine was fifth with 6%.

Tweets primarily linked to straight news accounts instead of opinion pieces, although to a slightly lesser extent than on blogs. On Twitter, 82% of the links went to news reporting, while 18% went to opinionated columns or stories.

The higher tech orientation of Twitter users also came through in the stories they linked to, with a greater tendency toward multimedia stories (almost one-fifth of the links). For example, on June 23, more than 500 tweets linked to a page that was primarily a photo collection produced by Boston.com of vivid images from the Iranian protests.

YouTube

On the video sharing site YouTube, the priorities are not as much the most important or pressing topic of the week, but rather what image or video was the most interesting to view. Often these came in the form of political gaffes or humorous acts captured on camera. And the geographic mix here was strongest with many videos from foreign lands.

The style of citizen participation differs as well. While there is a place for people to comment on a clip they are viewing, most do not. Instead, their involvement comes in selecting among all the millions of videos available and then sometimes sharing that choice with others. There does not need to be as much personal attachment to activities here. Partly as a result, clicks do not convey the same sense of public endorsement as in other types of social media.

This less personal quality may be part of YouTube's appeal. The total number of people viewing popular clips is far greater than the number of people who tend to link to and comment on news stories. Top news videos are often viewed millions of times in one week. For example, the October CNN interview with the "balloon boy" family was viewed more than 2.5 million times that week.[8] Popular stories in the blogosphere, on the other hand, garner somewhere around 300 to 500 links in a week. But they do not tend to stay popular any longer. Just 9% of these videos remained at the top for more than one week, versus 5% of top stories on Twitter and 13% on blogs.[9]

Topics

Like both Twitter and blogs, the news agenda on YouTube rarely coincided with that of the mainstream press. In only eight of the 49 weeks studied was the top video about the same subject that also led the traditional media. Of those eight occasions, three of them involved footage of discussing the health care reform bill (often with contentious opposition), and two of them were videos about the protests in Iran.

So if the most watched videos of the day are not similar to what is in the mainstream press, what news events are people choosing to view?

The answer is that most of the top videos have a visual and dynamic quality that makes people want to share them with other people.

In some instances, that quality can be of a politician's or celebrity's gaffe. For example, the week of August 10, during the heat of the town hall protests involving health care reform, the most viewed video was of Rep. Sheila Jackson Lee appearing rather callous by answering her cell phone while a constituent was sharing a personal story.

A number of the most popular videos are of a humorous nature. In March, for instance, the top video was of an unidentified city council meeting that was interrupted by the sounds of flatulence.

And many of the most watched videos are of things that are too good, or too bad, to be believed. The performance of British singing sensation Susan Boyle on the television show Britain's Got Talent was the most popular video one week in June and was estimated to have been viewed more than 100 million times in less than one month.

Topics of the Most Viewed News Videos on YouTube
January 19, 2009–January 15, 2010

	YouTube (% of videos)
Foreign Events (non-U.S.)	26
Government	20
Entertainment	8
Media	7
Health and Medicine	6
Accidents/Disasters	5
Other Domestic Affairs	4
U.S. Miscellaneous	4
Lifestyle	3
Crime	3
U.S. Foreign Affairs	2
Education	2
Sports	2
Race/Gender/Gay Issues	2
Politics and Campaigns	1
Economy	1
Environment	1
Science and Technology	1
Domestic Terrorism	<1
Business	<1
Transportation	<1

On the flip side, a surveillance tape of a drunk New York State bus driver endangering students was the most viewed in January 2010.

Other times, the leading videos were related to the popular subjects of the week. In January 2009, the most viewed clip was Obama's inaugural address while the second video was raw footage of the US Airlines plane that safely landed in the Hudson River without incurring any significant injuries.

Overseas issues gained the most attention among YouTube videos, something that reflects the international reach of the site. The second most view subject was President Obama.

More than a quarter (26%) of the top five most watched news videos in a given week were about things that happened overseas. Many of them were in foreign languages and were about issues that received virtually no attention in the American press or elsewhere in English-language social media.

For the week of May 4–8, for example, the four most viewed videos were of a crash at a Queen's Day parade in the Netherlands. The videos were all in Dutch and showed dramatic footage of the crash that occurred when a man tried to attack the Dutch royal family with his car and instead struck a crowd watching the parade.

Other non-U.S. events also gained viewers because they made for great video more than any other reason. For instance, the top video the week of November 2-6 was from a British news station and showed a video of a drunk fork lift driver in Russia who drove into a warehouse and the shelves that came crashing down on him.

After international events, the next largest subject on YouTube was government with 20%. More than half of those (11%) involved President Obama or his administration in some capacity, such as in early December when the top video was of White House Press Secretary Robert Gibbs getting into a feisty exchange with a reporter whom he compared to his young son. In a week in late January, two of the top videos featured Obama himself. The first clip was his weekly video address, and the fourth most watched clip was of his first interview with the Arab television station Al-Arabiya.

Videos featuring celebrities also made frequent appearances on the YouTube list, with 8%. For the week of July 6–10, for instance, all five of the top videos involved the death of music icon Michael Jackson. Two of those videos came from the eulogy service held in Jackson's honor. Even though Jackson was not on a major subject that week elsewhere on social media, the dramatic moments broadcast originally on television and archived online made it a dominating YouTube subject.

Sources

One of the unique aspects of YouTube is the ability of users to view raw footage that is not edited or posted by a news organization. Many of the most viewed news videos on YouTube are of this nature.

For example, for two consecutive weeks in September, the most viewed video was a first-person clip from a demonstration in Pittsburgh surrounding the G20 summit where an unidentified protestor is forced into a car by three men dressed in camouflage.

Clips such as these provide an open forum for anyone to post newsworthy videos, but there is often little verifiable information to accompany the video to provide context for the viewer.

Other popular YouTube videos are segments from news television programs. A July 25 interview from Fox News in which the guest was clearly flirting with the woman interviewing him was the most viewed one week.

Finally, a fair number of popular YouTube videos come from news organizations based overseas—often in languages other than English. In late August, a Brazilian news report about a teacher who was fired after a video of her dancing provocatively at a nightclub surfaced was the most viewed.

SOCIAL MEDIA'S AGENDA VERSUS THE MSM, WEEK TO WEEK

Differences between the social media and mainstream press come into clearer relief when we look at specific stories that get attention week to week. This level of analysis reveals first and foremost how infrequently social media and the traditional press share the same agenda. Blogs, as seen in other measures, match up most often but still only rarely.

It is also illuminating to examine the nature of the stories that *do* dominate both social and traditional media in a given week. They tend to be blockbuster events, and they cut across a wide variety of topic areas—the economy, health pandemics, the deaths of well-known figures. And many major national news events don't make it to the top of the social media agenda. The week of August 3–9, for example, while health care and the town hall protests led the mainstream press, blogs led with a story about a woman suing her college because they didn't do enough to help her find a job, and Twitter led with an outage of Twitter itself.

In the 49 weeks studied, blogs and the mainstream press shared the top story just 13 times. The storyline shared most was the U.S. economic crisis (five weeks in all). Other storylines that drove attention on both platforms included the initial H1N1 flu outbreak in late spring, the June protests in Iran, the death of Senator Edward Kennedy in late August, and the shootings at Fort Hood in early November.

On Twitter, the top story was even less likely to be the same as in the mainstream press—just four of the 29 weeks studied, or less than one seventh of the time. (Iran, Fort Hood and the NWA terror attempt, which closed out the year.) All but one of those was also a top story among the blogs that week.

Most weeks, however, blogs and Twitter led with different stories than the mainstream press.

The week of August 17–23, for example, the traditional press led with the health care debate for the fifth week in a row as the Obama administration appeared poised to pull back its support for the so-called "public option" to be included in a final bill. That story was not among those followed closely in social media that week. There, two scientific studies that received almost no mainstream media attention led the list. For bloggers, the top story was about Canadian researchers who conducted a mathematical exercise to see if a zombie attack would lead to the collapse of civilization. And Twitterers led with a story about research by a professor at the University of Massachusetts Dartmouth who discovered that 90% of U.S. paper money contained small traces of cocaine.

In another example, the week of November 30-December 6, more than a quarter (27%) of the traditional press' newshole was occupied with the war in Afghanistan as Obama delivered a major speech outlying his plans for the U.S. role there. In the blogosphere, Afghanistan was the third largest subject of the week, following two very different subjects. First was a vote in Switzerland to ban the building of minarets, which are distinctive structures associated with Islamic mosques. And second was the subject of global warming surrounding the "climate-gate" controversy. On Twitter, Afghanistan was not among the top five stories at all. Instead, an unfortunate error on a billboard in Mobile, Alabama, led the way as a television news station created a sign featuring pictures of three news anchors and a real-time Twitter feed of breaking events. Unfortunately, that created an embarrassing juxtaposition as one passerby took a photo of the billboard at a time when the text read, "3 Accused of Gang Rape in Monroeville."

CONCLUSION

As social media sites and tools evolve, so too will their impact on news information and citizens' relationship to the news. The interplay among new and traditional media will also almost certainly evolve. Even now, new partnerships and content sharing are being developed across platforms and outlets. The Project will continue to follow and study these emerging tools and trends for producing, consuming and sharing news information in our society. And the flow will be tracked weekly in PEJ's NMI.

NOTES

1. http://www.journalism.org/analysis_report/understanding_participatory_news_consumer
2. http://www.emarketer.com/Article.aspx?R=1007271
3. For the NMI, the priorities of bloggers and users of Twitter are measured in terms of percentage of links. Each time a news blog or social media Web page adds a link to its site directing

its readers to a news story, it suggests that the author places at least some importance on the content of that article. The user may or may not agree with the contents of the article, but they feel it is important enough to draw the reader's attention to it.

4. There were three weeks in 2009 when no NMI was produced: March 2–6, November 16–20, and December 14–18.

5. For the sake of authenticity, PEJ has a policy of not correcting misspellings or grammatical errors that appear in direct quotes from blog postings.

6. The data discussed in this section refers to all of the stories and links collected from blogs as part of the weekly NMI sample, regardless of whether that subject made the list of top stories in the given week.

7. The data discussed in this section refers to all of the stories and links collected from Twitter as part of the weekly NMI sample, regardless of whether that subject made the list of top stories in the given week.

8. This does not mean that 2.5 million people watched the clip because it is likely that a number of people viewed it multiple times.

9. PEJ's method of tracking the most popular topics on YouTube is different than the method for tracking blogs and Twitter. For YouTube, PEJ simply captures the top-five most frequently viewed news videos each week.

[*]The **Pew Research Center's Project for Excellence in Journalism** is dedicated to trying to understand the information revolution. It specializes in using empirical methods to evaluate and study the performance of the press, particularly content analysis.

Pew Research Center, Project for Excellence in Journalism, "New Media, Old Media: How Blogs and Social Media Agendas Relate and Differ from Traditional Press" (Washington, D.C., Pew Research Center Publications, May 23, 2010), http://pewresearch.org/pubs/1602/new-media-review-differences-from-traditional-press.

Used by permission.

How to Save the News

*by James Fallows**

Everyone knows that Google is killing the news business. Few people know how hard Google is trying to bring it back to life, or why the company now considers journalism's survival crucial to its own prospects.

Of course this overstates Google's power to destroy, or create. The company's chief economist, Hal Varian, likes to point out that perhaps the most important measure of the newspaper industry's viability—the number of subscriptions per household—has headed straight down, not just since Google's founding in the late 1990s but ever since World War II. In 1947, each 100 U.S. households bought an average of about 140 newspapers daily. Now they buy fewer than 50, and the number has fallen nonstop through those years. If Google had never been invented, changes in commuting patterns, the coming of 24-hour TV news and online information sites that make a newspaper's information stale before it appears, the general busyness of life, and many other factors would have created major problems for newspapers. Moreover, "Google" is shorthand for an array of other Internet-based pressures on the news business, notably the draining of classified ads to the likes of Craigslist and eBay. On the other side of the balance, Google's efforts to shore up news organizations are extensive and have recently become intense but are not guaranteed to succeed.

That this campaign is under way is surprising in its own right, as is its strong emphasis inside the company as a significant strategic measure. Most Internet and tech businesses have been either uninterested in or actively condescending toward the struggles of what they view as the pathetic-loser dinosaurs of the traditional media. (What is the Craigslist vision for sustaining the news business? Facebook's? Microsoft's?) Google's projects have hardly been secret, since most of them involve collaboration with major newspapers, magazines, and broadcast-news organizations. This April, the company's CEO, Eric Schmidt, delivered a keynote address to the major news editors' convention, telling them "we're all in this together" and that he was "convinced that the survival of high-quality journalism" was "essential to the functioning of modern democracy." Last December, he wrote an op-ed in *The Wall Street Journal* announcing that Google would be going out of its way to devise systems that would direct more money toward struggling news organizations-rather than, as many in the news industry assumed, simply directing more of everyone else's money toward itself. Publishing this in

The Journal was a piquant touch, since the paper's owner, Rupert Murdoch, has frequently denounced Google's effect on the news industry.

Still, compared with what it could have been saying about its strategy toward news companies, Google has undersold its efforts and rarely talked about them as an overall program with a central guiding idea. Partly this is because of disappearing classified ads, "unbundling" of content—the list of what's killing journalism is long. But high on that list, many would say, is Google, the biggest unbundler of them all Now, having helped break the news business, the company wants to fix it—for commercial as well as civic reasons: if news organizations stop producing great journalism, says one Google executive, the search engine will no longer have interesting content to link to. So some of the smartest minds at the company are thinking about this, and working with publishers, and peering ahead to see what the future of journalism looks like. Guess what? It's bright. The highly decentralized nature of most innovative effort at Google, which often takes place in "20 percent time"—a workday per week when developers can concentrate on projects they choose themselves. Partly it is because of the "permanent beta" culture at Google, in which projects are viewed as tentative and experimental long after they have reached what others would consider a mature stage. (The company's wildly popular e-mail system, Gmail, officially graduated from beta-test status only last summer, after five years of operation by tens of millions of users worldwide.) And the news organizations that are trying out experimental approaches at Google's suggestion and with its support have themselves chosen to be quiet.

But after talking during the past year with engineers and strategists at Google and recently interviewing some of their counterparts inside the news industry, I am convinced that there is a larger vision for news coming out of Google; that it is not simply a charity effort to buy off critics; and that it has been pushed hard enough by people at the top of the company, especially Schmidt, to become an internalized part of the culture in what is arguably the world's most important media organization. Google's initiatives do not constitute a complete or easy plan for the next phase of serious journalism. But they are more promising than what I'm used to seeing elsewhere, notably in the steady stream of "Crisis of the Press"–style reports. The company's ultimate ambition is in line with what most of today's reporters, editors, and publishers are hoping for—which is what, in my view, most citizens should also support.

That goal is a reinvented business model to sustain professional news-gathering. This is essential if the "crowd sourcing" and citizen journalism that have already transformed news coverage—for instance, the videos from inside the Iranian protests last summer—are not to be the world's only source of information. Accounts like those are certainly valuable, but they will be all the more significant if they are buttressed by reports from people who are paid to keep track of government agencies, go into danger zones, investigate and analyze public and private abuse, and generally serve as systematic rather than ad hoc observers. (I am talking about what journalism should do, not what it often does.)

Google's likely route toward this destination, however, differs in crucial and sometimes uncomfortable ways from the one the existing news business would probably choose on its own. The differences are natural, given the cultural chasm that separates a wildly successful, collectively cocky, engineer-dominated, very internationally staffed West Coast tech start-up from a national news establishment that is its opposite in all ways: East Coast-centric, liberal arts-heavy, less international in staff and leadership (more Brits and Australians than in the tech industry, fewer Indians, Chinese, and Russians), dominated by organizations founded in the distant past, and at the moment strikingly downcast and even panicked.

Here's an important illustration of the difference: people inside the press still wage bitter, first-principles debates about whether, in theory, customers will ever be willing to pay for online news, and therefore whether "pay walls" for online news can ever succeed. But at Google, I could hardly interest anyone in the question. The reaction was: Of course people will end up paying in some form —why even talk about it? The important questions involved the details of how they would pay, and for what kind of news. "We have no horse in that race or particular model in mind," Krishna Bharat, one of the executives most deeply involved in Google's journalistic efforts, told me, in a typical comment. His team was already working with some newspapers planning to put their content behind paywalls, others planning to remain free and hoping to become more popular with readers annoyed when paywalls crop up elsewhere, and still others planning a range of free and paid offerings. For Bharat and his colleagues, free-versus-paid is an empirical rather than theological matter. They'll see what works.

The deeper differences involve Google's assumptions about what the news business will have to do to "engage" readers again—that is, make them willing to spend time with its printed, online, or on-air products, however much they cost. One Google employee who asked not to be named mentioned another report on journalism's future and pointed out a section called "Focus on the User." "They just mean, 'Get money out of the user.'" he said. "Nowhere do they talk about how to create something people actually want to read and engage with and use." On the topic of engaging modern users, Google feels very confident right now, and the news business feels very nervous. Apart from anything else, that certainty gap makes Google important to the future of the news. Before describing how Google came to this point, what its engineers are trying to do, and where it all might lead, a full-disclosure note. Eric Schmidt of Google is an important figure in this saga. By chance, and because he and his wife were *Atlantic* readers, Schmidt and his family had become friends of my family long before he joined Google as CEO in 2001, and we have stayed in touch. For this story, I did not talk with him except in one official on-the-record interview in late March, after I had finished my other reporting at Google HQ.

Let's start with the diagnosis: If you are looking at the troubled ecology of news from Google's point of view, how do you define the problem to be solved? You would accept from the outset that something "historic," "epochal," "devastating," "unprecedented," "irresistible," and so on was happening to the news business—all terms I heard used in interviews to describe the challenges facing newspapers in particular and the journalism business more broadly.

"There really is no single cause," I was told by Josh Cohen, a former Webnews manager for Reuters who now directs Google's dealings with publishers and broadcasters, at his office in New York. "Rather, you could pick any single cause, and that on its own would be enough to explain the problems—except it's not on its own." The most obvious cause is that classified advertising, traditionally 30 to 40 percent of a newspaper's total revenue, is disappearing in a rush to online sites. "There are a lot of people in the business who think that in the not-too-distant future, the classified share of a paper's revenue will go to zero," Cohen said. "Stop right there. In any business, if you lose a third of your revenue, you're going to be in serious trouble."

You can't stop right there, Cohen said, and he went through the list of the other, related trends weighing on newspapers in particular, each pointing downward and each making the others worse. First, the relentless decline of circulation—"fewer people using your product," as he put it. Then, the consequent defection of advertisers from the lucrative "display" category—the big ads for cars, banks, airlines—as well as from classifieds. The typical newspaper costs much more to print and deliver than a subscriber pays. Its business rationale is as an advertising-delivery vehicle, with 80 percent of the typical paper's total revenue coming from ads. That's what's going away. In hopes of preserving that advertising model, newspapers have decided to defend their hold on the public's attention by giving away, online, the very information they were trying to sell in print. However that decision looks in the long run, for now it has created a rising generation of "customers" who are out of the habit of reading on paper and are conditioned to think that information should be free.

"It's the triple whammy," Eric Schmidt said when I interviewed him. "Loss of classifieds, loss of circulation, loss of the value of display ads in print, on a per-ad basis. Online advertising is growing but has not caught up."

So far, this may sound familiar. To me, the interesting aspects of the Google diagnosis, which of course sets the stage for the proposed cure, were these:

First, it was strikingly not moralistic or mocking. This was a change, not simply from what I'd grown used to hearing at tech conferences over the past decade-the phrase "dead-tree edition" captures the tone-but also from the way Americans usually talk about distressed industries. Think of the connotations of "Big Auto" or "Rust Belt." Whatever the people at Google might privately think, that is not how they talked about the news business. What was happening to the press, they said, was happening because of huge, historic technological forces rather than because of short-sightedness or backward thinking by publishers, editors, and owners. "This is a fundamental disruption of an industry," Nikesh Arora, who joined Google six years ago and is now president of its global sales operations, told me, before detailing the top-to-bottom pressure on every part of the modern journalistic business model.

Next in the Google assessment is the emphasis on "unbundling" as an insurmountable business problem for journalism. "Bundling" was the idea that all parts of the paper came literally in one wrapper—news, sports, comics, grocery-store coupons—and that people who bought the paper for one part implicitly subsidized all the rest. This was important not just because it boosted overall revenue hut because it kept publishers from having to figure out whether enough people were reading stories from the statehouse or Mexico City to pay the costs of reporters there.

"Newspapers never made money on news,'" Hal Varian said, "Serious reporting, say from Afghanistan, has simply never paid its way. What paid for newspapers were the automotive sections, real-estate, home-and-garden, travel, or technology, where advertisers could target their ads." The Internet has been one giant system for stripping away such cross-subsidies. Why look to the newspaper real-estate listings when you can get more up-to-date, searchable info on Zillow—or better travel deals on Orbitz, or a broader range of movie showtimes on Yahoo? Google has been the most powerful unbundling agent of all. It lets users find the one article they are looking for, rather than making them buy the entire paper that paid the reporter. It lets advertisers reach the one customer who is searching for their product, rather than making them advertise to an entire class of readers.

Next, and significantly for the company's vision of the future, nearly everyone at Google emphasized that prospects look bleak for the printed versions of newspapers—but could be bright for the news industry as a whole, including newspaper publishers. This could seem an artificial distinction, but it is fundamental to the company's view of how news organizations will support themselves.

"If you were starting from scratch, you could never possibly justify this business model," Hal Varian said, in a variation on a familiar tech-world riff about the print-journalism business. "Grow trees—then grind them up and truck big rolls of paper down from Canada? Then run them through enormously expensive machinery, hand-deliver them overnight to thousands of doorsteps, and leave more on newsstands, where the surplus is out of date immediately and must be thrown away? Who would say that made sense?" The old-tech wastefulness of the process is obvious, but Varian added a less familiar point. Burdened as they are with these "legacy" print costs, newspapers typically spend about 15 percent of their revenue on what, to the Internet world are their only valuable assets: the people who report, analyze, and edit the news. Varian cited a study by the industry analyst Harold Vogel showing that the figure might reach 35 percent if you included all administrative, promotional, and other "brand"-related expenses. But most of the money a typical newspaper spends is for the old-tech physical work of hauling paper around. Buying raw newsprint and using it costs more than the typical newspaper's entire editorial staff. (The pattern is different at the two elite national papers, *The New York Times* and The *Wall Street Journal.* They each spend more on edit staff than on newsprint, which is part of the reason their brands are among the most likely to survive the current hard times.)

Publishers would be overjoyed to stop buying newsprint if the new readers they are gaining for their online editions were worth as much to advertisers as the previous ones they are losing in print. Here is a crucial part of the Google analysis: *they certainly will be.* The news business, in this view, is passing through an agonizing transition—bad enough, but different from dying. The difference lies in the assumption that soon readers will again pay for subscriptions, and online display ads will become valuable.

"Nothing that I see suggests the 'death of newspapers,'" Eric Schmidt told me. The problem was the high cost and plummeting popularity of their print versions. "Today you have a subscription to a print newspaper," he said. "In the future model, you'll have subscriptions to information sources that will have advertisements embedded in them, like a newspaper. You'll just leave out the print part. I am quite sure that this will happen." We'll get to the details in a moment, but the analytical point behind his conviction bears emphasis. "I observe that as print circulation falls, the growth of the online audience is dramatic" Schmidt said. "Newspapers don't have a demand problem; they have a business-model problem." Many of his company's efforts are attempts to solve this, so that newspaper companies can survive, as printed circulation withers away. Finally, and to me most surprisingly, the Google analysis reveals something about journalism that people inside the business can't easily see about themselves. This involves a kind of inefficiency that a hard-pressed journalistic establishment may no longer be able to afford.

At a minor, practical level, today's news organizations generally seem clumsy, at least from Google's perspective, as they try to re-create their brand and business on the Internet. "The print world has gotten placing an ad in a newspaper or magazine down to a science." Neal Mohan of Google, who is in charge of working with publishers to develop online display ads, told me. He said that for TV or radio advertising, the overhead and administrative costs of placing an ad might be 2 or 3 percent of the ad's total value; but for the online news sites he knew about, simple, correctable inefficiencies might drive the cost to 25 or 30 percent. His team is working with publishers to reduce these "parasite costs."

It was Krishna Bharat who identified a more profound form of inefficiency. As a student at the Indian Institute of Technology in Madras, Bharat had written for the campus newspaper while taking his computer-science degree. "In a second life, I would be a journalist," he once told an Indian newspaper. (When the Indian newspaper asks me, I will say: In a second life, I would be a successful Google executive.) He got his Ph.D. at Georgia Tech and was an early Google hire, in 1999. After the 9/11 attacks two years later, he grew worried about the narrowness of news he was receiving through the U.S. media. "I felt that we really had to catch up with the world's news," he told me. "To get a broad understanding, you had to visit sites in Europe and Asia and the Middle East I was wondering if Google could do something to make the world's news information available."

This last statement is the kind of thing many people at the company say in utter earnestness. In Bharat's case, it meant devising a system that would collect news feeds from around the world, automatically and instantly cluster them by subject and theme, and move them up and down in prominence based on how many sources in various parts of the world were discussing the same topic. A few weeks later, such an automatic news-monitoring site was up and running as an internal demo at Google. In September 2002, it went public as Google News, initially covering 4,000 English-language news sources a day. Now it covers as many as 25,000 sources in some 25 languages, all by purely automated assessments of the main trends emerging in news coverage around the world.

Except for an 18-month period when Bharat founded and ran Google's R&D center in Bangalore, his original hometown, he has been guiding Google News ever since. In this role, he sees more of the world's news coverage daily than practically anyone else on Earth. I asked him what he had learned about the news business.

He hesitated for a minute, as if wanting to be very careful about making a potentially offensive point. Then he said that what astonished him was the predictable and pack-like response of most of the world's news outlets to most stories. Or, more positively, how much opportunity he saw for anyone who was willing to try a different approach.

The Google News front page is a kind of air-traffic-control center for the movement of stories across the world's media, in real time. "Usually, you see essentially the same approach taken by a thousand publications at the same time," he told me. "Once something has been observed, nearly everyone says approximately the same thing." He didn't mean that the publications were linking to one another or syndicating their stories. Rather, their conventions and instincts made them all emphasize the same things. This could be reassuring, in indicating some consensus on what the "important" stories were. But Bharat said it also indicated a faddishness of coverage—when Michael Jackson dies, other things cease to matter—and a redundancy that journalism could no longer afford. "It makes you wonder, is there a better way?" he asked. "Why is it that a thousand people come up with approximately the same reading of matters? Why couldn't there be five readings? And meanwhile use that energy to observe something else, equally important, that is currently being neglected." He said this was not a purely theoretical question. "I believe the news industry is finding that it will not be able to sustain producing highly similar articles."

With the debut of Krishna Bharat's Google News in 2002, Google began its first serious interactions with news organizations. Two years later, it introduced Google Alerts, which sent e-mail or instant-message notifications to users whenever Google's relentless real-time indexing of the world's news sites found a match for a topic the user had flagged. Two years after that, in the fall of 2006, Google began scanning the paper or microfilmed archives of many leading publications so that articles from their pre-digital era could be indexed, searched for, and read online.

Up to this point, the company's attitude was that it was doing the news business a favor, whatever the publishers themselves thought. "Our anecdotal evidence was that [these and other news efforts] were driving users to better stories," Eric Schmidt told me. "There was a set of publishers who recognized that with these tools, users were more likely to visit their Web sites"—and in turn increase the publisher's online audience and make online ads easier to sell. "There was another set who believed we were stealing their content."

Google's rebuttal to the claim of stealing is that it doesn't sell ads on the Google News site, and moreover provides hardly any of the newspapers' original content. Indeed, in this practice it is the opposite of "aggregators" like the Huffington Post, which often "excerpt" enough of someone else's story that readers don't bother to click through to the source. Google News gives only a set of headlines and two-line links meant to steer traffic (and therefore ad potential) to the news organization that first ran the story.

With this approach, Google has in a curious way recreated the "bundled" approach that it has helped destroy for newspapers. Virtually all of Google's (enormous) revenue comes from a tiny handful of its activities: mainly the searches people conduct when they're looking for something to buy. That money subsidizes all the other services the company offers—the classic "let me Google that" informational query (as opposed to the shopping query), Google Earth, driving directions, online storage for Gmail and Google Docs, the still money-losing YouTube video-hosting service. Structurally this is very much like the old newspaper bargain, in which the ad-crammed classified section, the weekly grocery-store pullout, and other commercial features underwrote statehouse coverage and the bureau in Kabul. Bundling worked for newspapers, as long as they offered things that readers couldn't get elsewhere, to a wide swath of the public. Google's version depends on its loss-leader services, like search and mail, being so central to modern online life that, when people do their less frequent but more valuable commercial searches, they'll stay inside Google's world. This in turn depends on the existence of information worth searching for, which brings us back to the predicament of the press.

"About two years ago, we started hearing more and more talk about the decline of the press," Schmidt told me. "A set of people [inside the company] began looking at what might be the ways we could help newspapers."

Why should the company bother? Until recently, I would have thought that the answer was a combination of PR concerns and Schmidt's personal interest. On the PR front, one news official recounted a conversation two years ago in which Schmidt said that whether or not Google was responsible for journalism's business problems, it did not want to be seen as "the vulture picking off the dead carcass of the news industry." Unlike the two Google founders, Larry Page and Sergey Brin. Schmidt is well connected in the news business and at ease with the media. His wife, Wendy, has a degree from the Graduate School of Journalism at UC Berkeley. Brin's family experience with repression in the old Soviet Union is universally assumed to have shaped his uncompromising stance toward repression in today's China. His parents brought him from Moscow to Maryland when he was a child; by all accounts, it was Brin who drove the recent change in Google's policy toward China. Schmidt is just as widely assumed to have driven Google's efforts on the press. But, significantly, he's no longer the only one.

Before this year, when I asked Google employees about the health of the news business, their answers often seemed dutiful. During my interviews this year, people sounded as if they meant it. Google is valuable, by the logic I repeatedly heard, because the information people find through it is valuable. If the information is uninteresting, inaccurate, or untimely, people will not want to search for it. How valuable would Google Maps be, if the directions or street listings were wrong?

Nearly everyone I spoke with made this point in some way. Nikesh Arora's version was that Google had a "deeply symbiotic relationship" with serious news organizations. "We help people find content," he told me. "We don't generate content ourselves. As long as there is great content, people will come looking for it. When there's no great content, it's very hard for people to be interested in finding it. That's what we do for a living." As Chris Gaither, a former technology reporter for the *Los Angeles Times* who joined Google last year as a communications manager for the news team, put it, "We believe in making information accessible. The surest way to make it inaccessible is if it doesn't get created in the first place. That is why it is in our interest to deal with the problems of the industry." (Small-world department: Gaither worked at The Atlantic as an intern in the mid-1990s and was a student in a class I taught at Berkeley's journalism school nine years ago.)

"For the last eight years, we mainly focused on getting the algorithms better," Krishna Bharat said, referring to the automated systems for finding and ranking items in Google News. "But lately, a lot of my time has gone into thinking about the basis on which the product"—news—"is built. A lot of our thinking now is focused on making the news sustainable."

So how can news be made sustainable? The conceptual leap in Google's vision is simply to ignore print. It's not that everyone at the company assumes "dead tree" newspapers and magazines will disappear. Schmidt and others talk about how much easier and more efficient it is to assess, at a glance, stories on a broadsheet newspaper page than to click through to see the full text on a screen. Steve Ballmer, the CEO of Microsoft, told the *Washington Post* editorial board two years ago, "There will be no newspapers, no magazines, that are delivered in paper form" by 2020. (Ballmer later made clear that there might be small exceptions.) No one I spoke with at Google went quite that far. But all of their plans for reinventing a business model for journalism involve attracting money to the Web-based news sites now available on computers, and to the portable information streams that will flow to whatever devices evolve from today's smart phones, iPods and iPads, Nooks and Kindles, and mobile devices of any other sort. This is a natural approach for Google, which is, except for its Nexus One phone, a strictly online company.

The three pillars of the new online business model, as I heard them invariably described, are distribution, engagement, and monetization. That is: getting news to more people, and more people to news-oriented sites; making the presentation of news more interesting, varied, and involving; and converting these larger and more strongly committed audiences into revenue, through both subscription fees and ads. Conveniently, each calls on areas of Google's expertise. "Not knowing as much about the news business as the newspapers do, it is unlikely that we can solve the problems better than they can," Nikesh Arora told me. "But we are willing to support any formal and informal effort that newspapers or journalists more generally want to make" to come up with new sources of money.

In practice this involves projects like the ones I'm about to describe, which share two other traits beyond the "distribution, engagement, monetization" strategy that officially unites them. One is the Google concept of "permanent beta" and continuous experimentation—learning what does work by seeing all the things that don't. "We believe that teams must be nimble and able to fail quickly," Josh Cohen told me. (I resisted making the obvious joke about the contrast with the journalism world, which believes in slow and statesmanlike failure.) "The three most important things any newspaper can do now are experiment, experiment, and experiment," Hal Varian said.

In fact, such advice is both natural and inconceivable for most of today's journalists. Natural, in that every book, every article, every investigative project, every broadcast is its own form of pure start-up enterprise, with nothing guaranteed until it's done (if then). Inconceivable, in that news businesses themselves are relatively static, and the very name "Newspaper Guild" suggests how tradition-bound many journalists are. We pride ourselves on defending standards of language, standards of judgment, and even a form of public service that can seem antique. Whether or not this makes for better journalism, it complicates the embrace of radical new experiments.

The other implicitly connecting theme is that an accumulation of small steps can together make a surprisingly large difference. The forces weighing down the news industry are titanic. In contrast, some of the proposed solutions may seem disappointingly small-bore. But many people at Google repeated a maxim from Clay Shirky, of New York University, in an essay last year about the future of the news: "Nothing will work, but everything might."

In all, Google teams arc working with hundreds of news organizations, which range in scale from the Associated Press, the Public Broadcasting System, and *The New York Times* to local TV stations and papers. The last two efforts I'll mention are obviously different in scale and potential from all the others, but these examples give a sense of what "trying everything" means.

Living Stories. News reporting is usually incremental. Something happens in Kabul today. It's related to what happened there yesterday, plus 20 years ago, and further back. It has a bearing on what will happen a year from now. High-end news organizations reflect this continuous reality in hiring reporters and editors who (ideally) know the background of today's news and in the way they present it, usually with modest additions to the sum of established knowledge day by day.

The modest daily updating of the news—another vote in Congress, another debate among political candidates matches the cycle of papers and broadcasts very well, but matches the Internet very poorly, in terms of both speed and popularity rankings. The *Financial Times* might have given readers better sustained coverage of European economic troubles than any other paper. But precisely because it has done so many incremental stories, no one of them might rise to the top of a Google Web search, compared with an occasional overview story somewhere else. By the standards that currently generate online revenue, better journalism gets a worse result.

This past winter, the Google News team worked with *The New York Times* and *The Washington Post* to run the Living Stories experiment, essentially a way to rig Google's search results to favor serious, sustained reporting. All articles about a big topic—the war in Afghanistan, health-care reform were grouped on one page that included links to all aspects of the paper's coverage (history, videos, reader comments, related articles). "It is a repository of information, rather than ephemeral information," Krishna Bharat said, explaining that it was a repository designed to prosper in what he called "today's link economy." In February, Google called off the *Times-Post* experiment—and declared it a success, by making the source code available free online, for any organization that would like to create a Living Stories feature for its site.

"If you are asking, 'Has this moved the needle for us yet in a financial way?' the answer is no," Vijay Ravindran, chief digital officer of the *Washington Post Company*, said when I asked him about the experiment. "But it has brought to the surface many different ideas for changing our technology, changing our user interface. The idea that [Google] would work with us on a product and take feedback was very positive. It's almost unique, compared with working with technologists who view 'content creators' as raw-material suppliers and nothing more." He said that simply being able to work directly with Google engineers was a plus, for the implicit lessons in how they develop products and what they know about user behavior.

Richard Tofel, the general manager of ProPublica, a new nonprofit news organization that conducts investigative journalism projects, described a similar collaboration. When an article or documentary by a ProPublica staffer is ready, it is carried by an existing news organization as well as on ProPublica's site. Tofel met Don Loeb, another Google manager working with news companies, at a journalism conference in Berkeley last year and mentioned that Google News and Google Web searches often featured the paper that ran the story but not ProPublica. "He was receptive to the argument, and said that if the search algorithm was not rewarding creators, they would view it as defective," Tofel told me. Loeb and his Google colleagues later asked for illustrations of searches that slighted ProPublica's role. Whether or not there was ever an adjustment (Google never discusses such matters publicly), ProPublica's results now come higher up.

Fast Flip. The Internet is a great way to get news but often a poor way to read it. Usually the longer the item, the worse the experience; a screenful is fine, clicking through thousands of words is an ordeal. Moreover, the gap between the print and online experiences is greatest for those high-end publications that put a lot of thought and expense into elements other than words themselves: the glossy photos of a fashion magazine, the info charts and pull quotes of a mainly text magazine like this.

The Fast Flip project, which began last summer and has now graduated to "official" status, is an attempt to approximate the inviting aspects of leafing through a magazine. It works by loading magazine pages not as collections of text but as highly detailed photos of pages as a whole, cached in Google's system so they load almost as quickly as a (human) reader can leaf through them. "It was an experiment in giving you a preview of an article that was more than just a link to the title," Krishna Bharat said. "It gives you a sense of the graphics, the emphasis, the quality, the feel. Whether you would like to spend time with it." Spending time with an article, whether in print or online, is of course the definition of "engagement" and the behavior advertisers seek. The online manager for a well-known consumer magazine, who asked not to be identified "because Google is too central to our existence," said that each day, Fast Flip was sending his magazine tens of thousands of clicks, which in turn had increased his site's ad revenue. "What we don't know is how many people are staying just at the Google site, and how the money is divvied up, which makes us a little nervous about the proportional value."

"We're not saying we have worked out exactly the right model," Krishna Bharat said when I asked about Fast Flip details. "We just want news to be available, fast, all over the place on the Internet."

YouTube Direct. Projects like Living Stories and Fast Flip are tactical in their potential. Google's hope is that broader use of YouTube videos could substantially boost a news organization's long-term ability to engage an audience. Amateur-produced video is perhaps the most powerful new tool of the Internet era in journalism, making the whole world a potential witness to dramas, tragedies, achievements almost anywhere. The idea behind the various YouTube projects is that the same newspapers that once commanded an audience with printed reports of local news, sports, crime, and weather could re-create their central role by becoming a clearinghouse for video reports.

Steve Grove, a former ABC news staffer (and another onetime intern for *The Atlantic*) has worked at Google since just after it acquired YouTube, three years ago. His team has tried to establish YouTube as a news operation on its own, for instance as a center for footage from Haiti after the earthquake in January. But Grove is also working with newspapers and broadcast-news stations to encourage them to use YouTube clips (while Google bears the storage and upload costs) as a way of reestablishing their role in their communities. For instance, Google offers, for free, the source code for YouTube Direct, which any publication can put on its own Web site. Readers can then easily send in their video clips, for the publication to review, censor, combine, or shorten before putting them up on its site. After a blizzard, people could send in clips of what they had seen outside. Same for a local football game, or a train wreck, or a city-council meeting, or any other event when many people would be interested in what their neighbors had seen. The advertising potential might be small, for YouTube and the local paper alike. The point would be engagement. Al Jazeera used YouTube Direct during the elections in Iraq this spring to show footage from around the country.

If YouTube Direct had existed when I was living in China, I could have set it up to receive videos from people who had seen something worth sharing: the aftermath of a huge event, like the Sichuan earthquake; local effects of pollution; new buildings going up or old ones being torn down; the other daily dramas of modern China. Of course some sites already carry videos. And of course YouTube is often blocked by Chinese censors, so people inside the country might not see what their neighbors posted. Such complications aside, I could quickly see the potential of a tool with which people could easily share information in a new way. Setting up such a site is next on my to-do list.

Another tool extends the lessons of the YouTube Debates during the 2008 presidential campaign, in which Grove invited YouTube users from around the country to send in clips of brief questions for the candidates. Anderson Cooper of CNN then introduced YouTube clips of the questions CNN had chosen to use. They ranged from serious to silly and included one asking Barack Obama whether he was "black enough." YouTube has added a feature that lets users vote for the questions they want asked and has used the method effectively many times since then, including for an interview Grove conducted with Obama at the White House early this year. "We feel this is a tool with tremendous potential for connecting newspapers with their audiences," Grove told me. "There is tremendous leverage to this kind of reporting."

Whatever comes of these experiments, two other broad initiatives are of unquestionable importance, because they address the two biggest business emergencies today's news companies face: they can no longer make enough money on display ads, and they can no longer get readers to pay. According to the Google view, these are serious situations, but temporary.

Display ads. The idea for improving display-ad prospects begins with insignificant-sounding adjustments that have great potential payoff. For instance: Neal Mohan of Google pointed out that news organizations now typically sell their online ad space in two very different ways. Premium space—on the home page, facing certain featured articles or authors handled by "direct sales," through the publication's own sales staff. "Remnant" space, anything left over, is generally franchised out to a national sales network or "exchange" that digs up whatever advertisers it can. Publications decide on the division of space ahead of time, and hope the real-world results more or less fit.

One of Google's new systems does for online ad space what the airlines' dreaded "yield management" systems do for seats on a plane. Airlines constantly adjust the fares on a route, and the size of the planes that will fly it, toward the goal of making each plane as full as it can be before it takes off. The Google system does the same thing, allowing publishers to adjust the allocation of high- and low-priced space, second by second. "Your top salesperson might just have had dinner with the biggest client, who decides to run a big campaign," Mohan told me. The dynamic allocation system ensures that the publisher doesn't lose a penny of potential ad revenue to avoidable supply/demand glitches. If an advertiser wants to spend more on "premium" ads, the necessary space will be automatically redeployed from lower-value sections. "We think publishers should always monetize for the highest value," Mohan said. He could tell that my reaction was "Duh!" so he went on to say, "Day by day, across billions of ad impressions, this makes a tremendous difference." Yield management has allowed airlines to survive; according to Mohan, the advertising equivalent in Google's new system "has generated a lift for publishers of 130 percent, versus what they did when dividing the space themselves."

Mohan suggested a variety of other small but significant operational improvements, which together led to a proposal so revolutionary that it challenges all despairing conclusions about the economic future of the press. Newspaper and magazine publishers have felt trapped by the death of print, he says, because display ads in print have been such a crucial cash cow. The switch to online display ads has not offset the losses in print, since the "per eyeball" revenue from online display ads has been so much lower. ("Is that because they're so much less attractive?" I interrupted to ask, adding, "A good print ad can look better than the article next to it, while an online display ad can just be a nuisance." "No offense taken!" he said wryly: his life's work is these ads.) Online display ads may not be so valuable now, he said, but that is because we're still in the drawn-out "transition" period. Sooner or later—maybe in two years, certainly in 10—display ads will, per eyeball, be worth more online than they were in print.

How could this be? In part, he said, today's discouraging ad results simply reflect a lag time. The audience has shifted dramatically from print to online. So has the accumulation of minutes people choose to spend each day reading the news. Wherever people choose to spend their time, Mohan said, they can eventually be "monetized"—the principle on which every newspaper and magazine and television network) has survived until today. "This [online-display] market has the opportunity to be much larger," he said. It was about $8 billion in the U.S. last year. "If you just do the math—audience coming online, the time they spend—it could be an order of magnitude larger." In case you missed that, he means tenfold growth.

The best monetizing schemes are of course ones that people like—ads they enjoy seeing, products for which they willingly pay. Online display ads should be better on these counts too, Mohan said. "There are things we can do online that we simply can't do in print," he said. An ad is "intrusive" mainly if it is not related to what you care about at that time. (I pore over unadorned tiny-print ads in hobbyist publications I care about; I skip past beautiful pictures for, say, women's fashion, which I don't know about.) "The online world will be a lot more attuned to who you are and what you care about, and it will be interactive in a way it never has been before." Advertising has been around forever, Mohan said, "but until now it has always been a one-way conversation. Now your users can communicate back to you." His full argument is complex, but his conclusion is: eventually news operations will wonder why they worried so much about print display ads, since online display will be so much more attractive.

Hal Varian pointed out that people who read printed newspapers report spending an average of about 30 minutes a day with them, whereas online users flit in and out of news sites in an average of 70 seconds. Eventually they'll spend more, if never quite as much as with a newspaper. At that point, he said, "you'll be as valuable to advertisers as you ever were—if anything, more so, since advertisers can probably have a better-focused ad." They won't be telling me about strollers and toddlers' clothes when my children are in college; they won't be telling families with young children about leisure cruises.

"I am a growing-pie guy," Mohan said, referring to the total ad money that flows toward news sites. (As a physical specimen, he is reasonably trim.) "The audience is there, and the dollars will follow. I would argue that publishers will ultimately do better in the digital world. That bodes well for everybody who is going through this shift."

When I later spoke with Eric Schmidt, I asked whether this growing-pie proposition was a widely shared view. "It is my view," he said. Maybe such statements will prove inaccurate, but considering the source, they can't be ruled out as naive.

Designing the paywall. The other hugely consequential effort Google is exploring involves reviving the idea of "subscriptions"—the quaint old custom of an audience paying for what it receives. Most Google people I spoke with had zero interest in the paywall question as an abstraction, because it seemed so obvious that different publications in different circumstances with different business models will make different decisions about how customers should pay.

"If you go back through history, content has always been monetized across a broad spectrum," Nikesh Arora said. "You could buy a journal for a $1,000 subscription price and an audience of 1,000. Or you could pick up a newspaper that is given out free on the Metro. People have adjusted their cost curves to their own form of monetization. The *Harvard Business Review* is not fretting about a loss of advertising [most of its revenue comes from subscribers]. The free Metro paper is not fretting about low subscription income. They have different business models, and the same principle will apply on the Internet." Before, "publishing" meant printing information on sheets of paper: eventually, it will mean distributing information on a Web site or mobile device. That shift, according to Arora and others, will not force news companies into a limited range of business choices. If anything, it should allow for even more variety.

"We don't want to encourage anyone to start charging for content, or not to charge for content," Chris Gaither said. "That is entirely up to them." But Google teams based in Mountain View and New York have been working with newspapers and magazines on the surprisingly complex details of making any kind of payment system work. Paywalls themselves come in a wide variety: absolute barriers to anyone who is not a subscriber, metered approaches that allow nonsubscribers a certain number of free views per day or month, "first click free" schemes to let anyone see the start of an article but reserve the full text for subscribers, and many more. Each involves twists in how the publication's results show up in Google searches and on Google News. For instance: if you are a paid subscriber to the *Financial Times*, any Web search you run should include *FT* results—and indeed rank them all the higher, since your status as a subscriber means you place extra value on the paper's reports. If you don't subscribe, those links should come lower in the search results, since you won't be able to read them—but the results should still appear, in case you decide you want them enough to subscribe. But when you run the search, how can Google tell whether or not you subscribe? How can it know that you are you, whether you're using your computer, or a friend's, or one at an Internet café, or an iPhone? And how can its Web crawlers index the *FT*'s stories in the first place, if they're behind the paywall? All these questions have answers, but they're not always obvious.

"We often hear from publishers saying, 'We're thinking of this approach, and we want to understand it fully,'" Josh Cohen told me. "'We want to be sure this works the way we intend it to work. Can you give it a look?' We will tell them how their ideas would turn out with our system." Then, without giving the newspaper's name or the proprietary details of its specific plan, the Google team will also post its findings and advice on its public Web site. And for publications thinking of the "E-ZPass" approach—some automatic way to collect small per-article charges without slowing the user down or involving cumbersome forms—another Google team is working on the practicalities.

As for the very idea of paid subscriptions: How can they have a future in the Google-driven world of atomized spot information? "It is probable that unbundling has a limit," Eric Schmidt said. Something basic in human nature craves surprise and new sources of stimulation. Few people are "so monomaniacal," as he put it, that they will be interested only in a strict, predefined list of subjects. Therefore people will still want to buy subscriptions to sources of information and entertainment—"bundles," the head of the world's most powerful unbundler said—and advertisers will still want to reach them. His example:

"It's obvious that in five or 10 years, most news will be consumed on an electronic device of some sort. Something that is mobile and personal, with a nice color screen. Imagine an iPod or Kindle smart enough to show you stories that are incremental to a story it showed you yesterday, rather than just repetitive. And it knows who your friends are and what they're reading and think is hot. And it has display advertising with lots of nice color, and more personal and targeted, within the limits of creepiness. And it has a GPS and a radio network and knows what is going on around you. If you think about that, you get to an interesting answer very quickly, involving both subscriptions and ads."

This vision, which Schmidt presented as utopian, helps illustrate the solution Google believes it will find; the problem it knows it can't solve; and another problem that goes well beyond its ambitions.

The solution is simply the idea that there can be a solution. The organization that dominates the online-advertising world says that much more online-ad money can be flowing to news organizations. The company whose standard price to consumers is zero says that subscribers can and will pay for news. The name that has symbolized disruption of established media says it sees direct self-interest in helping the struggling journalism business. In today's devastated news business, these are major and encouraging developments, all the more so for their contrast with what other tech firms are attempting.

The problem Google is aware of involves the disruption still ahead. Ten years from now, a robust and better-funded news business will be thriving. What next year means is harder to say. I asked everyone I interviewed to predict which organizations would be providing news a decade from now. Most people replied that many of tomorrow's influential news brands will be today's: *The New York Times, The Wall Street Journal,* the public and private TV and radio networks, the Associated Press. Others would be names we don't yet know. But this is consistent with the way the news has always worked, rather than a threatening change. Fifteen years ago. Fox News did not exist. A decade ago, Jon Stewart was not known for political commentary. The news business has continually been reinvented by people in their 20s and early 30s—Henry Luce when he and Briton Hadden founded *Time* magazine soon after they left college, John Hersey when he wrote *Hiroshima* at age 32. Bloggers and videographers are their counterparts now. If the prospect is continued transition rather than mass extinction of news organizations, that is better than many had assumed. It requires an openness to the constant experimentation that Google preaches and that is journalism's real heritage.

The challenge Google knows it has not fully coped with is a vast one, which involves the public function of the news in the broadest sense. The company views the survival of "premium content" as important to its own welfare. But Schmidt and his colleagues realize that a modernized news business might conceivably produce "enough" good content for Google's purposes even if no one has fully figured out how to pay for the bureau in Baghdad, or even at the statehouse. This is the next challenge, and a profound one, for a reinvented journalistic culture. The fluid history of the news business, along with today's technological pattern of Google-style continuous experimentation, suggests that there will be no one big solution but a range of partial remedies. Google's efforts may have bought time for a panicked, transitional news business to see a future for itself and begin discovering those new remedies and roles.

*James Fallows** is a national correspondent for *Atlantic Monthly* and has worked for the magazine for more than 25 years, writing on a wide range of topics. His blog can be found at jamesfallows. theatlantic.com.

James Fallows, "How to Save the News," *The Atlantic Magazine*, June 2010: 44–46, http://www.theatlantic.com/business/archive/2010/05/google-powerpoint/56360.

DISCUSSION QUESTIONS

1. Are new media opportunities or threats to traditional journalism?

2. What is the role of the professional journalist in the new media age?

3. What role should the nonprofessional play in modern journalism?

4. Bloggers are now competing with professional journalists to cover important events, but bloggers' information is often unsubstantiated or incomplete. How should the media address this challenge?

5. Do new media, like Google, have a role in saving traditional media?

Part 3:

How Traditional Media Can and Are Fighting Back

This section addresses what traditional media are or could be doing to meet the challenges they face. In the first article, "*The Associated Press v. All Headline News*," Daniel Park explains how the Associated Press (AP) used a 91-year-old law to guard its intellectual property from an online news aggregator that was rewriting AP stories and posting them with no credit. To protect its property, AP revived the hot news doctrine, first recognized by the Supreme Court in 1918. This doctrine asserts that while facts cannot be copyrighted, news outlets can sue a rival for re-reporting "time sensitive" material. Park believes that the willingness of a modern court to accept the doctrine will protect traditional media and help shape customary practices in online journalism.

The next two articles in this section examine suggested changes that could restore journalism to solid economic footing. In an excerpt from "Clues in the Rubble: A User-First Framework for Sustaining Local News," Bill Mitchell of the Poynter Institute argues that media should use a multipronged approach to discover the best ways to create new value for news products. For example, news organizations might provide smart phone apps that users might be willing to pay for. He also suggests that newspapers include a simple donate button on their websites for people who want to support good journalism. In "Bad Public Relations or Is This a Real Crisis?: YES," Lauren Rich Fine provides an overview of the financial problems facing the news industry and offers a number of prescriptive measures to solve them. She argues that newspapers must consider themselves "part public service and part consumer packaged good," maintaining their watchdog function while employing new strategies to reach out to readers, making their product so compelling that they buy it.

The next two articles see a role for government in helping the media. In "Getting Media Right: A Call to Action," Federal Communications Commissioner Michael J. Copps contends that, encouraged by misguided FCC policies, the traditional media have traveled down "a suicidal road of hyper-speculation, creativity-stifling consolidation, and Wall Street pandering that gutted journalism's ranks and resources." In the process, the ethos of the business changed as the ideals of stewardship were pushed aside by business considerations—at a heavy cost not only to the industry but to American democracy. Copps argues that traditional media are disappearing and that new media have not found the sustaining resources they require. During this period of change, the FCC can play a role in fostering a renewed commitment to serious news and journalism by keeping new media open and innovative and by preventing them from repeating the mistakes of traditional media.

The second article is an excerpt from "Saving the News: Toward a National Journalism Strategy" by Victor Pickard, Josh Stearns, and Craig Aaron. They point out that traditional media, particularly newspapers, have been battered by a perfect storm: the rise of the Internet, a deep recession, the decline in advertising revenues (on which their financial model was based), and bad economic decisions. The authors recommend solving the journalism crisis by viewing it as a public policy issue. They call for the development of a national journalism strategy that would foster innovation and provide ongoing support for emerging news models and a shift to a public service paradigm for the press.

Finally, some have asserted that education is vital for the survival of traditional media. While many have emphasized the need to provide journalists with the technological skills and techniques needed to utilize new media, Susan King, in "Improving How Journalists Are Educated and How Their Audiences Are Informed," also emphasizes the need for a greater focus on intellectual rigor in journalism schools. She contends that journalism needs better critical thinkers with a strong sense of ethics and argues for more specialized expertise in complex subjects like medicine and economics, as well as firsthand knowledge of languages, religions, and cultures.

The Associated Press v. All Headline News: How Hot News Misappropriation Will Shape the Unsettled Customary Practices of Online Journalism

by Daniel S. Park*

I. Introduction

The newspaper industry has entered "something perilously close to a free fall."[1] Profits are declining,[2] daily newspapers have lost about 17% of their staff since 2001,[3] and some fear deterioration into a vicious cycle of lost quality and further cost cutting.[4] In a recent interview, President Obama worried that a failing industry would adversely affect the quality of reporting to the point that the news would become "all blogosphere, all opinions, with no serious fact-checking."[5] He emphasized that "serious investigative reporting . . . is absolutely critical to the health of our democracy."[6] The president echoed a growing—and increasingly shared—concern about the future of the media. Rep. Henry Waxman observed recently that "[a] vigorous free press and a vigorous democracy have been inextricably linked . . . . We cannot risk the loss of an informed public and all that means because of a 'market failure.'"[7]

The ease of disseminating information over the Internet has caused deep structural distress within the reporting industry.[8] News aggregators have become a prominent new player, gathering articles written by news reporting agencies and offering a combination of headlines, ledes, summaries, and links back to the original story. In so doing, aggregators provide a useful service to consumers and generate their own ad revenue. Newspapers, however, struggle to capture a larger share of the ad revenue attached to their stories since large portions now go to aggregators.[9] In short, customary practices in the news-reporting world are in a state of flux.

The Associated Press ("AP"), the largest and oldest news organization in the world,[10] took one news aggregator to court for copying its news. In January 2008, AP sued All Headline News ("AHN") for copying, rewriting, and reselling AP's news.[11] AP alleged that AHN committed, among other improprieties,[12] the tort of "hot news" misappropriation.[13] Judge Castel of the Southern District of New

York denied AHN's motion to dismiss the misappropriation claim.[14] He found that the action, though originating from an old case of federal common law, was viable under New York law.[15]

The parties settled in June 2009. Although the terms of the agreement were confidential, an AP spokesperson emphasized in a joint press release that the settlement would "safeguard[] AP's investments in journalism, and [would] serve[] as notice to others that AP will fully defend its intellectual property rights against unfair competition."[16] AHN also acknowledged its improper use of AP's content and that the tort of hot news misappropriation had been ruled viable and applicable in the case.[17] Implicit in the settlement, particularly when coupled with AP's earlier announcement that it would aggressively pursue claims of misappropriation to protect its content,[18] was AP's underlying theory that an enforceable claim of hot news misappropriation strongly serves its news reporting interests.

This Note argues that the doctrine of hot news misappropriation will play an important role in shaping the online newspaper journalism landscape. Cases like *All Headline News* signal to an adapting industry that some behaviors are unsustainable and cannot become customary practices. Part II of this Note describes how the newspaper industry once thrived, now struggles, and is poised to adapt in the Internet age. Part III explains that the doctrine of hot news misappropriation reflects the customary practices of traditional newspaper journalism. Part IV argues that hot news misappropriation in *All Headline News* will serve as a significant but behind the-scenes anchor as new customary practices develop in online journalism.

II. Journalism: Then and Now

A. Traditional Newspaper Journalism

Historically, media industries—including newspapers, magazines, and television —delivered regular content to a stable audience and faced little competition for readers across local markets or for advertiser dollars.[19] They were able to turn consistently exceptional profits, almost regardless of the quality of their product.[20]

About 80% of newspaper revenue traditionally derived from advertising dollars, most of it from classified and retail ads.[21] Subscription prices accounted for only a minority of newspaper revenue; in other words, newspapers were sold to readers at a price that did not offset the costs of gathering the news, writing and editing articles, and printing the paper.[22] This pricing model worked because reader and advertiser demand were interdependent: a lower subscription price attracted more readers, which attracted advertisers who wanted to target those readers. Newspapers could reinvest advertising revenue to improve their product and thus attract even more readers. In short, advertising dollars heavily cross-subsidized investigative reporting.

B. Journalism Today

Print media today is characterized by reduced circulation,[23] fewer advertising dollars,[24] and increased layoffs.[25] These trends began well before the Internet boom in the mid-1990s,[26] but the huge shift to online media and the recession exacerbated the trends.[27] It remains unclear where the bottom lies: as David Evans noted, print is either going the way of the typewriter or settling into the reduced but stable existence of the bicycle.[28]

A primary driver of print media's downward trend has been vastly increased competition for readers' eyes on the Internet.[29] As sources of the news, newspapers face competition from myriad low-cost entrants into the news reporting and commenting sphere—namely, bloggers. But newspapers also must indirectly compete for advertising dollars with websites such as Craigslist and careerbuilder.com[30] and even video games.[31] These alternative channels are especially attractive to advertisers because their targeted audiences facilitate more focused advertising.

The downward trend is worrisome because it reflects far more than the cyclical problems brought by a recession. Newspapers, as Rep. Waxman noted, may be falling into a vicious cycle of cost-cutting and reduced quality attracting fewer readers and less revenue.[32] The fear is that the downward trend will be permanent, because "[a] serious, protracted economic crisis can result in changes in consumer behavior that persist after the end of the crisis. A change in consumption, even in some sense involuntary, can be a learning experience. . . . [Readers and businesses] may never go back."[33]

Newspapers also struggle because they failed to monetize online distribution methods.[34] *The New York Times* ("NYT"), for example, has until recently[35] adopted the free distribution model,[36] perhaps under the assumption that, like in traditional print media, the revenue generated from online advertising would offset the costs of gathering, writing, and distributing the news. This calculus proved faulty. When factoring in online readers, readership of newspapers has in fact increased in recent years.[37] Half of those readers, however, obtain their news online where the industry produces only 10% of its revenue.[38]

The Wall Street Journal ("WSJ") chose a different approach and offered its content over the Internet for a yearly subscription fee.[39] Rupert Murdoch claims that WSJ's subscriber model has largely succeeded[40] and plans to extend the pay-to-read model to his other holdings,[41] such as *Times of London*.[42] Other papers such as *The Economist* employ alternative steps to charge for content, such as for older or premium articles.[43] Note, however, that although the charging model may perform better than the free model, *WSJ*'s subscription fee has increased over the years at a rate far outstripping the rate of inflation,[44] suggesting uncertainty in *WSJ*'s ability to value its own model.

Those problems and models aside, online reporting raises another new challenge to traditional newspaper journalism: the news aggregator. News aggregators gather stories from content originators and repackage it for a reader. Many aggregators exist. For example, Google News is a large aggregator that automatically gathers headlines and ledes and provides links to the original stories.[45] Others, such as Huffington Post or Breitbart.com, contribute opinion reporting or editorial summaries of the news items in addition to or in place of links to the source of the original story.[46] Individual bloggers can also act as small-scale aggregators, providing summaries of stories and links, usually to a very specialized audience.[47] And some outfits behave as All Headline News once did, by copying, rewriting, and repackaging others' news stories as their own.[48]

News aggregators are easy to establish due to the low cost of entry into the market. The majority of newspapers adhered to the free model and made their content available for free online. Ease of access to content combined with the low cost of aggregation and linking provided aggregators the means to build a new industry. Aggregators provide a useful and valuable service by catering to consumers' limited time and have quickly proven profitable.

Moreover, news aggregators provide economic value to content originators because most aggregators link to original sources. Linking is more than a courtesy to the original source; it lies at the heart of Internet economics as the "distinguishing feature of the Web."[49] News aggregators generate their own revenue by displaying ads alongside aggregated or summarized content. Newspapers frequently argue that aggregators take more than their fair share of the advertising revenue attached to a story.[50] Nonetheless, the majority of newspapers' online readers arrive via search engines and news aggregators.[51] Although online revenue contributes only 10% of the newspaper industry's revenue, and in its current form cannot alone sustain the costs of news gathering, newspapers are loath to lose any readers at all. For example, although major news sites could remove themselves from Google's search results,[52] they generally do not.[53]

C. The Multi-Pronged Effort to Save Newspaper Journalism

Commenters have pitched various approaches to preserving the quality of journalism in the Internet age. None are panacean. Instead, each approach may contribute to a sustainable, multi-pronged ecosystem that supports quality news-gathering and profitable dissemination. The most frequently discussed approaches include: (1) protecting news content through sui generis legislation, (2) focusing on niche or hyperlocal reporting, which can lead to new pay models, (3) sharing revenue with aggregators, (4) controlling unauthorized dissemination through technological means, (5) offering new payment models, and (6) receiving public support.

1. Legislative Proposals

One proposed legislative solution would bolster federal copyright law either to award reporters temporary rights in the news they gather,[54] or to provide a federal cause of action for hot news misappropriation.[55] In 2009, for example, Judge Richard Posner wrote that it might be necessary to "[e]xpand[] copyright law to bar online access to copyrighted materials without the copyright holder's consent, or to bar linking to or paraphrasing copyrighted materials without the copyright holder's consent."[56]

Senator Benjamin L. Cardin (D-MD) recently introduced a different kind of bill called the Newspaper Revitalization Act of 2009.[57] This bill targets only small local newspapers and allows them to operate as non-profits, thereby exempting them from paying taxes on advertising and subscription revenue. Newspapers electing to take on tax-exempt status would be prohibited from making political endorsements, but would retain independence in all other operations,[58] and would essentially be treated like public broadcasting stations.[59]

2. Niche and Hyperlocal Reporting

Niches offer a promising target for many smaller newspapers and subsidiaries of larger newspapers. By offering news keyed to a particular location or a specialized audience, newspapers can create monopolies with a stable audience, albeit on a smaller scale than in the heyday of traditional journalism.[60] These monopolies would enable niche newspapers to secure steady advertising revenue, and perhaps even adopt new subscription models. Arguably, *WSJ*'s pay-to-subscribe model has succeeded[61] because *WSJ* offers specialized financial news not otherwise readily obtainable.[62]

A recently developing joint venture between private equity founder Warren Hellman, KQED-FM public broadcasting, and the Berkeley Graduate School of Journalism is working to create a nonprofit local news website.[63] The website would fill a local niche and be paid for by benefactors, similar to public broadcasting.[64] The project emerged during an effort to save the existing area paper, The *San Francisco Chronicle,* but quickly shifted toward an entirely new direction in order to "support[] local journalism in any form, [and] to pick up some of what newspapers have dropped."[65] Discussions have included a possible alliance with *NYT.*[66]

Hyperlocal reporting in the context of the Hellman-Berkeley endeavor refers to the creation of a neighborhood-specific website, or one specific to a single type of news, such as the arts in the Bay Area. Once established as a community fixture, these kinds of sites could enjoy customer loyalty.[67] Sites like these also benefit from a lead time advantage over competitors,[68] if competitors exist.[69]

3. Sharing Revenue with Aggregators

Another major effort of the news industry has focused on developing relationships with aggregators to recapture advertising revenue directed at aggregators' sites. For example, Google pays AP an undisclosed license fee to aggregate AP's content on Google News.[70] The parties are actively negotiating compensation schemes going forward. AP considers receiving the licensing fee akin to being "thrown a bone" in lieu of receiving the much larger compensation possible through sharing advertising revenue.[71]

Google, however, has showcased new technologies in addition to its existing AdSense service[72] that could change the way that content producers earn revenue. Three technologies in particular may change the game for revenue sharing: FastFlip, the DoubleClick Ad Exchange, and a micropayments platform.[73] FastFlip is an automated aggregator that acts as a hub for news from many different sources, but notably offers a share of associated advertising revenue to the content originator. DoubleClick Ad Exchange is a real-time auction for Internet ads that allows publishers to increase the number of advertisers. The micropayments platform facilitates the monetization of digital content. Such technologies have the potential to more fairly distribute advertising dollars to news companies.

But Google will not be monopolizing the future of content aggregator relationships. News Corp has reportedly been in talks with Microsoft about creating an exclusive partnership for the Bing search engine: News Corp would block other search engines from displaying its stories, and Bing would link only to News Corp stories.[74] Apple made headlines as well when it recently announced the upcoming iPad, which is designed to integrate closely with print media.[75]

Newspapers and aggregators face a substantial hurdle: overcoming an Internet-is-free mentality,[76] or at least a consumer expectation for free news that newspapers may have themselves created by adopting the free online distribution model.[77] A basic tenet of the Internet link economy is that the aggregation of content by linking generates ad revenue both for the aggregators and the linked-to sites. Furthermore, some scholars contend that anyone who posts content to the web naturally consents to linking, at least to some reasonable degree.[78] The problem with the link economy is that being linked to is far less lucrative than being the linker.[79] Aggregators receive far more ad revenue, especially when they provide enough of a headline or summary that readers need not click through to the originating site.

4. Controlling Unauthorized Dissemination through Technological Means

AP and others sponsor a Digital Rights Management approach to controlling and monetizing their content. In July 2009, AP announced that it would build a news registry to "encapsulate AP and member content in an informational 'wrapper' that includes a digital permissions framework."[80] In other words, AP would track all of its content to assure compliance with terms of use.[81]

Attributor offers a similar line of products called "FairShare" that periodically scans billions of web pages to look for unauthorized copies of a copyrighted work to help a copyright holder enforce its rights.[82] FairShare works by digitally fingerprinting the essential features of protected content. AP is counted among its customers.[83]

5. New Payment Models

Some newspapers attempt to generate revenue directly from readers. The charge model requires an annual subscription to gain access to the paper's full content.[84] Other newspapers have attempted partial subscription models, such as the short-lived *NYT* "TimesSelect" program, which required a subscription to access editorial content.[85] Some commenters have encouraged the development of a micropayments model much like iTunes,[86] emphasizing the smaller unit of consumption typical with consumers' use of the Internet.

However, a newspaper largely subsidized by readers' direct payment for content—as opposed to traditional newspapers' cross-subsidization by advertising revenue—raises the question of whether the quality of reporting could decline as a result. Rupert Murdoch extolled News Corp's "good record" in "looking for ways—whether better content or delivery—to meet [its] customers' needs and interests."[87] News Corp gives readers what they want to read, but at what cost?

The market for newsworthy but unpopular stories diminishes when those stories can no longer be bundled with merely popular stories.[88]

6. Public Funding

An October 2009 report entitled *The Reconstruction of American Journalism* makes several recommendations to save local media, one of which would enable public funding through a system similar to the National Endowment for the Arts.[89] Funding could flow from a surcharge for radio and television licenses, spectrum auctions, or Internet service provider fees.[90] The report downplayed a potential counterargument in the loss of reporters' autonomy by highlighting public broadcasting's resilience to political pressure.[91]

III. HOT NEWS MISAPPROPRIATION REFLECTS CUSTOMARY PRACTICES IN TRADITIONAL JOURNALISM

A. The Origin of Hot News Misappropriation in *International News Service*

In 1918, AP was a large cooperative organization, gathering news from all over the world and distributing it daily to its 950 member newspapers.[92] Under AP's bylaws, members agreed to publish in their newspapers only the news disseminated by AP.[93] Members could make no other use of that news.[94] The International News Service ("INS") directly competed in newsgathering and dissemination though at a somewhat smaller scale, reaching 400 newspapers across the nation.[95]

At issue in the case was INS's practice of copying news from AP's published bulletins during World War I.[96] This practice emerged in light of two developments —the first technological and the other political. First, the invention of the telegraph enabled INS to take the news from bulletins published in eastern cities and transmit it to western papers for instant publication.[97] Second, Britain and France banned INS from reporting from the front lines because the Hearst papers—then in control of INS—showed sympathy for the German cause.[98] INS's inability to otherwise report on the War notwithstanding, AP filed a bill to restrain INS's "pirating of [its] news"[99] for constituting an unfair competition in business and for violating AP's property right in the news.[100]

The Supreme Court's analysis turned on the unusual nature of the business at issue—that news has a "peculiar value . . . in the spreading of it while it is fresh; . . . [a value that] cannot be maintained by keeping it secret."[101] Making the news of current events known to the world was an "innocent but extremely useful" trade.[102] Due to the character and circumstance of this valuable trade, the Court accepted as unquestionable the right of the public to uncopyrighted news after the moment of first publication.[103] The Court focused instead on the relative right of exclusion between AP and INS. "[A]s between them, [the news] must be regarded as quasi property, irrespective of the rights of either as against the public."[104]

The Court held that AP had earned a temporary "quasi property" right against INS, for such duration as to prevent INS from "reaping the fruits of [AP's] efforts and expenditure."[105] The Court perceived INS's free-riding conduct as inequitable: "[News] has all the attributes of property necessary for determining that a misappropriation of it by a competitor is unfair competition because [it is] *contrary to good conscience*."[106] The Court, standing in equity, assigned to the news an evaporating property right to reward the great cost in acquiring it and the great value in its distribution and exchange.[107]

The Court's decision was accompanied by a partial concurrence by Justice Holmes[108] and a somewhat longer dissent by Justice Brandeis. In his concurrence, Justice Holmes stressed that property, a creation of law, does not necessarily flow from the exertion of labor.[109] He agreed with the majority that INS was engaged in potentially fraudulent and unfair appropriation of AP's news, but concluded that an accurate acknowledgement of the source of news by INS would defeat a claim of misappropriation.[110]

On the other hand, Justice Brandeis dissented from the majority's creation of a quasi property right in news because he viewed property as a positive legal construct that had never before "conferred the attributes of property" to the news.[111] Brandeis conceded that INS's practice of appropriating AP's news and using it for profit "may be inconsistent with a finer sense of propriety" but separated this notion of propriety from the law's definition of property.[112] According to Brandeis, absent a showing of malice or intent to commit fraud, "the law sanctions, indeed encourages, the pursuit."[113] He allowed that there were some instances where public policy would require awarding property rights to knowledge, but noted that such cases typically included artistic creations, inventions, or discoveries.[114] He saw no merit in protecting the "mere record of isolated happenings, whether in words or by photographs not involving artistic skill."[115] He argued that only legislatures, and not the courts, were equipped to decide matters of public policy that could have such far-reaching effects in an increasingly complex society.[116]

B. Misappropriation Reapplied in *All Headline News*

Ninety years later, AP once again alleged misappropriation of its content in *All Headline News*.[117] AP was still a newsgathering and disseminating organization, albeit on a larger scale than at the time of *International News Service*.[118] The notable difference between the cases is that AHN, unlike INS, did no original reporting.[119] As AP alleged, AHN hired "poorly paid individuals" to find news stories on the Internet, copy or rewrite them, and resell them in competition with AP.[120] AHN sold those rewritten stories as their own product either without attributing AP as an original source, or by attributing stories to AP and giving the false impression that it was a licensed member of AP.[121]

AP filed a bill in the Southern District of New York to restrain AHN from "free riding" on AP's original stories.[122] AP brought its complaint against AHN on six counts: (1) hot news misappropriation; (2) copyright infringement; (3) violation of the Digital Millennium Copyright Act ("DMCA") by altering or removing copyright-management information; (4) trademark infringement of the trademarks "AP," "ASSOCIATED PRESS," and "THE ASSOCIATED PRESS"; (5) unfair competition under the Lanham Act; and (6) unfair competition under New York common law. AHN moved to dismiss all claims but the second, copyright infringement.[123] This Note only examines count one.[124]

The *All Headline News* court first noted that International News Service turned on federal common law and was consequently non-binding after Erie.[125] Hot news misappropriation, however, still appears in the laws of some states. Therefore, two issues remained: whether *All Headline News* should be decided under New York law, which recognizes hot news misappropriation, and if so, whether AP had a valid hot news misappropriation claim.

AHN argued that the law of Florida, which lacks a state hot news misappropriation claim, should apply because AHN located its servers there.[126] The district court applied New York law because it was the state where AP was incorporated and headquartered, where it suffered economic loss, and where AHN maintained an office.[127]

The court then turned to the Second Circuit's decision in *National Basketball Association v. Motorola, Inc.*,[128] which "unambiguously held that [hot news misappropriation under New York law] is not preempted by federal law."[129] The Second Circuit defined the claim as surviving preemption if it met five elements:

> (i) a plaintiff generates or gathers information at a cost; (ii) the information is time-sensitive; (iii) a defendant's use of the information constitutes free riding on the plaintiff's efforts; (iv) the defendant is in direct competition with a product or service offered by the plaintiffs; and (v) the ability of other parties to free-ride on the efforts of the plaintiff or others would so reduce the incentive to produce the product or service that its existence or quality would be substantially threatened.[130]

After acknowledging the existence of the New York claim for misappropriation and noting AHN's failure to address this claim, the district court denied AHN's motion to dismiss count one.[131] The court did not adjudicate AP's claim on the merits.

In July 2009, five months after the district court denied AHN's motion to dismiss the hot news misappropriation claim, the parties settled on terms favorable to AP.[132] AHN agreed to cease making competitive use of AP's content, paid AP an unspecified sum, admitted to using AP's content improperly, and acknowledged the validity and applicability of the tort of hot news misappropriation.[133] AP also used the joint press release as an opportunity to declare its willingness to "fully defend its intellectual property rights against unfair competition,"[134] echoing its statement in April that it would "take all actions necessary to protect the content of the Associated Press . . . from misappropriation on the Internet."[135]

C. Criticisms of the Doctrine of Hot News Misappropriation

International News Service has been questioned and criticized ever since its publication. The criticism comes from two corners. First, some argue the case depends on non-binding federal common law and is preempted by federal copyright law. Second, some argue the Pitney majority simply got it wrong and that Holmes's or Brandeis's dissents were either more cohesive with intellectual property law or represented better policy.

After *Erie*, the federal courts abandoned the authority to create federal common law, which rendered *INS* "no longer . . . legally authoritative."[136] The *INS* doctrine, however, persists in some states,[137] and was never specifically overturned by the Supreme Court in any later decision. Some have argued that the misappropriation doctrine was never adopted into federal copyright statutes and therefore Congress intended to preempt the doctrine.[138] The Second Circuit nonetheless held that a narrowly constructed, five-element hot news misappropriation claim survives.[139]

Another criticism derives from the exclusion of facts from the protection of copyright.[140] As the Supreme Court explained, facts are unoriginal, not copyrightable, and "free for the taking."[141] Copyright law would allow a news aggregator to use the facts underlying a reported story, though mere reproduction would violate the copyright in the writing of the story. Critics argue that hot news misappropriation runs counter to a primary purpose of copyright: to "encourage[] others to build freely upon the ideas and information conveyed by a work."[142]

One response to this criticism is that the extreme time-sensitivity of the news adds an extra element that sets it apart from typical, uncopyrightable facts.

Intellectual property often struggles to balance the interests of rights holders against those of the public; here, the public has a strong interest in preserving the quality of news reporting agencies, and those agencies depend on being able to profit from the timeliness of its news.[143]

Other critics focus on the case's creation of a cause of action without clearly defining any boundaries.[144] In 2003, Judge Posner argued that *International News Service* was not only invalid law, but also based only on the vague and unproven assumption that free-riding constituted significantly harmful activity and therefore made it difficult to calculate the proper duration of an injunction against misappropriation.[145] Such critics prefer that the legislature and not the courts determine the proper lead time.

Some of the loudest criticism of misappropriation comes from the bloggers' corner. Bloggers responded clamorously to Judge Richard Posner's 2009 posting, which supported misappropriation; they argued the misappropriation cause of action would "outlaw linking"[146] and that Posner was "out of touch with social media."[147] They argued that a strengthened copyright law and the application of hot news misappropriation would lead to absurd results,[148] that such a change would harm newspapers more than help them,[149] and that newspapers should be allowed to fail in order to make way for new and better substitutes.[150]

Rep. Henry Waxman voiced the primary counterargument in his recent address to the FTC:

> Journalism on the Internet could try to fill the void. But it is not certain that it can generate replacement revenues of such an extent as to ensure a restoration of the resources devoted to journalism by mainstream media over the past several decades—or anything close to it.[151]

It remains to be seen whether newspapers are too important to fail.

D. Hot News Misappropriation in *International News Service* Reflects Customary Practices

This Note adopts Richard Epstein's view that Justice Pitney's majority opinion in *International News Service*, whether purposefully or not,[152] created a rule that aligned with customary practices within the news industry.[153] The relevant custom, as AP described it in its brief in *International News Service*, was that taking a story in whole or in part without independent investigation was improper, whereas using a story as a basis for independent investigation or verification is proper.[154] Pitney's rule essentially added that custom to federal law by creating a temporary, quasi property right enforceable against competitors—but only to the extent that no independent investigation occurred.

This custom likely developed from the fact that AP and INS were frequent competitors with repeated interactions.[155] It was a classic prisoner's dilemma: if either INS or AP defected and began misappropriating the other's news, then the other would retaliate in kind, and both would suffer. Thus INS and AP followed conventional rules of independent investigation in order to avoid upsetting the equilibrium, the benefit being that they could use each other's stories as tips for independent investigation.[156]

The resilience of this self-enforced system is highlighted by INS misappropriating AP's news about the war in Europe. INS limited its acts of misappropriation only to those cases where it could claim necessity[157] due to its political ban from reporting in Europe.[158] But this does not represent a breakdown in self-enforcement; on the contrary, AP sued instead of misappropriating INS's news in kind.[159] AP's lawsuit represented not retaliation, but rather reinforcement of the established antipathy toward misappropriation.[160]

As scholars noted, however, courts should not always defer to customary practices.[161] Mark A. Lemley argues that customary practices change over time,[162] only work for homogeneous groups,[163] have no clear enforcement mechanism,[164] and may not account for externalities that affect those outside the industry.[165]

Perhaps the strongest response to these criticisms is simply that customary practices are particularly useful when "there are repeat and reciprocal interactions between the same parties, for then their incentives to reach the correct rule are exceedingly powerful,"[166] but should only apply to situations where customary practice was developed by directly competing parties.[167] Also, when externalities affecting those outside of the industry trigger the public's interest, then courts should not blindly follow customary practices.

IV. THE ROLE OF HOT NEWS MISAPPROPRIATION IN SHAPING UNDEVELOPED CUSTOMARY PRACTICES IN ONLINE JOURNALISM

Part IV.A explains how *All Headline News* is similar to *International News* and that both cases represent a manifestation of strong customary practices. Part IV.B argues that, going forward, hot news misappropriation actions should apply when the defendant's behavior leads to unsustainable practices. On the whole, however, the doctrine will serve as a quiet influence as the news industry adapts to online journalism.

A. *All Headline News* and *International News Service* Both Mirror Customary Practices

AP's strategy in *All Headline News* becomes apparent after answering the following questions: (1) Why AHN and why now? and (2) Why settle? Many news aggregators, large and small, perform functions similar to AHN. And yet content originators rarely raise claims of hot news misappropriation.[168] This Note argues that the similarities between the *International News Service* and *All Headline News* cases, coupled with AP's other litigious endeavors, exemplify AP's attempt to shape industry custom—a process that must occur between parties and not solely through the courts.

1. *AHN Was a Perfect Candidate*

The similar facts in *All Headline News* and *International News Service* bridge a ninety-year gap. Both cases feature the same party, AP, a news-gathering entity that today continues to practice independent investigation when verifying tips gleaned from outside sources.[169] Both cases also feature the right to control the news a party has gathered, at least against a competitor. The main differences are that the technology underlying the misappropriation has shifted from the telegraph to the Internet and that the defendant in *All Headline News* does not perform its own independent news gathering.

AHN's status as a pure aggregator deserves further scrutiny because a vital element in a hot news misappropriation claim is that the parties must compete directly.[170] At a glance, AHN and AP may not seem like direct competitors because the former engages only in news aggregation and the latter invests heavily in original reporting. But this difference is illusory. A defendant need not follow the exact same business model as the plaintiff in order to be a direct competitor; as *National Basketball Association* shows, a direct competitor is in competition with a product or service offered by the plaintiffs,[171] so it does not need to employ the same means.

This result—that a misappropriator and a news gatherer may in fact compete directly—is in accord with the development of customary practice, in which the essential requirement is that the parties have repeated and reciprocal interactions.[172] AHN, and news aggregators like it, reciprocates with AP by potentially offering tips to stories it takes from sources other than AP. Additional reciprocity occurs when aggregators direct readers via links to the original stories, and newspapers, by allowing indexing of their stories, generate hits for the aggregators.

The difference between *All Headline News* and *International News Service* is one of degree: AHN acted worse than INS. Both directly competed with AP, but only INS actually performed its own news gathering and therefore had a very strong incentive to maintain a good relationship with AP going forward. INS could even try to argue that it acted out of necessity.[173] AHN, in unscrupulously performing an almost entirely free-riding service in competition with AP, was an apt target for applying *International News Service*.[174] AHN's behavior is an outlier, which helps to explain why it suffered the lawsuit instead of any number of other news aggregators.

2. AP Endeavored to Shape Industry Practice

AP tried to apply hot news misappropriation in other cases before it sued AHN.[175] In *Associated Press v. Drudge Retort*, a suit that lasted all of one week, AP sued a news aggregator that published quotations of 33 to 79 words from several AP stories for the purpose of creating a liberal parody of the conservative Drudge Report.[176] AP sued under theories of copyright infringement and hot news misappropriation.[177]

In a "quick about-face," AP caved to pressure from well-known bloggers and withdrew its lawsuit.[178] AP stated that it would "challenge blog postings containing excerpts of AP articles 'when [it] feel[s] the use is more reproduction than reference, or when others are encouraged to cut and paste.'"[179] AP promised to issue guidelines for fair use by bloggers,[180] but those standards are still forthcoming.

Drudge Retort reveals a persistent but remarkably cautious effort by AP to shape the industry custom. Jim Kennedy, the vice president and strategy director of AP, said, "We don't want to cast a pall over the blogosphere by being heavy-handed, so we have to figure out a better and more positive way to do this."[181] Kennedy displayed awareness of a reciprocal relationship that AP shared with bloggers and aggregators.

In contrast with *Drudge Retort*, AP's persistence in *All Headline News* indicates that AP felt compelled to show that hot news misappropriation claims remained viable. It is rare enough that hot news misappropriation cases surface at all, and commenters frequently criticize those that do.[182] Nonetheless, AP, by carefully picking its target, and not retreating, reaffirmed an old and controversial doctrine.

But why would AP settle rather than win, or attempt to win, on the merits? This question lies at the heart of the theory that an industry's customary practices should guide the law: competitors develop customs.[183] AP's actions, whether consciously or not, represent a step toward creating a sustainable relationship with news aggregators instead of allowing a judge—who may not fully understand the newspaper industry—to interfere by imposing rules of positive law.[184] The risk of allowing a court to interfere on the merits is too high.

B. The Role Hot News Misappropriation Will Play in Online Journalism

With *All Headline News* and the subsequent settlement, AP struck a powerful blow against at least one unsustainable online model: an aggregator that commits large-scale copying, rewriting, and reselling of a newspaper's stories. The role that the case will play going forward is to remind industry participants that in order to develop customary practices, repeated and reciprocal interactions are required, and those interactions have to be sustainable.

This role, however, should not encourage AP to spring off its success in *All Headline News* to engage in more litigation. On the contrary, it should serve only as a warning to particularly aggressive aggregators like AHN. Aggregators and newspapers must both understand that, like it or not, they are in it for the long haul. Aggregators provide an extremely useful service for the public. Newspapers will continue to provide content valuable to a functioning democracy. They need each other to survive.

Because they are engaged in a repeating and reciprocal relationship, both newspapers and aggregators have a very strong incentive to create efficient and sustainable customary practices.[185] And there is plenty of reason to be optimistic that this can and will occur.[186]

V. CONCLUSION

The future landscape of news reporting is still evolving. The newspaper industry has suffered a tremendous drop in revenue due to both the recession and the advent of news dissemination online. The industry has actively pursued new methods of saving quality journalism, such as emphasizing niche reporting and implementing new revenue streams through subscription models. There is hope that such new methods, in concert, will help chart the future of the industry.

Another, more controversial method has been to establish a working relationship with news aggregators, which raises the question of whether and to what extent aggregators may use the content generated by reporters and agencies such as the Associated Press. The boundary between fair appropriation and misappropriation remains unclear despite the recent decision in *All Headline News*.

The very presence of *All Headline News* will influence the future relationships of newspapers and aggregators. Its primary significance, however, is as an indication of the evolving customary practices that, in combination with other newspaper-saving methods, will help create a sustainable equilibrium of news-gathering and dissemination.

Notes

1. Pew Project for Excellence in Journalism, *Newspapers*, The State of the News Media 2009: An Annual Report on American Journalism, http://www.stateofthemedia.org/2009/printable_newspapers_chapter.htm [hereinafter PEW, Newspapers].

2. Pew Project for Excellence in Journalism, *Overview*, The State of the News Media 2009: An Annual Report on American Journalism, http://www.stateofthemedia.org/2009/printable_overview_chapter.htm ("Newspaper ad revenues have fallen 23% in the last two years. Some papers are in bankruptcy, and others have lost three-quarters of their value.") [hereinafter Pew, Overview].

3. Pew, Newspapers, *supra* note 1.

4. Representative Henry Waxman, Chairman, Comm. on Energy and Commerce, Remarks to the Federal Trade Commission News Media Workshop (Dec. 2, 2009), http://www.ftc.gov/opp/workshops/news/docs/waxman.pdf.

5. Dave Murray, *Newspaper Journalism Gets Words of Praise; Print Media's Role Vital, Obama Says*, Toledo Blade, Sept. 20, 2009, http://www.toledoblade.com/apps/pbcs.dll/article?AID=/20090920/NEWS16/909200326; *see also* Pew, *Newspapers*, *supra* note 1 ("Fewer people and less space equates to significant erosion of the serious, accountability reporting that newspapers do more than any other medium.").

6. Murray, *supra* note 5.

7. Waxman, *supra* note 4

8. Pew, *Newspapers*, *supra* note 1 (estimating that roughly half of newspapers' recent distress can be attributed to cyclical problems such as the recession, with the rest of it due to structural problems).

9. *Id.*

10. Complaint ¶ 2, The Associated Press v. All Headline News Corp., 608 F. Supp. 2d 454 (S.D.N.Y. Jan. 14, 2009) (No. 08 Civ. 323), *available at* http://www.citmedialaw.org/sites/citmedialaw.org/files/2008-01-14-AP%20v.%20AHN%20Complaint.PDF [hereinafter Complaint].

11. *Id.*

12. The other claims are briefly described *infra* Part III.B, but are outside this Note's scope.

13. Complaint, *supra* note 10, ¶ 2.

14. The Associated Press v. All Headline News Corp., 608 F. Supp. 2d 454, 461 (S.D.N.Y. 2009).

15. *Id.* at 458–59.

16. Joint Press Release, The Associated Press and AHN Media, AP and AHN Media Settle AP's Lawsuit Against AHN Media and Individual Defendants (July 13, 2009), http://www.ap.org/pages/about/pressreleases/pr_071309a.html.

17. *Id.*

18. *See* Dean Singleton, Chairman, The Associated Press, Remarks at the AP Annual Meeting (Apr. 6, 2009), http://www.ap.org/pages/about/pressreleases/pr_040609c.html.

19. *See* Susan Athey, Presentation at the Federal Trade Commission News Media Workshop: Economics of Publishing in the Age of the Internet 3 (Dec. 1. 2009), http://www.ftc.gov/opp/workshops/news/docs/athey.pdf.

20. Letter from Warren E. Buffett, Chairman of the Bd., Berkshire Hathaway Inc., to Shareholders of Berkshire Hathaway Inc. (Feb. 28, 1992), *available at* http://www.berkshirehathaway.com/letters/1991.html (observing that newspaper, television, and magazine properties were what he described as "franchises"—needed or desired, not easily substitutable, and not subject to price regulation—and therefore earned high returns regardless of the quality of management or product).

21. Jon Leibowitz, Chairman and Comm'r of the Fed. Trade Comm., Opening Remarks at the Federal Trade Commission News Media Workshop: "Creative Destruction" or Just "Destruction":

How Will Journalism Survive the Internet Age? (Dec. 1, 2009), http://www.ftc.gov/speeches/leibowitz/091201newsmedia.pdf; PEW, *Newspapers, supra* note 1.

22. Some scholars call this kind of industry a "two-sided platform market." *See, e.g.*, David S. Evans, *The Antitrust Economics of Multi-Sided Platform Markets*, 20 YALE J. ON REG. 325, 329 (2003). Other examples of two-sided platform markets include video game consoles (players and game developers), shopping malls (shoppers and retailers), and payment cards (cardholders and merchants). *Id.* at 328.

23. PEW, *Newspapers, supra* note 1 ("The print circulation slide from 2001 to 2008 totals roughly 13.5% daily and 17.3% Sunday.").

24. *Id.* (finding that the advertising revenue has fallen 23% in two years).

25. *Id.* (giving a *low* estimate of "roughly 25% of the industry's news workforce lost in nine years").

26. Bruce C. Greenwald, et al., *The Moguls' New Clothes*, THE ATLANTIC, Oct. 2009, *available at* http://www.theatlantic.com/doc/200910/moguls* ("[Media companies], as a group, had... underperformed the S&P for much of the previous decade, *before* the Internet upended their industry.") (emphasis in original).

27. *See generally* PEW, *Newspapers, supra* note 1.

28. David S. Evans, Presentation at the Federal Trade Commission News Media Workshop: Advertising-Supported Journalism 13 (Dec. 1, 2009), http://www.ftc.gov/opp/workshops/news/docs/evans.pdf.

29. PEW, *Newspapers, supra* note 1. Note, however, that "roughly half of the downturn in the last year was...related to the economic downturn." *Id.*

30. *Id.* (highlighting the effect of these sources of competition on newspaper advertising revenue).

31. *See* Erika Brown, *Product Placement on the Rise in Video Games*, FORBES, July 21, 2006, http://www.msnbc.msn.com/id/13960083/.

32. Waxman, *supra* note 4.

33. Posting of Richard Posner to The Becker-Posner Blog, The Future of Newspapers, http://www.becker-posner-blog.com/2009/06/the_future_of_n.html (June 23, 2009) [hereinafter Posner, The Future of Newspapers].

34. PEW, *Newspapers, supra* note 1 ("[A] mistake may have been to make website content, much of it still drawn from big and expensive legacy newsroom operations, available for free.").

35. Eliot Van Buskirk, New York Times *Plans to Charge for Articles*, WIRED, Jan. 20, 2010, http://www.wired.com/epicenter/2010/01/new-york-times-plans-to-charge-forarticles/.

36. David Carlson's Virtual World, The Online Timeline, http://iml.jou.ufl.edu/CARLSON/1995s.shtml#1996 ("Jan. 21[, 1996]: The New York Times on the Web opens to the public. Registration is required, but access is free to U.S. residents.").

37. PEW, *Newspapers, supra* note 1.

38. *Id.; see also* Peter R. Kann, *Quality Reporting Doesn't Come Cheap: The Decline of Newspapers is a Tragedy for Democracy. How Can It Be Stopped?*, THE WALL STREET JOURNAL, Sept. 26, 2009, http://online.wsj.com/article/SB10001424052970203440104574400582081349944.html ("Online edition ad rates and online edition ad revenues are only small fractions of those in traditional print."); Posner, The Future of Newspapers, *supra* note 33 ("Online viewership and revenue have grown but not nearly enough to offset the decline in ad revenues.")

39. *WSJ's* online edition was released in May 1996 at the price of $49 annually, *see* Carlson, *supra* note 36, which was considerably more expensive than the print subscription of $29 annually, *see* Media Advisory, Dow Jones & Company, Inc., The Wall Street Journal Interactive Edition Introduces E-Mart, the Internet Version of the Wall Street Journal's Popular Classified Section, BUSINESS WIRE, July 29, 1996, *available at* http://www.thefreelibrary.com/Media+Adisory%2FThe+Wall+Street+Journal+Interactive +Edition+introduces...-a018531210. Today, however, a subscription to the online edition is cheaper than for the print edition. *See* The Wall Street Journal Online, Subscribe Now, https://order.wsj.com/sub/f3 (last visited Jan. 31. 2010).

40. Rupert Murdoch, Presentation at the Federal Trade Commission News Media Workshop: From Town Crier to Bloggers: How Will Journalism Survive the Internet Age? 11 (Dec. 1, 2009), http://www.ftc.gov/opp/workshops/news/docs/murdoch.PDF (stating that WSJ.com had one million subscribers and Barrons.com has 150,000 subscribers).

41. Paul McIntyre, *News Corp Moves Up A Gear for Pay Sites*, SYDNEY MORNING HERALD, Sept. 25, 2009, http://www.smh.com.au/technology/biz-tech/news-corp-movesup-a-gear-for-pay-sites-20090925-g5s1.html.

42. Salamander Davoudi, *Times and Sunday Times Unveil Membership Schemes*, FINANCIAL TIMES, Oct. 5, 2009, http://www.ft.com/cms/s/0/5627d30c-b1b6-11de-a271-00144feab49a.html.

43. Robert Andrews, *Economist.com Builds Its Pay Wall Higher, But All The New Stuff Stays Free*, PAIDCONTENT.ORG, Oct. 6, 2009, http://paidcontent.org/article/419-economist.combuilds-its-pay-wall-higher-but-all-the-new-stuff-stays-free/.

44. *Compare* Media Advisory, Dow Jones, *supra* note 39 (showing that in 1996 WSJ's online subscription price was $49 annually), *with* Wall Street Journal, Subscribe Now, *supra* note 39 (showing an increase in online subscription price by 210% to $103 annually). Comparatively, a dollar in 1996 now has the buying power of approximately $1.41, showing a total inflation of 37%. *See* Dollar Times, Inflation Calculator, http://www.dollartimes.com/calculators/inflation.htm (last visited Jan. 31, 2010).

45. *See* Google News, http://news.google.com (last visited Jan. 31, 2010).

46. *See* Huffington Post, http://www.huffingtonpost.com (last visited Jan. 31, 2010); Breitbart, http://www.breitbart.com, (last visited Jan. 31, 2010); *see also* Drudge Report, http://www.drudgereport.com (last visited Jan. 31, 2010).

47. *See, e.g.*, Nuts & Boalts, http://boaltalk.blogspot.com (last visited Jan. 31, 2010).

48. *See* Complaint, *supra* note 10, ¶ 5.

49. Maureen A. O'Rourke, *Property Rights and Competition on the Internet: In Search of an Appropriate Analogy*, 16 BERKELEY TECH. L.J. 561, 617 (2001). *See also* Wikipedia Entry for PageRank, http://en.wikipedia.org/wiki/PageRank (describing how Google's ranking of search results depends in part on the number of hyperlinks to a searched item).

50. *See, e.g.*, Bobbie Johnson, *Murdoch Could Block Google Searches Entirely*, GUARDIAN, Nov. 9, 2009, http://www.guardian.co.uk/media/2009/nov/09/murdoch-google.

51. PEW, Newspapers, *supra* note 1 ("Newspapers are reconciled to having many visitors arriving by search or from sites that aggregate news reports from many sources, at the same time hoping to have enough to offer that local users will linger. The companies seem to be betting that online advertising, disappointing in the last several years, will increase in volume and command higher rates with better targeting.").

52. Josh Cohen, Presentation at the Federal Trade Commission News Media Workshop: Innovation and the News Industry 13 (Dec. 1, 2009), http://www.ftc.gov/opp/workshops/news/docs/cohen.pdf (explaining to industry workshop participants how to remove content from Google searches).

53. Rupert Murdoch has stated that he will be removing News Corp content from Google's search. Johnson, *supra* note 50, at 1.

54. *See, e.g.*, Ryan T. Holte, *Restricting Fair Use to Save the News: A Proposed Change in Copyright Law to Bring More Profit to News Reporting*, 13 J. TECH. L. & POL'Y 1, 32–33 (2008)(proposing that the Copyright Act be amended to give news reporters rights in their gathered facts for 24 hours).

55. *See, e.g.*, Connie Schultz, *Tighter Copyright Law Could Save Newspapers*, CLEVELAND.COM, June 28, 2009, http://www.cleveland.com/schultz/index.ssf/2009/06/tighter_copyright_law_could_sa.html.

56. Posner, The Future of Newspapers, *supra* note 33. Note that this blog entry marks a significant shift from Posner's position in 2008 that "copyright law cannot prevent [the freeriding behavior of bloggers], because a newspaper can prevent the copying of its articles—that is, the verbal

form in which the information in an article is expressed—and not the information itself." Posting of Richard Posner to The Becker-Posner Blog, *Are Newspapers Doomed?*, http://www. becker-posner-blog.com/archives/2008/06/are_newspapers.html (June 29, 2008) [hereinafter Posner, Are Newspapers Doomed].

57. S. 673, 111th Cong. (2009), *available at* http://thomas.loc.gov/cgi-bin/query/z?c111:S.673:.

58. *Id.* § 1.(k).

59. Press Release, Senator Benjamin Cardin, Senator Cardin Introduces Bill That Would Allow American Newspapers to Operate as Non-Profits, (Mar. 24, 2009), http://cardin.senate.gov/ news/record.cfm?id=310392.

60. *See, e.g.,* www.WickedLocal.com, which features over a hundred hyperlocal blogs in Massachusetts (last visited Jan. 31, 2010).

61. As indicated by Rupert Murdoch, *supra* note 40, at 11, and Peter Kann, *supra* note 38, at 2.

62. Kann, *supra* note 38 (*WSJ*'s content was "distinctive and very largely unduplicated").

63. Richard Pérez-Peña, *In San Francisco, Plans to Start a New Web Site*, THE NEW YORK TIMES, Sept. 24, 2009, http://www.nytimes.com/2009/09/25/business/media/25 bay.html?_r=1.

64. *Id.*

65. *Id.*

66. *Id.*

67. *See also* Smith, *supra* note 62.

68. *See, e.g.,* Robert Weisman, *NYT, Gatehouse Release Settlement Details*, BOSTON.COM, Jan. 26, 2009, http://www.boston.com/business/ticker/2009/01/nyt_gatehouse_r.html (describing the settlement in which Boston.com agreed not to post excerpts taken from GateHouse Media's "Wicked Local" blogs that covered Massachusetts communities).

69. Note, however, that a potential drawback to a lack of competition could be a lack of quality checks.

70. Dirk Smillie, *AP's Curley Has Fightin' Words For Google*, FORBES, Apr. 30, 2009, http://www. forbes.com/2009/04/30/associated-press-google-business-media-apee.html.

71. *Id.*

72. AdSense allows website owners to place third party ads on their page for a share of the revenue that Google receives from the third parties. Wikipedia Entry for AdSense, http://en.wikipedia. org/wiki/AdSense (last visited Jan. 31, 2010). Some have criticized the program for being a "'black box' in which users can't figure out how much of the cash Google is pocketing for any particular ad." Nate Anderson, *"Tech Tapeworms": Bloggers Denounce "Parasite" Label at FTC*, ARS TECHNICA, Dec. 1, 2009, http://arstechnica.com/techpolicy/news/2009/12/tech-tapeworms-bloggers-denounce-parasite-label-at-ftc.ars (quoting blogger Danny Sullivan).

73. James Temple, *Google Fast Flip May Not Be Great for Media*, SAN FRANCISCO CHRONICLE, Sept. 27, 2009, at D1.

74. Sarah Rabil & Dina Bass, *News Corp. Said to Talk to Microsoft on News Search*, BLOOMBERG.COM, Nov. 23, 2009, http://www.bloomberg.com/apps/news?pid=20601103&sid=aRbJZSQRVjEM.

75. Brian Lam, *Apple Tablet Aiming to Redefine Newspapers, Textbooks, and Magazines*, GIZMODO: THE GADGET BLOG, Sept. 30, 2009, http://gizmodo.com/5370252/appletablet-aiming-to-redefine-newspapers-textbooks-and-magazines.

76. *See* O'Rourke, *supra* note 49, at 615. ("The Internet is rooted in a tradition of openness and information sharing, and the web is intentionally designed to facilitate this through linking.").

77. PEW, Newspapers, *supra* note 1.

78. *See* O'Rourke, *supra* note 49, at 620.

79. PEW, Newspapers, *supra* note 1.

80. Press Release, The Associated Press, *Associated Press to Build News Registry To Protect Content* (July 23, 2009), http://www.ap.org/pages/about/pressreleases/pr_072309a.html.

81. *Id.*

82. Attributor, *Your Full Service Anti-Piracy Solution*, http://www.attributor.com/products/products.php (last visited Jan. 31, 2010).

83. Attributor, *About Us*, http://www.attributor.com/about_us.php (last visited Jan. 31, 2010).

84. *See* Wall Street Journal Online, Subscribe Now, *supra* note 39.

85. NYTimes.com, *Frequently Asked Questions About TimesSelect*, http://www.nytimes.com/membercenter/faq/timesselect.html (last visited Jan. 31, 2010).

86. *See, e.g.,* Walter Isaacson, *How To Save Your Newspaper*, Time, Feb. 5, 2009, http://www.time.com/time/printout/0,8816,1877191,00.html.

87. Murdoch, *supra* note 40, at 6.

88. *See* Oscar Wilde, The Soul of Man Under Socialism (Kessinger Publishing 2004) ("The fact is, that the public have an insatiable curiosity to know everything, except what is worth knowing.") (emphasis omitted).

89. Mac Slocum, *Downie and Schudson's 6 Steps Toward "Reconstructing" Journalism*, Nieman Journalism Lab, Oct. 19, 2009, http://www.niemanlab.org/2009/10/downie-andschudsons-6-steps-toward-reconstructing-journalism/(summarizing the Leonard Downie & Michael Schudson's report, The Reconstruction of American Journalism).

90. Leonard Downie, Jr. & Michael Schudson, The Reconstruction of American Journalism 92 (Columbia University School of Journalism 2009), *available at* https://stgcms.journalism.columbia.edu/cs/ContentServer/jrn/1212611716674/page/1212611716651/JRNSimplePage2.htm.

91. *Id.* at 86.

92. Int'l News Serv. v. Associated Press, 248 U.S. 215, 229 (1918).

93. *Id.* at 230.

94. *Id.*

95. *Id.*

96. *Id.* at 231.

97. *Id.* at 238–39. The Court explained:

> [S]ince in speed the telegraph and telephone easily outstrip the rotation of the earth, it is a simple matter for defendant to take complainant's news from … eastern cities and at the mere cost of telegraphic transmission cause it to be published in western papers … sometimes simultaneously with the service of competing Associated Press papers, occasionally even earlier.

> *Id.*

98. Richard A. Epstein, *International News Service v. Associated Press: Custom and Law as Sources of Property Rights in News*, 78 Va. L. Rev. 85, 91–92 (1992).

99. *Int'l News Serv.*, 248 U.S. at 231.

100. *Id.* at 231–32. AP also filed for restraint to stop INS from bribing employees to obtain news earlier and from inducing AP members to violate the AP by-laws. Those matters were not argued before the Court. *Id.* at 232.

101. *Id.* at 235.

102. *Id.*

103. *Id.* at 236.

104. *Id.*

105. *Id.* at 241.

106. *Id.* at 240 (emphasis added).

107. The Court further treated INS's practice as fraudulent, even though it conceded that INS had not clearly attempted to palm off its goods as those of AP. The Court instead determined that INS had been fraudulent in a more "direct and obvious" manner, by selling AP's goods as its own. *Id.* at 240.

108. Holmes's concurrence is arguably a dissent. LexisNexis refers to Holmes' contribution as a concurrence, unlike Westlaw, which refers to it as a dissent. *Compare Int'l News Serv.*, 1918 U.S. LEXIS 1664 *with Int'l News Serv.*, 248 U.S. 215.

109. *Int'l News Serv.*, 248 U.S. at 246 (Holmes, J., concurring).

110. *Id.* at 248.

111. *Id.* at 251 (Brandeis, J., dissenting).

112. *Id.* at 257.

113. *Id.* at 259.

114. *Id.* at 251.

115. *Id.* at 254.

116. *Id.* at 264.

117. The Associated Press v. All Headline News, 608 F. Supp. 2d 454, 457–58 (S.D.N.Y. 2009).

118. *See* Complaint, *supra* note 10, ¶ 2.

119. *See Id.*

120. *Id.*

121. *Id.*

122. *All Headline News*, 608 F. Supp. 2d at 458.

123. *Id.* at 457.

124. The court handled the remaining motions to dismiss for each count as follows: (3) denied because AHN did not show that the copyright management information section of the DMCA would not apply here; (4) granted because AP's trademark claim was thin and AP's conclusory allegations of confusion among clients lacked factual support; (5) granted because AP's unfair competition claim should not be extended to situations of no consequence to purchasers; and (6) denied because AHN failed to support its motion and because preemption of New York unfair competition law was unclear. *Id.* at 454–55.

125. *Id.* at 458–59 (citing Erie R. Co. v. Tompkins, 304 U.S. 64 (1938)).

126. *Id.*

127. *Id.* at 460–61.

128. Nat'l Basketball Ass'n v. Motorola, Inc., 105 F.3d 841 (2d Cir. 1997).

129. *All Headline News*, 608 F. Supp. 2d at 461.

130. *Nat'l Basketball Ass'n*, 105 F.3d at 845.

131. *All Headline News*, 608 F. Supp. 2d at 461.

132. Joint Press Release, The Associated Press and AHN Media, *supra* note 16.

133. *Id.*

134. *Id.*

135. Singleton, *supra* note 18.

136. Richard A. Posner, *Misappropriation: A Dirge*, 40 HOUS. L. REV. 621, 627 (2003) [hereinafter Posner, Misappropriation].

137. *Id.* at 629.

138. *See, e.g., Nat'l Basketball Ass'n*, 105 F.3d 841, 843 (2d Cir. 1997).

139. *Nat'l Basketball Ass'n*, 105 F.3d at 845.

140. *See* Feist Publ'ns, Inc. v. Rural Tel. Serv. Co., 499 U.S. 340, 349 (1991).

141. *Id.*

142. *Id.* at 350.

143. *See Int'l News Serv.*, 248 U.S. 215, 241 (1918).

144. *See, e.g.*, Posner, Misappropriation, *supra* note 136, at 637–38. Again, however, note that Judge Posner has as recently as July 2009 viewed misappropriation in a more positive light. *See* Posner, *Are Newspapers Doomed, supra* note 56.

145. Posner, Misappropriation, *supra* note 136, at 637–38.

146. Posting of Kevin O'Keefe to Real Lawyers Have Blogs, *Lawyers Ill Equipped to Advise on Intersection of Social Media and Copyright Laws*, http://kevin.lexblog.com/2009/06/articles/blog-law-and-ethics/lawyers-ill-equipped-to-advise-on-intersection-of-social-mediaand-copyright-laws/ (June 28, 2009).

147. Posting of Dave Rein to Owners, Borrowers & Thieves 2.0, *Judge Posner's Copyright Proposal To Save Newspapers—A Cosmic Paperboy?*, http://iplitigator.huschblackwell.com/2009/07/articles/copyright/judge-posners-copyright-proposal-to-save-newspapers-acosmic-paperboy/ (July 1, 2009); see also Dan Kennedy, *Should Linking Be Illegal?*, THE GUARDIAN, July 1, 2009, http://www.guardian.co.uk/commentisfree/cifamerica/2009/jul/01/richard-posnercopyright-linking-newspapers.

148. Posting of Danny Sullivan to Daggle, *Justice Richard Posner's Copyright Law No One Can Talk About (Or Link To)*, http://daggle.com/posner-copyright-law-798 (June 29, 2009) (describing as ludicrous a situation in which the first person to report Michael Jackson's death would be the only one to report it).

149. *See* posting of Erick Schonfeld to TechCrunch, *How to Save the Newspapers, Vol. XII: Outlaw Linking*, http://www.techcrunch.com/2009/06/28/how-to-save-the-newspapers-volxii-outlaw-linking/(June 28, 2009) ("A link on its own is valuable. . . . [N]ewspaper sites get their readers . . . through links, not direct traffic.").

150. Posting of Gary Becker to the Becker-Posner Blog, *The Social Cost of the Decline of Newspapers*, http://www.becker-posner-blog.com/2009/06/the_social_cost.html (June 23, 2009) ("Although the printed newspaper industry is doomed, . . . they are being replaced by good substitutes in the form of blogs, social networks like Facebook and Twitter, online news gathering by various groups, including newspapers, and other electronic forms of communication.").

151. Waxman, *supra* note 4, at 2.

152. Epstein, *supra* note 98, at 124 ("[T]he INS decision . . . reached results consistent with the custom of the news-gathering industry, although [Justice Pitney] did not purport to derive [his] rules from custom.").

153. *Id.* at 115.

154. *Id.* at 98 (citing AP's brief).

155. *Id.* at 101.

156. *Id.* at 102.

157. *Id.* at 105.

158. *Id.* at 91–92.

159. *Id.* at 105–06.

160. Professor Epstein notes that INS perhaps should have prevailed with a defense of necessity, or at least that Justice Pitney should have left open such a defense to hot news misappropriation in certain cases. *Id.* at 118.

161. *See, e.g.,* Jennifer E. Rothman, *The Questionable Use of Custom in Intellectual Property*, 93 Va. L. Rev. 1899 (2007).

162. Mark A. Lemley, *The Law and Economics of Internet Norms*, 73 Chi.-Kent L. Rev. 1257, 1267 (1998).

163. *Id.* at 1270.

164. *Id.* at 1284.

165. *Id.* at 1277.

166. Epstein, *supra* note 98, at 126.

167. *Id.* at 122.

168. Posting of Arthur Bright to Citizen Media Law Project, *Associated Press v. Drudge Retort*, http://www.citmedialaw.org/threats/associated-press-v-drudge-retort (June 16, 2008) (noting *National Basketball Association* was "one of the few cases to address a 'hot news' claim").

169. *See* Press Release, The Associated Press, Statement of News Values and Principles, Feb. 16, 2006, http://www.ap.org/newsvalues/index.html ("We must satisfy ourselves, by our own reporting, that the material [used from any source] is credible.").

170. *Int'l News Serv.*, 248 U.S. 215, 239 (1918) (applying quasi property in consideration of the "rights of complainant and defendant, *competitors in business*, as between themselves") (emphasis added); *Nat'l Basketball Ass'n, Inc.*, 105 F.3d 841, 845 (2d Cir. 1997) (stating that the fourth factor to be considered is whether "the defendant is in direct competition with a product or service offered by the plaintiffs.").

171. *Nat'l Basketball Ass'n*, 105 F.3d at 845.

172. Epstein, *supra* note 98, at 126.

173. *Id.* at 105.

174. *See Int'l News Serv.*, 248 U.S. at 240 (finding that a competitor committing misappropriation to the disadvantage of complainant is behavior "contrary to good conscience").

175. AP also sued Moreover Technologies, a headline and news aggregation service, under copyright infringement and misappropriation theories, but the case settled on undisclosed terms. *See* Press Release, The Associated Press, AP Settles Lawsuit Against Moreover and VeriSign (Aug. 18, 2008), http://www.ap.org/pages/about/pressreleases/pr_081808a.html.

176. Bright, *supra* note 168.

177. *Id.*

178. Saul Hansell, *The Associated Press to Set Guidelines for Using its Articles in Blogs*, New York Times, June 16, 2008, http://www.nytimes.com/2008/06/16/business/media/16ap.html?_r=1&ref=business.

179. *Id.*

180. *Id.*

181. *Id.*

182. *See supra*, Section III.C.

183. Lemley, *supra* note 162, at 1270.

184. *See* Epstein, *supra* note 98, at 117 ("The risk of seeking out the immutable rules of positive law is that, had the composition of the Supreme Court been different, the three dissenting voices in [*International News Service*] would have established the legal norms for an industry whose internal operation they scarcely understood.").

185. *See Id.* at 126.

186. *See supra* Section II.C.3.

*Daniel S. Park, attended college at Harvard and law school at Berkeley. In 2011, he began working at Gibson, Dunn & Crutcher, a law firm in Los Angeles.

Clues in the Rubble: A User-First Framework for Sustaining Local News

by Bill Mitchell*

[...]

PAID CONTENT

Shift the debate from what publishers might charge to what users actually want.

The debate over paid content is approaching a key turning point, especially in terms of a growing awareness of the sort of content that might support payment and the technical infrastructure to charge in ways that can be easily adjusted based on user response. News organizations will soon have at their disposal mechanisms that will enable much more aggressive experimentation with user fees than has been possible thus far. Equipped with tools to charge, all that publishers need now is a framework for creating or packaging products and services that customers will want to pay for. The most promising areas fall into two main categories: sites or applications that facilitate an *experience* of interacting with content that surpasses what's available without charge and/or a type of high-value content that users need to do their job or enjoy a hobby or personal passion. Perhaps increased experimentation will move the paid content debate from that of "dogma . . . to something scientifically studied," as analyst Vin Crosbie urged way back in 2003.[35]

In a much-anticipated move, *The New York Times* announced January 20, 2010, that it would begin charging for news online at the beginning of 2011.[36] *The Times* said it would rely on a meter providing users with access to a certain number of articles each month before requiring payment of a flat fee to read unlimited content. The paper's executives said they had not decided how many articles would be free or what the fee will be. Among other things, they said they needed a year to prepare the software required to coordinate online payment with its database of print subscribers, who will get free access to online articles. One of the paper's biggest challenges will be preserving its 13 relationship with its most loyal, online-only readers—the users bearing the biggest burden of its new pay plan.[37]

Key to preserving that relationship will be creating sufficient new value to support new charges. "It is not enough to make content informative, relevant, interesting and believable," media economist Robert G. Picard, has written. "To gain loyal audiences willing to provide the financial support needed for the future, news organizations must provide engaging, pleasing and memorable experiences to their users."[38]

Sharing the stage with Apple CEO Steve Jobs during the January 2010 introduction of the iPad, Martin Nisenholtz, senior vice president of digital operations for The New York Times Company, claimed the user experience enabled by the paper's iPad application reflects "the best of print and the best of digital, all rolled up into one." Interestingly, Apple Senior Vice President Scott Forstall envisioned a user experience drawn more from the analog than digital worlds: "IPad is the best way to browse the Web for the same reasons that *it just feels right* to hold a book or a magazine or a newspaper as you read them. It just feels right—to hold the Internet in your hands as you surf it."[39]

It's unclear whether interacting with *New York Times* content on the iPad will become the kind of "memorable experience" called for by media economist Picard, but it does suggest the wisdom of publishers creating "paid experience" as a substantial portion of whatever content they limit to paying customers.

Subscription services on news Web sites typically fall into two main categories: blunt and less so. The former limits all or most online content to print subscribers or customers paying an online surcharge. The latter includes several variations, including targeted services aimed at such hobbies as sports; memberships designed to serve users' professional as well as high-stakes personal interests such as investing; metered access that permits a certain number of stories to be viewed in any given period; donations on a one-time or ongoing basis.

The biggest downside to walling off content is the loss of advertising revenue caused by reduced traffic. That's the problem that prompted The New York Times to lift user fees on its Times Select service for columnists in September 2007, despite 227,000 paying 14 customers and $10 million in annual subscription revenue.[40] As new technology enables greater flexibility for subscription services, publishers are hoping to leverage the additional demographic information they'll gather about paid users to support higher prices for advertising they're exposed to.[41]

The History of Paid Content

News has enjoyed such convenient subsidy for so long, in the form of advertising, that journalists have had a tough time finding other ways of paying for it. This was a problem for local news, it turns out, even before advertising began paying the bills in the 19th century. In his landmark history of American journalism, *The Creation of the Media,* Princeton professor Paul Starr says publishers of rural papers in New York in the late 1700s and early 1800s didn't believe their "readers would pay for information which they could secure by word of mouth from their neighbors."[42]

But with insufficient commerce to support substantial advertising, the burden of paying for news fell almost entirely on readers. And they eventually came around—at least the group of "elites made up of the royals, nobility and wealthy landholders and merchants"—until a business model based on advertising showed up with the industrial revolution and increased literacy.[43]

The revenue share borne by newspaper advertisers eventually rose as high as 82 percent in 2006,[44] but it's now on the way down, shifting the burden back to readers. *The New York Times*—an unusual case because of high subscription fees for its print edition and limited classified advertising—reported recently that it's approaching a 50–50 split of advertising and circulation revenue. Some metropolitan dailies are headed in the same direction, if not quite as quickly. The Detroit Newspapers, for example, hope to achieve a 60–40 percent split of advertising and circulation after doubling the single copy price of their daily papers from 50 cents to a dollar last year.[45]

Online, no one is suggesting that subscription or other user fees will make up all the revenue lost from diminished advertising. Research indicates that most readers say they won't pay,[46] underlining the importance of providing users with something more than just the news—a service or experience worth paying for. Even then, user fees are seen as just one stream among several.

The Money Goes to the Niches

Consumers are spending a lot of money for information online, but not much on local news. Forrester Research projected spending of nearly $3 billion in 2009 on information and services from such sites as *The Wall Street Journal,* Match.com and ConsumerReports.org.[47]

Forrester's Sarah Rotman Epps estimated that only 3 percent of Internet users in the U.S. have paid to access digital information—and that the average household income of those who have is nearly $100,000. She urged publishers to be sure their offers satisfy three requirements before attaching an online price tag: compelling content, the right targeting (customers already predisposed to spend money on such products) and "smart device integration" on iPhones, Blackberries and other tools in common use.[48]

In a separate Forrester report, researcher Nick Thomas warned against viewing "the Web as a panacea for the historic decline in print," adding: "It would be nice to see online revenues making up for the shortfall in print subscriptions, thus allowing publishers to carry on as they are, but that's not going to happen any time soon. The Web is a separate, increasingly important medium and must evolve on its own terms."

Thomas steered publishers toward specialized content: "News will be free, but paid opportunities will arise around niche verticals. Smart publishers and advertisers will focus on content channels where brand values and expertise coincides with readers' passions or their needs: This could be around wine, books, music or travel, for example—or around personal finance or content for professionals."[49]

James Hamilton, director of the DeWitt Wallace Center for Media and Democracy at Duke University, suggests, "One way to make sense of the many different types of news offered in the market is to categorize demands for information by the types of decisions that give rise to the demands." In his 2004 book, *All the News That's Fit to Sell*, he recounts earlier research by Anthony Downs that sorts people's desire for information into four functions: "consumption, production, entertainment and voting."[50]

Government information has been a lucrative part of the information industry for decades, but powered mostly by users combining special interests beyond citizenship and the wherewithal to pay high prices for the information. I found at least a couple of examples of successful entrepreneurs in this segment interested in tweaking their business models to direct some of that government news to a wider audience of users. In Denmark, former TV reporter Rasmus Nielsen makes available, without charge, a portion of his niche reports about the Danish Parliament to a general readership.[51] Craig Sandler, who publishes similar, high-priced services tracking state government in Florida and Massachusetts, is also working on a consumer edition with more modest fees.[52]

Foundations have been helpful in encouraging nonprofit initiatives aimed at filling some of the gaps users are finding in government news and information as a result of cutbacks. Sites like Connecticut Mirror, which launched in January 2010, are also taking significant strides in making sense of government reporting. Among its features: An Editor's Choice service that provides users with a one-stop aggregation of news about government and politics throughout the state, similar to Jim Romenesko's news about news on Poynter Online. Connecticut Mirror says it does not anticipate charging users.[53]

Among the paid content experiments in the entertainment area was the 2003 decision by *The Los Angeles Times* to put its popular CalendarLive entertainment section behind a pay wall. In a mini case study of the initiative, the Nieman Journalism Lab's Tim Windsor reported that the move generated about $63,000 from the $39.95-a-year subscription fee and attracted about 19,000 registered users, 15,000 of them print subscribers who paid no online fee. Windsor noted an audience drop from 729,000 visitors in July 2003 to the 19,000 registered visitors after the subscription requirement was imposed. Losses in ad revenue were not reported, but *The Times* removed the pay wall about 21 months after it went up. "If it was a success," he added, "there was never a press release heralding that fact."[54]

The latest test of the paid content model is underway on Long Island, where *Newsday* installed a $5 per week subscription fee in November 2009. Two months after imposing the pay wall, *Newsday* reported that only 35 people had purchased an online-only subscription. The idea of the pay wall in this case, though, is not generating new revenue from out-of-market customers but securing the site's value to users on Long Island.[55]

The paper kept the site free for subscribers to the print edition and subscribers to the various services of Cablevision, which owns *Newsday*.[56] Since newspaper and Cablevision subscribers account for about 75 percent of the households on Long Island, it's unclear how much other news organizations will be able to learn from the *Newsday* initiative. But MediaPost Communications provided an early impression, citing Nielsen data showing a 21-percent traffic drop from October to November after the pay wall was installed.[57]

Since they typically enjoy a more exclusive hold on local news than larger news organizations do, it's not surprising that smaller papers are doing somewhat better with online subscriptions. The *Lima* (Ohio) *News*, which sells 32,000 papers a day during the week and about 40,000 on Sundays, placed all locally produced news behind a pay wall August 10, 2009. By year's end, the paper had added more revenue via subscription fees than it lost from the reduced views of online ads, according to publisher Jim Shine. Readers with seven-day print subscriptions are invited to register for the paper's site without charge, and about 4,000 have registered so far. The paper has sold about 800 online subscriptions, most of them at the monthly rate of $4.95.[58]

Shine urged colleagues considering such a move to prepare themselves for "some pretty harsh feedback from readers," but said he's also heard from Web readers who had cancelled their print subscriptions but had no quarrel with the paper's decision to charge online. "They told me they knew this day was coming," he said.

Shine said he doesn't know whether the pay wall will "become a long-term solution." But he described several valuable lessons learned in the meantime:

- Breaking local news continues to drive online subscriptions. He said he thought both registrations and online subscriptions would subside after the first couple of months, but he said both are experiencing slow, steady growth. In the past month, he said the paper had added 96 new online subscriptions and 400 registrations of existing print subscribers.

- The pay wall resulted in an immediate 28-percent drop in traffic, but has not erased all of the site's traffic gains on a year-over-year basis.

- The increased demographic information collected from registered and paying users has not yet enabled the paper to increase its online ad rates.

- The pay wall appears to have had little impact, so far, in protecting print circulation.

Especially given economic conditions, Shine said he was not surprised by either of the last two developments.

Pay Walls as Defenders of Print Circulation

An October 2009 study of paid content by the American Press Institute found that 11 of 16 small- to medium-circulation papers listed protection of print circulation as one of the main goals of their pay walls.[59] Walter Hussman, publisher of the *Democrat Chronicle* in Arkansas, has become a spokesman for that approach, citing statistics indicating that the average value of a print subscriber dramatically exceeds that of an online visitor.[60]

In a time when newspaper circulation is falling nationwide, Edward L. Seaton, publisher and editor-in-chief of the 10,304-circulation Manhattan (Kansas) *Mercury* told API that a pay wall erected in May 2009 was responsible for driving up print subscriptions nine percent over the previous year.

E. Mayer Maloney, publisher of the 26,433-circulation *Herald-Times* in Bloomington, Indiana, said he and his colleagues expected "the earth to open up and the fires of hell to consume us" when they imposed a pay wall in October 2003.[61]

Instead, the paper attracted about 2,100 paying, online-only subscribers at $5.95 a month and managed to help protect print circulation. With those results in mind, he has introduced pay walls on two smaller papers he manages, the 12,500-circulation *Times-Mail* in Bedford, Ind., and the 6,000-circulation *Reporter-Times* in Martinsville, Ind. The *Times-Mail* has 600 online-only subscribers, and the *Reporter-Times* about 300, according to the API report.

Maloney's boss, Schurz Communications president and CEO Todd Schurz, said in a telephone interview that he encourages experimentation with pay models at all of his company's 11 daily newspapers, eight weeklies and TV stations in six markets.

But he confessed to what he termed his "single biggest worry" about pay walls: "In instituting a pay wall, you want to stop the slide in print circulation. But in making the decision to defend the old model you may be handicapping the new one. And while the [print circulation] you protect will save the newspaper money, it will not save the newspaper."

New Charges for New Services

Other experiments involve paid sites providing content and services not available either in the paper or on the paper's Web site.

Jim O'Shea, the former *Los Angeles Times* editor who now heads the start-up Chicago News Cooperative, makes a point of insisting that the $2 weekly fee he envisions charging "is not fee for content." The Co-op, launched in the fall of 2009, provides content for a regional edition of *The New York Times* as well as its own Web site, where stories are freely available to all.

But O'Shea hopes membership in the co-op will provide sufficient additional benefits—beyond the news itself—to support the fee he describes as "less than a cup of Starbucks." Within five years, he hopes to support an annual newsroom budget of $3 to $4 million by collecting those two dollars a week from 30,000 to 40,000 people—about one half of one percent of the population of metropolitan Chicago. But before he can get to the stage of seeking those co-op fees, he says he needs an additional $2 million in philanthropic help to sustain the operation in the meantime.

The co-op model is at the heart of an ambitious plan developed by veteran journalist Tom Stites to create a news service aimed at "less-than-affluent Americans" in communities around the country. Like the Chicago News Co-op, Stites' Banyan Project would not sell its journalism but rather the online community services it would create *around* the news—its benefits of ownership. Also still in the stages of seeking foundation funding to get started, Stites hopes for a half million shareholders who, at "a dime a day," could generate annual revenues of $18 million.[62]

The key to the Banyan's strategy is an approach to news and users that Stites describes as "relational journalism." He explains: "It's the relational approach that makes possible Banyan's value proposition—that the less-than-affluent Banyan public will find its journalism relevant to their lives, respectful of them as people, and worthy of their trust. Consumer co-op ownership is at the heart of this in that it makes the 20 editors accountable to the reader/owners—this is user-first not just in aspiration, but in structure."[63]

In Pittsburgh, the *Post-Gazette* has introduced a new online service built on the concept of extra fee for extra service. This one does include some pay walls. PG+, introduced in September 2009, spotlights special sports material but also provides a range of features and blogs focused on politics, music and life in Pittsburgh. *Post-Gazette* editor David Shribman says more than 90 percent of the content is original to PG+—as opposed to material previously available free online and then walled off. The site also includes the kind of user perks that many publications are making available to home delivery customers—discounts at area museums, two-for-one specials at restaurants, etc.

Shribman declined to reveal how many users have signed up for the service, which costs $3.99 a month or $35.88 a year. His assessment: "We're making steady progress and we're not going to abandon it."

Part of the experiment involves exploration of new markets, including a group he calls the "Pittsburgh Diaspora." Shribman said the paper is trying to see how it might tweak PG+ to provide special services to the estimated 500,000 former Pittsburgh residents "who live elsewhere—except for Thanksgiving and Christmas and the Web—and who care about their hometown and their hometown teams."

The Mystery of Who Pays for What and Why Online

Among the data points PG+ is still trying to sort out: "We have the oddest surge in subscribers on Tuesdays. Maybe it's because it's the day after the day after (the Steelers' games on Sundays), and people are saying, 'Did you see that on Plus?' But we really have no idea. It's a mystery."[64]

Steve Brill, co-founder of one of several vendor services in development to help publishers collect user fees, says that's the nature of paid content.

"I guarantee that in six or nine months," he told Poynter Online's Steve Myers in November 2009, "we can look at these 16 [ways of monetizing content] and we can declare together that five of them were totally stupid, ridiculous, and why were we screwing with them?"[65]

In addition to charging by niche, the new online subscription services enable publishers to adjust free/paid dials based on number of articles viewed and the timing of publication. Some may also invite readers to set their own price, depending on the value they attach to the content at hand.

A chart from a Journalism Online presentation shows how a publisher might decide to reserve access to certain articles to paying customers for a period of, say, one hour after publication. For big news of widespread interest, the publisher could remove the meter and make the story available immediately to all. Whether restricted by timestamp or not, the advantage of such an approach is that it avoids sealing news off behind a pay wall and thwarting the ability to build as big an audience as possible.[66]

Audience building—or content swiping, depending on your point of view—is at the heart of the dispute between Google and some news executives. That controversy is beyond the scope of this paper, but Google's "First Click Free" service is worth noting in the context of emerging pay wall options.

In a December 1 post, Jeff Cohen, a senior business product manager for Google, said the search engine had updated the service to enable publishers to limit readers to no more than five articles per day.[67] This approach enables the so-called metered approach used by the *Financial Times* and planned by *The New York Times*.

The idea, according to U.S. FT managing editor Chrystia Freeland, "is to be simultaneously open to visits from the occasional and casual newcomer while assuring that the addict has to pay for his addiction." In practical terms, this means you can visit FT.com 10 times in a month before a pay wall pops up in front of article #11.

Differentiating the Lookie-Lou's from the Regulars

The capacity to differentiate among users who show up only now and then and others who might hit the site, say, 50 or 100 times in a month, is critical. Steve Yelvington, digital strategist for Morris Communications, points out that blocking those occasional visitors—he calls them "Lookie-Lou's"—with a pay wall would mean forfeiting ad revenue, however modest it might be. He says it's an even worse idea to block the more frequent visitors, people who are more likely to be local and are much more valuable to advertisers. But not just to advertisers. It's critical to understand what keeps them coming back to the site so frequently before blocking them with a pay wall, Yelvington says. Once understood, it might be possible to persuade them "to pitch in some cash" one way or another, he says.[68]

At the *Financial Times*, the percentage of occasional users who decide to subscribe when they encounter the pay wall is very small—"single digits," Freeland told me a in brief interview—"but that's OK."

The metered approach is useful for several reasons. It generates some advertising revenue from those occasional visitors and it provides a taste of the publication that might one day prompt subscriptions in print or online. In the case of visitors who do subscribe when the meter runs out, Freeland points out: "Generating subscriptions like that is very cheap."

Freeland argues that "pay walls clearly do work for niche publications—and your niche can be sports, maybe technology, it might even be entertainment." She adds: "The bigger question is, 'Can you charge for general news?'" Freeland says she hopes her local paper—*The New York Times*—will figure out a way to do so and proposes one example of not-exactly-general news that she'd be willing to pay for: "I would pay to know about schools. There's nothing that parents are more obsessive about."

Jim O'Shea plans to put Freeland's theory to the test with the first of many "news interest networks" he hopes to introduce at the Chicago News Cooperative. He and his colleagues met Jan. 19, 2010 with a group of about 34 people with special interest in education and asked them what should go into the co-op's education network: "What's something they'd place high value on, and how might it play out journalistically?"

O'Shea plans similar meetings with the Chicago Council on Global Affairs, an organization with about 7,000 members especially interested in international issues. Since the *Chicago Tribune* has closed all of its foreign bureaus, O'Shea says he's anxious to see how the Chicago News Cooperative might collaborate with the Council to meet the needs of its members—and grow membership in both organizations.

Among the advantages of paid content, in Freeland's mind, is "becoming less advertiser-dependent."

A wide distribution of subsidy has always been important to journalism's independence. If a news organization attracts enough advertisers, no single one should be able to carry enough weight to influence coverage. As the number of advertisers shrinks along with total overall ad revenue, increased payments from users and other sources can provide a valuable antidote to the potential influence of the big spending advertisers that remain. As Ken Auletta notes in his new book, *Googled*, over-reliance on advertising can deposit too much influence over the news in too few hands.[69]

More Civil Comments—Plus a $1.99 Fee—on the iPhone App

Robert Picard, the media economist, points out that the value of what's created in new services around news "does not necessarily translate" into the revenue needed to sustain journalism. But without something new that's distinctive and compelling enough to separate people from their cash, all the new paid content tools in the world will leave journalism hopelessly underfunded.[70]

News organizations are having some success in raising prices for existing products. But framing the paid content issue, as Picard does, as the creation of new value is quite different from simply imposing a fee today on content that yesterday was free.

Instead of installing a pay wall in front of its online coverage of the Miami Dolphins, for example, *The Miami Herald* created a new iPhone app for Dolphins fans. By October 2009, the app had generated about 13,000 sales at $1.99 each. More significantly, it paved the way for the paper to offer similar apps for college teams throughout Florida and to develop a small but growing new revenue stream.[71]

Herald executive editor Anders Gyllenhaal said the *Herald* considered commissioning an outside contractor to develop the app, but decided that the relatively modest time investment of its own programmers in the project would pay off in the long run. As with the *Post-Gazette*'s Tuesday subscriber surge, the *Herald* is noticing trends with its iPhone apps that it doesn't quite get. Noting the nasty comments that the Dolphins' unexceptional record has provoked on the *Herald*'s Web site, he said: "For some reason that we don't really understand, the comments attached to articles on the iPhone app are a lot more elevated."

Maybe it has something to do with the kind of community created by a paid membership? As anyone with an iPhone will tell you, the decision to purchase a news-related app is not simply about news. It's also about the experience.

Finding Ways to Monetize the Most Fully Engaged Customers

When Philip Balboni wrote his business plan for GlobalPost, he included subscription fees—a pay wall. He backed off the plan before launch—"I just didn't think that as a new brand we could pull it off"—but insists that user fees of some sort are an essential ingredient of digital publishing.

"There has to be some sort of a bond with the community," he says, arguing that advertising and syndication revenue will never be enough to sustain his enterprise. Rather than require subscriptions to read the bulk of GlobalPost content, the site introduced Passport, a premium membership service that debuted at $199 a year.

The price was cut to $99 with a half-price option for academics, and subsequently to $49.99 for all individual memberships.

So far, only about 500 of the site's users have purchased a membership—a long way from the 25,000 to 50,000 that Balboni says he believes will eventually join.

Mulling his site's prospects, he asked: "Is it the content or being a member of the community" that will drive allegiance to the site in the long run? His answer: "I tend to believe it's more a matter of community. But like any community it probably takes time to get that interaction going. And we're not experts in this."

Among GlobalPost's most important challenges, Balboni believes, is figuring out how to more fully engage the 15 percent of its audience that visits the site 100 times or more each month. "That's a heavy level of engagement," he says, noting that the site needs to "track those particular users and at the appropriate moment display an invitation to become Passport members."

I joined Passport at the $50 level and took part in one of the benefits that membership provides: participation in a conference call with one of the more than 65 correspondents working for GlobalPost in nearly 50 countries around the world. I joined a half dozen other members in an early December conference call with GlobalPost Dubai reporter Tom Hundley, a veteran foreign correspondent who worked overseas for the *Chicago Tribune* for 18 years. Dubai was much in the news after its debt problems tumbled stock markets around the world. Among the Passport members with a clear business interest on the call was David Riedel, who advises mutual funds on their investments in 15 emerging countries around the world.

Riedel engaged Hundley in a conversation about whether Abu Dhabi might supplant Dubai as the economic center of the Emirates—just the sort of insiderish info that he could later pass along to his clients.

"I'm surprised so few people participate," Riedel told me in a follow-up phone chat about the correspondent conversations. "Any little tidbit that helps me have that conversation with fund managers can be valuable. GlobalPost is an undiscovered jewel in terms of the insights that can help me help my clients."

Riedel's experience with Passport illustrates how a freely accessed consumer site can carve out a paid, premium service for users who have clear, work-related needs. For customers like Riedel, even the original Passport fee of $199 a year seems like a bargain. Less so, even at $50, for more casual members like me.

Perhaps part of the answer is creating two levels of membership—professional and personal. But how to create a premium *personal* service compelling enough to sustain fees of $50 or even $25 a year? The key may lie in people's attachment to place, a concept with as much to offer local news sites as operations like Global-Post. What killer app, for example, might GlobalPost's man in Dubai develop to make the service essential for expat families living in the United Arab Emirates? What might PG+ create for displaced Pittsburghers that would render a modest monthly fee a no-brainer? Could GlobalPost and the *Post-Gazette* monetize social networking tools—as the Chicago News Cooperative hopes to—and create interactive communities of interest around geography, schools and topics?

Donations: Why Not Just Ask—and Receive?

Few organizations seek donations as effectively as NPR. But even there, a breakdown of its revenues shows that user gifts is just one revenue source among many:[72]

- 31% from listeners via pledges, memberships and other donations
- 20% from businesses via corporate underwriting
- 11% from the federally funded Corporation for Public Broadcasting (CPB)
- 10% from licensee support
- 9% from foundations and major gifts
- 5% from local and state governments, and
- 14% from all other sources.[73]

When the wife and husband team of Morgan and Askins founded their Ann Arbor Chronicle site, they anticipated drawing all of their revenue from advertising. But then a funny thing happened to them—something that also happened to *The New York Times* some months later—readers began telling them that them they wanted to pay for the news they provided. They just needed a way to do so.[74]

The *Chronicle* installed both a DONATE button (for one-time gifts) and a SUBSCRIBE button. Subscriptions include both a minimum ($10-a-month) and maximum ($250-a-year) rate, the latter to prevent individual subscribers from claiming too big a stake in the enterprise. Unless subscribers request anonymity, their names are listed on the site.

Other than saying they're covering their costs and paying their bills, Morgan and Askins don't reveal their revenues. The site includes a list of subscribers indicating payments by 15 to 25 people a month, and a list of 54 advertisers—paying monthly rates of $100 or $200 or $300 a month—for the period of October through December 2009.[75]

The Miami Herald began soliciting donations—right next to its pitch for print subscriptions—in mid-December.[76] Media analyst Steve Outing provided a detailed critique, concluding that the Herald had been way too subtle in its pitch—criticism that Gyllenhaal noted in the comments section attached to his weekly column. Perhaps news organizations could learn a lesson from Wikipedia founder Jimmy Wales, who appeared safe from charges of subtlety with the pitch he tacked on the top of Wikipedia pages: *"Please read: A personal appeal from*

Wikipedia founder Jimmy Wales." The banner linked to a page encouraging donations in any of 18 national currencies.[77]

The result? The fundraising drive exceeded its $7.5 million goal by more than $500,000.[78]

No DONATE button has appeared on nytimes.com yet or the vast majority of Web sites maintained by legacy news organizations. But Kachingle, a new service designed to facilitate donations, is inviting publishers, bloggers and users to test their system for distributing donations among users' favorite sites.[79]

Joel Kramer didn't wait for that sort of special donation service to begin soliciting donations at MinnPost, the local news site he founded two years ago in the Twin Cities.

"Serious journalism is a community asset, not just a consumer good," Kramer argues, "and people (and foundations) should support it, as they support museums. We'll see if that argument persuades enough people."[80]

His focus may be on serious journalism, but he avoids taking himself too seriously in his fundraising. To raise sponsorship money for the blog written by David Brauer, Kramer solicited both $10 LoBrau and $25 HighBrau gifts.[81] The site lists contributors as members at various ranks, including "night police reporters" (the site boasts more than 200 of them, at a donation rate of $100 to $250) and "media moguls" (there are only 10 donations at that level—$5,000 to $10,000). MinnPost lists the names of its contributors online and includes a "Donors' Wall" where they're invited to explain their gifts.[82]

MinnPost added 500 first-time donors in 2009, increasing its revenue from individual donors and the organization's annual MinnRoast event from $356,000 in 2008 to $458,000 in 2009. With expenses down 20 percent year over year, the growing revenue burden carried by the donors and the roast in 2009 is even more striking.[83]

[…]

NOTES

[…]

35. "The Albuquerque Journal as a Bad Content Model," Vin Crosbie, Digital Deliverance LLC, Nov. 6, 2003.

36. "The Times to Charge for Frequent Access to its Web Site," Richard Perez-Pena, *The New York Times*, Jan. 20, 2010.

37. "New York Times Pay Plan to Target Most Loyal, Online-Only Users," Bill Mitchell, Poynter Online, Jan. 19, 2010, http://www.poynter.org/column.asp?id=131&aid=176180.

38. Picard, Robert G., cited above.

39. "What Apple's iPad Means for Journalism Design, Multimedia and Business," Steve Myers, Poynter Online, Jan. 27, 2010, http://www.poynter.org/column.asp?id=101&aid=176756

40. "Times to Stop Charging for Parts of its Web Site," Sept. 18, 2007, Richard Perez-Pena, *The New York Times*, http://www.nytimes.com/2007/09/18/business/media/18times.html

41. "How to Increase Ad Revenue with Paywalls, Higher Rates, Content Tracking," Steve Myers, Poynter Online, Dec. 11, 2009, http://www.poynter.org/column.asp?id=101&aid=174056

42. Starr, Paul, *The Creation of The Media*, p. 67.

43. Picard, Robert G., cited above, p. 28.

44. Picard, Robert G., *Journalism, Value Creation and the Future of News Organizations*, Shorenstein Center, Spring 2006, p. 28.

45. "Detroit Free Press, News Shifting Revenue Burden from Advertisers to Readers," Bill Mitchell, Poynter Online, Oct. 23, 2009, http://www.poynter.org/column.asp?id=131&aid=172280 See also: "Audience," Rick Edmonds, The State of the News Media 2009, http://www.stateofthe media.org/2009/narrative_newspapers_audience.php

46. "What's Your Online Content Worth? Global Consumers Say: It Depends," Nielsenwire, Jan. 5, 2010, http://blog.nielsen.com/nielsenwire/consumer/whats-your-online-content-worth-global-consumers-say-it-depends/

47. Forrester Research, "USB2C Online Paid Content: Five-Year Forecast," Dec. 3, 2008.

48. "Who Pays for Online Content?" Sarah Rotman Epps with Mark Mulligan and Dan Wilkos, Forrester Research, March 9, 2009.

49. "Evaluating Online News Sites Using The Forrester Content Strategy Review," Nick Thomas with Mark Mulligan and Erik Hood, June 2, 2009.

50. Hamilton, James, *All the News That's Fit to Sell*, 2004, p. 10

51. "Another Nielsen Goes Niche in Pursuit of Profit," Bill Mitchell, Poynter Online, Sept. 14, 2009, http://www.poynter.org/column.asp?id=131&aid=169796.

52. Sandler, Craig, telephone interview with author, Jan. 13, 2009.

53. "Nonprofit Connecticut Mirror Targets Gaps in Political Coverage and Data," Bill Mitchell, Jan. 25, 2010, Poynter Online, http://www.poynter.org/column.asp?id=131&aid=176435

54. "Will paid content work? Two cautionary tales from 2004?" Tim Windsor, Nieman Journalism Lab, Feb. 10, 2009, http://www.niemanlab.org/2009/02/will-paid-content-work-two-cautionary-tales-from-2004/

55. "Newsday Said It Wasn't Putting up a Paywall to Sell Online Subscriptions—and It Isnt," Staci D. Kramer, Content, Jan. 26, 2010, http://paidcontent.org/article/419-newsday-said-it-wasnt-putting-up-a-paywall-to-sell-online-subscriptions/. See also "Newsday exec: We don't measure success by how many people sign up to pay $260 a year for our website," Romenesko Memos, Jan. 28, 2010, Poynter Online, http://www.poynter.org/column.asp?id=45&aid=176825

56. "Newsday to Listen to Feedback on Paid Model," Joe Strupp, *Editor & Publisher*, Oct. 22, 2009 http://www.editorandpublisher.com/eandp/news/article_display.jsp?vnu_content_id=1004029591

57. "Pay Wall Drives Newsday Traffic Down, Paper Says According to Plan," David Goetzel, MediaDailyNews, Dec. 10, 2009, http://www.mediapost.com/publications/?fa=Articles.show Article&art_aid=118960

58. Shine, Jim, telephone interview with author, Dec. 23, 2009.

59. American Press Institute, "Profiles of Newspapers Charging for Online Content," October 2009.

60. "How to Sink a Newspaper," Walter Hussman, *The Wall Street Journal*, May 7, 2007, http://www.opinionjournal.com/editorial/feature.html?id=110010038

61. API study, "Profiles of Newspapers Charging for Online Content," October 2009.

62. Banyan Project, Co-op ownership, http://banyanproject.com/index.php?title=Co-op_Owner ship. Disclosure: I'm among more than two dozen unpaid advisors to the Banyan Project (listed in left rail of site).

63. Stites, Tom, e-mail to author, Jan. 22, 2010.

64. Shribman, David, interview with author cited above.

65. "Brill: Paid Content Debate Now about How, not If," Bill Mitchell, Poynter Online, Aug. 3, 2009, based on telephone interview.

66. "An Introduction to Journalism Online," http://www.journalismonline.com/media/Journalism_Online_Introduction.pdf

67. "Google and paid content," Jeff Cohen, Dec. 1, 2009 http://googlenewsblog.blogspot.com/2009/12/update-to-first-click-free.html

68. "Thinking about a paywall? Read this first," Steve Yelvington, Yelvington.com, Dec. 1, 2009

69. Auletta, Ken, Googled, 2009.

70. Picard, Robert G., cited above.

71. Hirsch, Rick telephone interview with Julia Kamin, Nov. 5, 2009.

72. Catone, Josh, "Why NPR is the Future of Mainstream Media," Mashable, June 3, 2009, http://mashable.com/2009/06/03/npr/. See also comments for discussion of NPR funding sources.

73. NPR.org, Annual Reports, Audited Financial Statements and Form 990s, http://www.npr.org/about/privatesupport.html

74. "Times Says It Will Cut 100 Newsroom Jobs," Richard Perez-Pena, Oct. 19, 2009 (see comments from readers volunteering to pay for online content to help avoid the layoffs)

75. Ann Arbor Chronicle, donation and subscription page, http://annarborchronicle.com/tip-jar/

76. "Figuring a way to pay for news that's read online," Anders Gyllenhaal, The Miami Herald, Dec. 20, 2009, http://www.miamiherald.com/news/issues-ideas/story/1389532.html

77. "This is where we protect Wikipedia, the encyclopedia written by the people," Jimmy Wales, Wikipedia, http://wikimediafoundation.org/wiki/Support_Wikipedia2/en?utm_medium=Appeal&utm_campaign=fundraiser2009&utm_source=2009 Jimmy Appeal9

78. "Annual Wikipedia Fundraiser Nets $8 Million," Mark Hefflinger, digitalmediawire, Jan. 5, 2010, http://dmwmedia.com/news/2010/01/05/annual-wikipedia-fundraiser-nets-8-million.

79. "Read All About Me on Kachingle: Where I'm Paying for News," Bill Mitchell, Poynter Online, Feb. 13, 2009. http://www.poynter.org/column.asp?id=131&aid=158396. And e-mail from Kachingle marketing director, Dec. 4, 2009 indicating the service is now ready for beta testing.

80. "Fewer Readers, Paying More," Joel Kramer, The New York Times Online, Feb. 10, 2009 http://roomfordebate.blogs.nytimes.com/2009/02/10/battle-plans-for-newspapers/?hp

81. "MinnPost-Harnisch High-Low Matched & Anonymous Contribution Model for News," Bill Mitchell, Poynter Online, March 11, 2009, http://www.poynter.org/column.asp?id=131 &aid=159920 See also MinnPost's End—of-year Wish List, December 2009 http://givemn.razoo.com/story/End-Of-Year-Wish-List-1

82. MinnPost donations page, January 2010, http://givemn.razoo.com/story/Minnpost

83. "2009: a remarkable year for MinnPost," Joel Kramer, http://www.minnpost.com/insideminnpost/2010/01/25/15209/2009_a_remarkable_year_for_minnpost (see full report linked as PDF from that url).

*Bill Mitchell heads the Poynter Institute's Entrepreneurial and International programs and serves as a member of its faculty. He was a Sagan Fellow at Harvard's Shorenstein Center the in Fall of 2009, where he prepared this report.

Bill Mitchell, "Clues in the Rubble: A User-First Framework for Sustaining Local News," Discussion Paper Series, #D-56 (Cambridge, Mass.: Joan Shorenstein Center on the Press, Politics and Public Policy, February 2010), 10–27.

Bad Public Relations or Is This a Real Crisis?: YES

*by Lauren Rich Fine**

Newspapers are suffering financially and many question their fate. Is this a case of bad public relations or is this a real crisis? I would contend it is both. This report is intended to provide a current look at the financial status of the industry, mostly using data on the public companies as they are the ones for which financial data is available, while incorporating industry data when possible. In addition to a snapshot of the industry, I also share a variety of thoughts on what can be done to improve the economics of the industry.

There are currently nine actively traded public newspaper companies: AH Belo, Gannett, Journal Communications, Lee Enterprises, McClatchy Newspapers, Media General, New York Times, F.W. Scripps, and Washington Post; the less actively traded names are Gatehouse Media and Journal Register. There is still some public data for Tribune and Media News Group. The combined circulation of these companies is roundly 22.4 million daily and 24.8 million Sunday, or 44% & 48% of total U.S. circulation as measured by the Newspaper Association of America (NAA). While the data isn't complete, this group generated roundly 35% of US ad revenues, again based on NAA data.

A number of newspapers have filed for bankruptcy over the last few months, in many cases, due to excessive debt, typically related to acquisitions. Among them are Tribune, Philadelphia Newspaper Holdings, Chicago Sun-Times, and the Minneapolis Star-Tribune. Some newspapers have folded, for example the Rocky Mountain News. Others have gone online only or some combination of print and online, such as the Christian Science Monitor and the Detroit Free Press. It is a dicey time. While many newspapers still have a lot of debt, it is not something I plan to address as it is company specific and typically was related to an acquisition.

REVENUES

Newspapers typically have two major revenue streams, advertising and circulation, which account for roughly 80% and 20% of revenues, respectively. Many newspapers offer commercial printing services, using their (increasingly) excess print capacity, and other related services such as custom publishing, direct marketing, etc.

Circulation: It would be easy to think that there are no newspaper readers left in the world if one were to read the popular press. While circulation trends are far from positive, there are still 50 million daily and Sunday newspaper readers in the United States (Table 1). Granted, they are aging, and unlike in past times, they are unlikely to be offset by new, younger readers. Younger people were never really newspaper readers, even historically, but typically, when a consumer bought their first house, they became a newspaper reader. That does not seem to be the case today.

Table 1. Newspaper Circulation Statistics

	Number of Daily Newspapers			Daily Circulation			Sunday	
Year	Morning	Evening	Total News- papers	Morning (000)	Evening (000)	Total (000)	Total News- papers	Total Circulation (000)
1940	380	1,498	1,878	16,114	25,018	41,132	525	32,371
1945	330	1,419	1,749	19,240	29,144	48,384	485	39,860
1946	334	1,429	1,763	20,546	30,382	50,928	497	43,665
1947	328	1,441	1,769	20,762	30,911	51,673	511	45,151
1948	328	1,453	1,781	21,082	31,203	52,285	530	46,308
1949	329	1,451	1,780	21,005	31,841	52,846	546	46,399
1950	322	1,450	1,772	21,266	32,563	53,829	549	46,582
1951	319	1,454	1,773	21,223	32,795	54,018	543	46,279
1952	327	1,459	1,786	21,160	32,791	53,951	545	46,210
1953	327	1,458	1,785	21,412	33,060	54,472	544	45,949
1954	317	1,448	1,765	21,705	33,367	55,072	544	46,176
1955	316	1,454	1,760	22,183	33,964	56,147	541	46,448
1956	314	1,454	1,761	22,492	34,610	57,102	546	47,162
1957	309	1,453	1,755	23,171	34,635	57,805	544	47,044
1958	307	1,456	1,751	23,161	34,258	57,418	556	46,955
1959	306	1,455	1,755	23,547	34,753	58,300	564	47,848
1960	312	1,459	1,763	24,029	34,853	58,882	563	47,699
1961	312	1,458	1,761	24,094	35,167	59,261	558	48,216
1962	318	1,451	1,760	24,563	35,286	59,849	558	48,888
1963	311	1,453	1,754	23,459	35,446	58,905	550	46,830
1964	323	1,452	1,763	24,365	36,048	60,412	561	48,383
1965	320	1,444	1,751	24,107	36,251	60,358	562	48,600
1966	324	1,444	1,754	24,806	36,592	61,397	578	49,282
1967	327	1,438	1,749	25,282	36,279	61,561	573	49,224
1968	328	1,443	1,752	25,838	36,697	62,535	578	49,693
1969	333	1,443	1,758	25,812	36,248	62,060	585	49,675

(continued)

	Number of Daily Newspapers			Daily Circulation			Sunday	
Year	Morning	Evening	Total News- papers	Morning (000)	Evening (000)	Total (000)	Total News- papers	Total Circulation (000)
1970	334	1,429	1,748	25,934	36,174	62,108	586	49,217
1971	339	1,425	1,749	26,116	36,115	62,231	590	49,665
1972	337	1,441	1,761	26,078	36,432	62,510	605	50,001
1973	343	1,451	1,774	26,524	36,623	63,147	634	51,717
1974	340	1,449	1,768	26,145	35,732	61,877	641	51,679
1975	339	1,436	1,756	25,490	35,165	60,655	639	51,096
1976	346	1,435	1,762	25,858	35,119	60,977	650	51,565
1977	352	1,435	1,753	26,742	34,753	61,495	668	52,429
1978	355	1,419	1,756	27,657	34,333	61,990	696	53,990
1979	382	1,405	1,763	28,575	33,648	62,223	720	54,380
1980	387	1,388	1,745	29,414	32,787	62,202	736	54,676
1981	408	1,352	1,730	30,552	30,878	61,431	755	55,180
1982	434	1,310	1,711	33,174	29,313	62,487	768	56,261
1983	446	1,284	1,701	33,842	28,802	62,645	772	56,747
1984	458	1,257	1,688	35,683	27,657	63,340	783	57,574
1985	482	1,220	1,676	36,362	26,405	62,766	798	58,826
1986	499	1,188	1,657	37,441	25,061	62,502	802	58,925
1987	511	1,166	1,645	39,124	23,702	62,826	820	60,112
1988	529	1,141	1,642	40,453	22,242	62,695	840	61,474
1989	530	1,125	1,626	40,759	21,890	62,649	847	62,008
1990	559	1,084	1,611	41,311	21,017	62,328	863	62,635
1991	571	1,042	1,586	41,470	19,217	60,687	875	62,068
1992	596	996	1,570	42,388	17,777	60,164	891	62,160
1993	623	954	1,556	43,094	16,718	59,812	884	62,566
1994	635	935	1,548	43,382	15,924	59,305	886	62,295
1995	656	891	1,533	44,310	13,883	58,193	888	61,229
1996	686	846	1,520	44,785	12,198	56,983	890	60,798
1997	705	816	1,509	45,434	11,290	56,728	903	60,486
1998	721	781	1,489	45,643	10,539	56,182	898	60,066
1999	736	760	1,483	45,997	9,982	55,979	905	59,894
2000	766	727	1,480	46,772	9,000	55,773	917	59,421
2001	776	704	1,468	46,821	8,756	55,578	913	59,090
2002	777	692	1,457	46,617	8,568	55,186	913	58,780
2003	787	680	1,456	46,930	8,255	55,185	917	58,495
2004	814	653	1,457	46,887	7,738	54,626	915	57,754
2005	817	645	1,452	46,122	7,222	53,345	914	55,270
2006	833	614	1,437	45,441	6,888	52,329	907	53,179
2007	867	565	1,422	44,548	6,194	50,742	907	51,246

Source: Editor and Publisher International Yearbook.

So, with 50 million readers, how could the industry be in trouble? Readers only contribute 20% of the revenues, that's why. Circulation has proven to be highly elastic, i.e. the cover price is raised, circulation volume goes down. Further, in the current environment, readers don't exactly need well-honed observation skills to know they are getting less content each day.

While it is imperative that newspapers find a way to attract younger generations, it can't be a primary focus today as circulation promotions are costly. Further, from an economic point of view, circulation revenues are unlikely to ever save the day (Table 2).

Table 2. Newspaper Circulation Revenues

Year	Weekday	Sunday	Total
1956	$ 961,507	$ 382,985	$1,344,492
1957	$ 989,574	$ 383,890	$1,373,464
1958	$1,064,760	$ 394,253	$1,459,013
1959	$1,131,744	$ 417,832	$1,549,576
1960	$1,168,627	$ 435,601	$1,604,228
1961	$1,233,592	$ 450,727	$1,684,319
1962	$1,350,763	$ 469,077	$1,819,840
1963	$1,418,540	$ 483,280	$1,901,820
1964	$1,486,318	$ 497,491	$1,983,809
1965	$1,501,332	$ 521,758	$2,023,090
1966	$1,580,811	$ 528,239	$2,109,050
1967	$1,643,068	$ 537,174	$2,180,242
1968	$1,732,427	$ 555,788	$2,288,215
1969	$1,799,116	$ 626,330	$2,425,446
1970	$1,921,404	$ 712,998	$2,634,402
1971	$2,088,520	$ 744,800	$2,833,320
1972	$2,138,653	$ 790,580	$2,929,233
1973	$2,206,430	$ 831,390	$3,037,820
1974	$2,641,020	$ 940,713	$3,581,733
1975	$2,886,978	$1,034,537	$3,921,515
1976	$2,973,894	$1,113,409	$4,087,303
1977	$3,129,901	$1,180,335	$4,310,236
1978	$3,289,526	$1,245,253	$4,534,779
1979	$3,519,008	$1,431,534	$4,950,542
1980	$3,863,822	$1,605,767	$5,469,589
1981	$4,359,244	$1,846,897	$6,206,141
1982	$4,689,837	$1,966,824	$6,656,661
1983	$4,895,936	$2,148,162	$7,044,098

(continued)

Year	Weekday	Sunday	Total
1984	$5,093,394	$2,274,764	$ 7,368,158
1985	$5,233,661	$2,425,636	$ 7,659,297
1986	$5,410,949	$2,641,199	$ 8,052,148
1987	$5,561,670	$2,837,362	$ 8,399,032
1988	$4,869,613	$3,176,674	$ 8,046,287
1989	$5,005,078	$3,365,246	$ 8,370,324
1990	N/A	N/A	N/A
1991	$5,455,070	$3,242,609	$ 8,697,679
1992	$5,745,052	$3,418,482	$ 9,163,534
1993	$5,704,671	$3,489,132	$ 9,193,802
1994	$5,846,897	$3,596,320	$ 9,443,217
1995	$6,007,134	$3,713,052	$ 9,720,186
1996	$6,157,735	$3,811,504	$ 9,969,240
1997	$6,227,741	$3,837,902	$10,065,642
1998	$6,352,295	$3,914,660	$10,266,955
1999	$6,475,426	$3,996,868	$10,472,294
2000	$6,507,803	$4,032,840	$10,540,643
2001	$6,689,745	$4,093,333	$10,783,078
2002	$6,830,230	$4,195,666	$11,025,896
2003	$6,974,530	$4,249,832	$11,224,362
2004	$6,832,315	$4,156,336	$10,988,651

Source: NAA

Advertising: The real economic crisis is on the advertising side of the business. Newspaper advertising is typically divided into three buckets: retail, classified, and national (Table 3)[1]. Retail historically has been the largest category, but classified has always been the most profitable. In fact, at the peak of the last boom cycle, classifieds contributed a purported 70% of pre-tax profits.

Classifieds: Classifieds (Table 4)[2] typically move in conjunction with GDP as it would be hard to have economic growth without gains in real estate, auto and jobs. Classifieds, however, came under pressure in advance of the economic cycle as classified auto ads started to decline in 2004 and as overall classifieds started their descent in 2006. There are many explanations for this. The most obvious is that print classifieds have lost share to online classifieds, on newspaper sites and certainly elsewhere. The other is that newspapers lost pricing power due to the competitive pressures of online. The likely answer is both; newspapers, after having enjoyed a virtual monopoly in classifieds, lost both pricing power and market share.

It is hard to know whether newspapers could have done a better job of holding on to their dominant position in classifieds. If they had united earlier as an industry and offered category killers along the line of what monster.com has done in recruitment, it could have made a big difference. Certainly there were some such efforts, Classified Ventures, cars.com, apartments.com, etc. However, the beauty and curse of the Internet is that there are no real barriers to entry and as such, rampant competition exists in every sector. There has been a more coordinated effort of late as a number of newspapers have allied themselves with Yahoo but it is still likely a futile effort. Newspapers are still poised to lose pricing power and market share. What is really a shame is that the industry refused to acknowledge the obvious and did not take the likely decline seriously enough and start to aggressively cultivate other revenues. In fact, there are still publishers who expect classified to enjoy its typical cyclical upturn when the economy improves.

In reality, when forecasting the future of the newspaper industry, it would be wiser to forecast excluding any classified ad revenues and hope for positive surprises. At the peak, classified ads contributed close to 50% of ad revenues; in 2008, they contributed 30–35% of ad revenues. Bottom line, it is hard to influence the purchase of a classified ad. Given the number of free alternatives, pricing cannot be used as a competitive tool. More importantly, newspapers can't influence when someone needs a car, job, or house.

Retail: Retail advertising (Table 5)[3] has been weak as well; retail has typically been the largest category hovering around 50% of the total. Retail's weakness began in advance of the current economic downturn due to rampant consolidation among department stores. A reduction in competition hurts both in terms of losing an advertiser as well as a softening in advertising by the remaining department store as they no longer have to spend against the competition. There is no question that the U.S. is over retailed based on studies of retail store square footage per consumer which is the likely reason we are starting to see bankruptcies and closures along the lines of Circuit City. Mall vacancy rates hit a 10-year high in the first quarter.

National: National advertising (Table 6)[4] has historically been a challenge for the industry, in part due to the difficulty in placing a national buy. The formats of daily metropolitan newspapers vary as do their pricing. While companies have emerged that facilitate the process, either rep firms or brand versioning firms, it remains a challenging category as it isn't typically influenced at the local level. It is, however, a category that remains enticing as it is under penetrated by the industry. *The Wall Street Journal, The New York Times,* and *USA Today* are the three most recognized national newspapers in the U.S.

Online: Online advertising has become more difficult of late, in part as a good portion of online is classified related and still often sold as an upsell to print. While online classifieds were late to turn as the share gains helped offset declines in the category overall, the full impact of the economic cycle is now being felt. This category probably will improve with an economic recovery although the pricing is a fraction of the print counterpart and, as such, will not have the power to really drive a solid recovery for overall newspaper ad revenues.

Other Revenues: Newspapers have attempted to generate other revenue streams through the years, among them commercial printing, direct marketing, archive sales and other merchandise sales. Ultimately, newspapers are doing a decent job of monetizing each of their assets whether it is their printing presses, distribution or editorial. While a small portion of revenues for most companies, it is growing in most cases.

COSTS

Turning to the cost side of the equation, newsprint, production and distribution are a major cost as is, of course, editorial. Labor constitutes about 50% of its segment costs, production and distribution 30% and other is 20%. Newsprint & ink represents about 12–13% of costs. Newsprint is a commodity; the paper industry has consolidated dramatically. Newspapers have very little control over pricing. Many newspapers have reduced their web width, i.e. size of the paper, in order to permanently reduce their newsprint consumption. Newspapers also manage the ratio of advertising and editorial as another method of expense control.

According to the site www.graphicdesignr.net/papercuts.com, buyouts and job eliminations reduced industry employment by 2,112 in the second half of 2007, 15,866 in 2008 and to date in 2009 by 8,097. Headcount reductions are a challenge in that the industry's obsession with itself leads to tremendous coverage and negative reactions to it, despite the fact that it is happening in every industry. Further, many papers have unions that make it more difficult than it otherwise might be to achieve the appropriate financial balance.

Newspapers have attempted to manage circulation to reduce costs by no longer distributing papers to outlying regions that advertisers don't value. They have promoted subscriptions v. single copy, thereby reducing the waste that typically ensues with single copy distribution. And, of course, papers are experimenting with online/print hybrids, online only publications and reducing home delivery.

Newspaper margins have compressed dramatically over the last few years. Based on the table below, it can be seen that industry margins peaked in the late 1990's at 29%; in 2008, the average was 13% with fairly sizable variances. The combination of a secular shift in classifieds combined with an economic downturn is proving devastating. Industry ad revenues have declined throughout

2006-2008 and are now back to where they were in 1996, including online ad revenues, or 1994 excluding them. The problem is that it is difficult to roll the costs back to that era.

What's the Industry to Do?

Put another way, industry revenues are down over $11 billion from the peak in 2005, predominately explained by the decline in classifieds. Even worse, there are relatively few direct costs associated with classified advertising, perhaps some minor commissions, making it difficult to react to the revenue decline.

Improve Revenues: Clearly, the obvious solution is to improve revenues. As ad revenues represent 75–80% of the total, it presents the biggest opportunity. I remain convinced of two things. Print classifieds will continue to go by the wayside and newspapers need to dramatically upgrade their ad sales departments. If I am right about classifieds, the industry could undergo another drop of $9 billion.

Aggressively Build Small Businesses Online Presence: I believe there is still the potential for a strong local online classified business. Newspapers have the ability to heavily promote their online classifieds. They could add a variety of related services and using the classifieds as content that drives page views, sell advertising around it. For example, on a local jobs site, they could link to the web sites of the potential employers so job seekers could investigate benefits, or corporate reputations. Perhaps links to MapQuest so a job seeker could evaluate their potential commute.

Local Online Listings: A strategy that the now bankrupt Chicago Sun-Times had employed struck me as the way to go and I am surprised more newspapers haven't tried it. In the early stages of the Internet, they offered a web site creation and hosting service for a nominal amount of money. The web sites were like brochure-ware but it was still the right strategy as it was a creative way to get smaller businesses online. Had it been aggressively pursued it could have created a comprehensive online local yellow pages business and would have been a natural way to drive online classifieds and display advertising.

Enter the Local Ad Network Business: No one has really cracked the local ad network code. This could still be a very healthy business over time as well and newspapers are well positioned, given their reach in the local market to achieve dominance. Newspapers could represent other mediums web sites as well.

Upgrade the Sales Department: Unfortunately, both the small business listing and local ad network businesses take strong sales forces. As an outside observer, and the daughter of a salesman, it is easy to be critical of newspapers' sales organizations. For years, they were order takers. Even when they started to get serious in the latter part of the 1990's and ventured into hiring commission only salespeople, they still weren't hungry or aggressive enough.

Perhaps due to the very thick wall between editorial and advertising, newspapers have never learned to sell their virtues or promote themselves, most likely for fear of being chastised. The radio industry always had the scrappiest, and most effective, sales force followed by television. Their respective willingness to put themselves out there and really help sell their clients' goods was something newspapers almost sneered at and often admonished for having "crossed the line."

This is a very important point. The very fact that so much press was given recently to the LA Times decision to run an advertorial on the front page is indicative of a mindset that still exists. Newspaper managements still don't fully get that this is a battle for survival and that the values they revere are not necessarily shared, or even prized, by their own customers. In fact, newspapers could be much more effective, even while retaining their values.

Notwithstanding the likely cultural reason newspapers have had mediocre sales organizations, now would be a good time to change. There is more talent available than in a long time. Retailers need solutions and a creative organization with the print and online reach of a newspaper should be able to provide the solution.

Learn to Better Promote the Paper: Newspapers need to sell from strength; they are still mass market in terms of their local penetration. It is one of the few mediums where the advertising is welcome, unobtrusive, and often construed as content. Some newspaper companies have had more success than others being aggressive in their markets, in particular, Lee. The company does local blitzes where they really try to penetrate the retail market. Aggressive sales people and aggressive goals are necessary.

When I look at the changes that have been made in my local paper, it is downright exciting. The investment in local investigative journalism has people buzzing. Yet, it is hard to change old impressions. I just had lunch with a friend and asked if she read the paper. She said yes but that she didn't think it was very good and only read it because it was the local paper. I asked if she had read a number of specific stories. By the end of the inquisition, she acknowledged that, in fact, I was right, the paper had improved. When the paper reaches out to people on a one on one basis, they convert their readers to loyal subscribers. The local public radio station has a great reputation; they reach out often and aggressively. Newspapers need to do the same.

I would like to see papers do a better job of getting their reporters back into the community and make them minor celebrities, in essence another form of promotion. Columnists achieve this but reporters can as well. Readers enjoy meeting reporters and reporters do a better job when they get to know readers. When readers can relate to the paper, it does better.

Charge for Online Content?: A lot has been written about the potential for newspapers to charge for their content online. Given consumers' reluctance to pay for the print product, I am hard pressed to get too optimistic about the potential for online payments. Much is made of The Wall Street Journal's success charging for their online content. They are a targeted publication with an audience that needs information to do their job; it isn't a fair comparison to other newspapers. Newspapers could undoubtedly create premium or niche products for which consumers will pay but for all of the effort in this debate, the economic result is likely to be small judging by the fact that circulation revenues represent less than 20% of most newspaper's total revenues.

Asking Loyal Subscribers for More: Given that the average newspaper reader is still happy with the print product they receive, another novel (to be read sarcastically) approach might be to convince this constituency to pay more. Unfortunately, even if consumer's paid twice as much for the paper, it might, at best, offset the potential reduction in print classifieds if they do go away entirely as I fear. Raising the cover price or subscription price isn't really what I am recommending. Instead, I am imagining a door to door campaign throughout the footprint of the publication whereby trained individuals try to explain to the community what is at stake if the newspaper were to fold (more on this later), what the economic issues are, and then find out what they might be willing to pay. Incorporated into this approach could be asking for a charitable contribution. While there are plenty of readers who, despite the unquestionable value they receive each day in the pages of the paper, believe they are paying too much, I suspect many of them have already canceled and moved to the Internet for their news. I genuinely believe there is an untapped market either for charitable contributions to support investigative journalism as well as readers who if faced with the prospect of an online only publication or no publication at all would pay more for the convenience of print.

Charitable Contributions: As indicated above, I do believe there are sufficient numbers of individuals who would support their local paper through charitable contributions. There is a growing recognition that newspapers provide a watchdog function. However, while there seems to be increasing awareness that newspapers are struggling financially, most consumers probably aren't as versed in what is at stake if a paper folds. This message needs to be delivered more clearly and broadly. ProPublica is a great example of philanthropy supporting investigative journalism, but it needs to happen locally as well. Moving to become a not for profit will not solve the financial challenges of the industry but finding a way to accept charitable contributions could be fruitful as a new source of revenues.

More Focused Content: Newspapers can no longer try to be everything to everyone. They need to focus their dwindling resources. While many still bemoan the loss of overseas news bureaus and DC bureaus, the fact is that the Internet and plethora of new news organizations no longer make it necessary for each local paper to have a presence in so many places. Local papers should focus on local events and let consumers supplement the paper's news with other sources. Regional efforts such as ONO, the Ohio News Organization, should proliferate. There should be more sharing of regional arts critics. Newspapers should devote their resources to providing a local watchdog effort, i.e. local investigative journalism. The Cleveland Plain Dealer has done an excellent job in this regard.

Stop Trying to Attract All Readers: I do not think print papers should spend a lot of money trying to entice younger readers to the paper; however, I think they can engage younger readers by getting them to contribute content that could appear online and eventually get integrated into print. At the end of the day, everyone loves to see their name in the paper. As younger people have never been big consumers of newspapers, there is no reason to think they would be any more so today, especially with so many other ways to get news and information. However, this should not be confused with a lack of interest in news and information. Cultivating relationships with students who work on their school papers (high school or college), especially covering sports, and perhaps giving them some coverage in the city paper is a great way to get them to get involved and perhaps virally market the paper, electronic version, and/or website.

Cautious Move to Online Only Papers: Many newspapers are trying to eliminate costs by moving more towards an online only model. The challenge, near term, is that the core newspaper constituency skews older and prefers a print publication. By moving online to reduce costs, papers risk losing their core reader. By not moving online to reduce costs, newspapers risk the entire franchise. The middle ground, from my point of view, is to slowly migrate folks online. It can be done by section or by day or both. Certain days of the week are more profitable than others. Sunday is by far the most profitable, so at the very least the Sunday print paper should survive. The move to online can best be done with an electronic version. An electronic version replicates the print paper online. It has all the virtues of the paper as I see it: it is edited, content can be located consistently, it retains the serendipity of the paper, and perhaps most importantly, it retains all of the ads. Importantly, if a paper were to move to an online only or electronic version instead of print, I would hope they would reach deep into the community to explain the decision.

Electronic Version Better Than a Website: While web sites serve a real purpose, they aren't the same as reading a paper. They are useful for individuals seeking specific content and/or more "snackable" content. The issue is that only the pages viewed can be monetized. Newspapers historically could monetize their entire circulation base as well as the assumption that each reader turned every page. Thus, the concept that print dollars are being turned into digital cents is really one of the inefficiency, from the advertiser's perspective, of the print publication which is eliminated online, i.e. advertisers only pay for the ads that are actually viewed. An electronic version retains all of the ad positions.

So realistically, even if all of a paper's readers followed it online, it is very unlikely that they could generate close to the same revenues as they did in print. Online ad rates are much lower than print and it is unlikely, given a typical three ad impressions per page view, that a paper could ever generate enough page views to replicate the number of ads, albeit dwindling, that is in the paper.

Several months ago, I did a simplistic analysis to see what it would take for *The New York Times* to generate the same revenues online as in print, which was both encouraging and discouraging. Encouraging because it isn't out of the realm of possibilities that they could achieve the number of 1.3 billion monthly pages views it might take. Discouraging as the assumptions might not be fully realistic and that the exercise doesn't necessarily apply to a more local franchise. At the time, we knew that October ad revenues for the New York Times Media Group (essentially the *New York Times*), were $113.9 million. We assumed the daily paper is about 100 pages a day and 200 on Sunday and that half the pages were advertising. On that basis, we backed into an ad rate cost per thousand (CPM) of $58. Based on ComScore data, nytimes.com had 173 million page views in October. At a $25 CPM, a premium to other sites due to the demographics, this would generate $13 million in ad revenues a month or $40 million in a quarter. In the third quarter, the New York Times Company generated $85 million in online revenues, of which almost $27 million was from About.com. Assuming that nytimes.com generated $40 million of the remaining $58 million is logical. So, on this basis, if nytimes.com could generate 1.3 billion (not too dissimilar from msnbc.com, Yahoo News or AOL News) at the time, it could generate $300 million a quarter, or what, at the time we were forecasting for the New York Times Media Group in the fourth quarter.

In Conclusion

So, in essence, I am recommending a variety of tactics. The business model for newspapers has changed dramatically by virtue of their near monopoly in print classifieds. At the peak, according to NAA statistics, it reached 40% of industry ad revenues in 1998 but perhaps more importantly it contributed close to 70% of pretax profits. I think it runs the risk of going pretty close to zero over time. On the other hand, I am highly critical of the newspaper industry on three fronts. They haven't learned how to promote themselves, both in terms of what they do to preserve our democracy, nor on how effective they are for marketers. They have never invested aggressively enough in their sales force and let them take risks. Finally, they haven't recognized that they can't produce the same breadth of editorial that was so nicely funded by classifieds through the years.

While newspapers stand for what is right about democracy and are fierce defenders of democracy, they were never asked to play that role. Interestingly, many readers will indicate that they don't read the paper because it is too negative or all bad news, or worse, yet, about things like war about which they don't want to read. Yet, there is still an expectation that newspapers will deliver after a major story, like 9/11, or will provide a watchdog function in the local community. The challenge is how to economically support the endeavor.

Newspapers need to view their brand as part public service and part consumer packaged good. The latter part tries to reach out and compel consumers to buy the paper, thus a front page that is enticing. The public service part of the paper is trying to create a common language for our society. Perhaps it doesn't matter how many people read the paper as long as the paper can continue to fund its watchdog function.

Bottom line, I think newspapers can survive but they are unlikely to be good investments. They are unlikely to be able to provide the breadth of coverage they do today. It would seem inevitable that they will have to adopt a hybrid strategy of print and online in order to reduce costs but ultimately, they need more revenues.

Notes

1. Ed. Note: Table 3 can be viewed at http://www.naa.org/Trends-and-Numbers/Advertising-Expenditures/Annual-All-Categories.aspx.
2. Ed. Note: Table 4 may be viewed at http://www.naa.org/Trends-and-Numbers/Advertising-Expenditures/Quarterly-Classified.aspx.
3. Ed. Note: The author can no longer provide the information for Table 5.
4. Ed. Note: To view Table 6, see print source.

*Lauren Rich Fine, CFA, is an executive search consultant at Howard & O'Brien Associates and was a practitioner in residence at Kent State University's College of Communication and Information. She previously served as a managing director at Merrill Lynch in Equity Research where she covered the publishing, information, advertising and online industries.

Lauren Rich Fine, "Bad Public Relations or Is This a Real Crisis?: YES" (paper presented at Duke Conference on Nonprofit Media, North Carolina, May 4–5, 2009).

Used by permission.

Getting Media Right: A Call to Action

by Michael J. Copps*

Thank you, Bill Moyers. When I heard the good news that you were going to introduce me tonight, I wasn't just pleased—I was thrilled. No one stands higher in my pantheon of citizen heroes than you, and I can think of no journalist, contemporary or at any time across the annals of our past, who has contributed so much to democracy's dialogue. I also thank Dean Nick Lemann and the Columbia University School of Journalism for bringing us together this evening and for all the great things they do to prepare the next generation of America's sentinels at the gate. Finally, my gratitude goes to Steve Coll and the New America Foundation for helping sponsor this event and for the path-breaking research the Foundation conducts across an impressively wide gamut of public policy issues.

We gather in the good and noble cause of sustaining American journalism in what I consider its hour of grave peril. "What," you say, "peril in a 500 channel universe? Peril when the touch of a search button delivers a veritable library of mankind's acquired knowledge to our various digitally-fueled devices? Peril when we can chat online with strangers on the other side of the planet as easily as our parents talked with their neighbors across the backyard fence?"

It's true there is much to celebrate. In fact, given what technology and innovation have wrought, this should be America's golden age of communications, news and information. Someone who is reading the New York Times on their iPad while watching live coverage from Afghanistan on their flatscreen HD TV might argue that the golden age is already reality. But the ecosystem is only as strong as its weakest link—and too many links are at the breaking point now. We should be riding on the cusp of an information and civic commons where anyone and everyone can engage, where bountiful news and information flow like water, where guaranteed openness trumps the threat of walled gardens, and where small "d" democracy is practiced on a town square paved with broadband bricks.

Alas, it is not thus. Our traditional media—newspapers, radio, television—have long since fallen victim to the excesses of a new Gilded Age. Media started earlier than most businesses down a suicidal road of hyper-speculation, creativity-stifling consolidation, and Wall Street pandering that gutted journalism's ranks and resources, cutting deep into the bone. What happened in media was prologue to the collapse of so many other industries and financial institutions. Even those station and newspaper owners who tried to resist—and there were many who wanted and still want nothing other than the chance to serve the public interest—came under often-irresistible pressure to cave. The ethos had changed; old ideals of stewardship were pushed aside and too often demolished; and the speculative fires burned on—at heavy and destructive cost to journalism, to the businesses themselves, and, most damaging of all, to our democracy.

Making it a perfect storm, this private sector debacle was aided and abetted by the public sector. This is the saddest part of the tale. The place where I work—the Federal Communications Commission—blessed it all, encouraged the consolidation mania, and went beyond even that to eviscerate just about every public interest responsibility that generations of reformers had fought for and won in radio and TV. One FCC Chairman summed up the agency's attitude that there was nothing special about the media by saying, "a television set is nothing but a toaster with pictures." So much for the people's airwaves and for any semblance of concern for the fragile news and information infrastructure that is the lifeblood of society's conversation with itself.

But "Wait!" you say, all this is talk of yesteryear—old Commissioner, old media and old technologies better consigned to the ash-heap of history. The Digital Age is upon us, we are assured, everything has changed, and our certain reward will be new and better media, more local news, enhanced global information, and a technology-fueled civic dialogue where all citizens are created equal.

Yet neither revolutions nor technologies come with guarantees, do they? One revolution creates a brave new nation that becomes democracy's best hope; another visits terror and destruction. New technologies can restore a brain or save a heart; others put our planet in peril or threaten to obliterate us all. Making technologies and revolutions serve the common good is, in every important way, up to us.

In his masterful new book, *The Master Switch*, Tim Wu revisits generations of media technologies, elucidating how each one's much-vaunted promise of unparalleled openness was eventually short-circuited—radio, film, TV and cable. And while he doesn't believe the Internet is necessarily doomed to tread the same destructive path, surely we see signs that it could. Consolidation is already well-advanced and businesses clearly dream about on-ramps with tollbooths dotting the information highway. Arguments rage over the right to secretly manage and prioritize content and to favor the affluent few at the expense of the many. Increasingly, the private interests who design and control our Twenty-first century information infrastructure resemble those who seized the master switch of the last century's communications networks.

Individual gatekeepers may change over time—tomorrow's might not be today's—but somehow the urge to be the keeper of the keys seems always to survive through generations of technology change. So it happened, as the doors were opened to the seemingly limitless prospects of the new media age, that public policy-makers once again became the willing accomplices of special interests. Indeed, the FCC spent the first eight years of the new century removing broadband from any meaningful public policy oversight, deregulating the telecom/cable duopoly, and blessing evermore competition-killing consolidations that narrowed consumer choice and inflated consumer bills. Other nations forged ahead of us in providing high-speed, value-laden broadband to their citizens. Perhaps one day we'll catch up. Perhaps one day we will harvest the full value of the Internet as an information and civic commons—but that will require some altered private sector aspirations and dramatically different public policy. I believe that happy outcome can come—but it is still years away.

Meanwhile, we find ourselves in perilous transition. The news and information journalism we depended upon is fast-disappearing from old media and has not found the sustaining resources it requires in the new. **FACT:** We've lost 35,000 members of the news industry in the past three years. **FACT:** Hundreds of newspapers have closed their doors and, last year alone, 367 magazines went out of business. **FACT:** Twenty-seven states have no full-time reporter accredited to Capitol Hill. Statehouse coverage has been slashed by a third in the past six years. How's that for our ability to hold the powerful accountable? **FACT:** Chris Dodd recently remarked that at one point in his 30-year Senate career, 11 reporters covered his activities on a day-to-day basis. In 2010, there were none. **FACT:** More money by far, more than $3 billion, was spent on political ads in the last election cycle than was spent on serious coverage of the issues that will determine the country's fate. **FACT:** The Annenberg School earlier this year released an in-depth report documenting that in the average 30-minute local news broadcast, less than 30 seconds is given over to cover hard local government news. If it bleeds it leads, but if it's democracy's life-blood, let it hemorrhage. **FACT:** Just this week, the Washington Independent, one of the really promising new media websites, folded. It could be just one of many if a sustainable model of financing is not found. **FACT:** Newspaper and broadcast newsrooms still provide the overwhelming bulk of the news citizens receive—whether they receive it in the paper, over the air, or online. Scholars of the trade tell us that 85% or 90%, perhaps even more, of the news people get online originates from these traditional sources. And it is on this shrinking diet of news and information that we are forced to rely to guide America through troubled waters.

What can we do about it? Let's recognize, up-front, that it gets harder all the time. Putting on my historian's hat, I subscribe to the theory that times of change and reform alternate with times of inaction and reaction. We had years of reaction and then a window of opportunity opened a couple of years ago. It provided a time—no one knew how long it would last—for us to address and redress mistakes of the past and to put in place right away a few interim safeguards as we set about developing longer-term solutions. These "down-payments," as I call them, are what I have come here to propose. I do not intend these as comprehensive fixes for what ails media old and new, but as ideas generated from having a front-row seat at the Commission for nearly a decade. My intent, rather, is to build some bridges to the future, some protections for what is still relevant in traditional news and information journalism—and couple these with safeguards to keep new media open and innovative and to prevent it from repeating the costly errors that short-circuited other generations of information infrastructure. I understand that what falls under the umbrella of the FCC's jurisdiction does not encompass the entirety of our broad and ever-expanding media ecosystem. But I believe that the FCC, by taking the kinds of action I am outlining here today, can play a vital role in catalyzing change and fostering a renewed commitment to serious news and journalism, with effects going far beyond the four corners of our traditional purview.

So here are a few mostly modest proposals to help media help democracy.

For traditional media that remains so critical to our news and information: The Federal Communications Commission should conduct a Public Value Test of every broadcast station at relicensing time—which should occur, I believe, every four years in lieu of the slam-dunk, no-questions-asked eight year renewals we dispense 100% of the time now. If a station passes the Public Value Test, it of course keeps the license it has earned to use the people's airwaves. If not, it goes on probation for a year, renewable for an additional year if it demonstrates measurable progress. If the station fails again, give the license to someone who will use it to serve the public interest.

The FCC's Public Value Test would include the following:

(1) **Meaningful Commitments to News and Public Affairs Programming.** These would be quantifiable and not involve issues of content interference. Increasing the human and financial resources going into news would be one way to benchmark progress. Producing more local civic affairs programming would be another. Our current children's programming requirements—the one remnant of public interest requirements still on the books—helped enhance kids' programming. Now it is time to put news and information front-and-center. At election time, there should be heightened expectations for debates and issues-oriented programming. Those stations attaining certain benchmarks of progress could qualify for

expedited handling of their license renewals. This requirement would have, by the way, important spill-over effects in a media environment where many newspapers are owned by broadcast stations—although such cross-ownership is something I hope the Commission will put the brakes on.

(2) **Enhanced Disclosure.** Requiring information about what programs a station airs allows viewers to judge whether their local station should be subsidized with free spectrum privileges. It opens a window on a station's performance. Right now the information we require on a station's public file is laughable and, believe it or not, the FCC generally does not even look at these files at re-licensing time. The public, too, has a right to easy access to this information so that its input counts at relicensing time. And citizens should be able to see the files on the Internet without spending a day tracking down and traipsing to the studio to go through the time-consuming and awkward motions of requesting and reviewing it. An enhanced disclosure proceeding has been before the Commission for two years. It may require some minor reworking but there is no reason not to complete this proceeding in the next 90 days.

(3) **Political Advertising Disclosure.** When the accounting is completed, we will likely find that nearly $3 billion was spent on media advertising in the recent campaign cycle. We the People have no idea who really paid for this political carpet-bombing. But we the people have a right to know who is bank-rolling these ads beyond some wholly uninformative and vapidly named group that appears on the bottom of the screen to mask the special interests it really represents. Both sides of the political spectrum are guilty of undemocratic sin here. The FCC worries, legitimately, about the dangers of placing a bottle of Coke or a tube of toothpaste on an entertainment program without disclosing who paid for the product's placement. Shouldn't we be even more concerned when unidentified groups with off-the-screen agendas attempt to buy election outcomes? I propose that the FCC quickly determine the extent of its current authority to compel release of what interests are paying for this flood of anonymous political advertising—and if we lack the tools we need to compel disclosure, let's go ask for them.

(4) **Reflecting Diversity.** This is not the place for a disquisition on how poorly America's minorities, women and other diversity groups are faring on our broadcast media. The fact that people of color own only about 3.6% of full power commercial television stations pretty much documents the shortfall. Diversity goes to how groups are depicted in the media—too often

stereotyped and caricatured—and to what roles minorities and women have in owning and managing media companies. The FCC's Diversity Advisory Committee has spent years providing us with specific, targeted recommendations to correct this injustice. How sad it is that most of these recommendations have not been put to a Commission vote. It is time to right this awful wrong.

(5) **Community Discovery.** The FCC, back when stations were locally-owned and the license holder walked the town's streets every day, required licensees to meet occasionally with their viewers and listeners to see if the programs being offered reflected the diverse interests and needs of the community. Nowadays, when stations are so often owned by mega companies and absentee owners hundreds or even thousands of miles away—frequently by private equity firms totally unschooled in public interest media—we no longer ask licensees to take the public pulse. Diversity of programming suffers, minorities are ignored, and local self-expression becomes the exception. Here's some good news: Community Discovery would not be difficult to do in this Internet age, when technology can so easily facilitate dialogue.

(6) **Local and Independent Programming.** The goal here is a more localism in our program diet, more local news and information, and a lot less streamed-in homogenization and monotonous nationalized music at the expense of local and regional talent. Homogenized music and entertainment from huge conglomerates constrains creativity, suppresses local talent, and detracts from the great tapestry of our nation's cultural diversity. We should be working toward a solution wherein a certain percentage of prime-time programming—I have suggested 25 percent—is locally or independently produced. Public Service Announcements should also be more localized and more of them aired in prime-time, too. And PEG channels—public, educational and government programming—deserve first-class treatment if we are to have a first class media.

(7) **Public Safety.** Every station, as a condition of license, must have a detailed, approved plan to go immediately on-air when disaster—nature-made or manmade—strikes. Stations, like government, have a solemn duty to protect the safety of the people. Preferably a station should be always staffed; if there are times when that is not possible, perhaps there are technology tools now that can fill in the gap and make the coverage instantaneous.

These few criteria for a Public Value Test are neither excessive nor onerous. But they would get us back to the original licensing bargain between broadcasters and the people: in return for free use of airwaves that belong exclusively to the people, licensees agree to serve the public interest as good stewards of a precious national resource. Importantly, these proposals are for the most part actions the FCC can take on its own authority. We can make this down payment on media democracy now. As the old question goes: If not now, when? If not us, who?

In the longer term, the Commission and Congress will need to examine rules governing the structure of media ownership and perhaps other parts of our enabling Telecommunications statute. I hope that as part of the dialogue leading up to possible legislative changes, the country will engage in a serious discussion about increasing support for public broadcasting—the jewel of our media land-scape. There will be those who will rail and rant to keep such a discussion from even starting. But the sad reality is that in this country, we spend, per capita, per annum, $1.42 supporting public media. In other democracies, citizens happily pay up to hundreds of dollars more than that. Public media enjoys high levels of public trust in our country, and investing in its future is investing in our future. It's a subject we should be able to discuss calmly and thoroughly.

Some will say that attempting to repair commercial broadcasting is a fool's errand. "Licensees will never agree," I am told, "so why not just hit them with a spectrum fee and put that money toward public news and media?" That has its temptations, I admit, but it also requires an act of Congress—and that's not the likeliest of outcomes just now. It further demands that if Congress would ever impose such fees—over strong industry objections, of course—that it must then direct the monies collected to broadcast purposes rather than to, say, reducing the deficit, building an interoperable broadband public safety network, or—even though we're told they are history—earmarking for various and sundry purposes. I would hesitate to predict that outcome!

As for new media, none among us can predict how it will look 5 or 10 or 20 years hence. But there are steps we can take now to avoid the mistakes that bedeviled earlier communications break-throughs and to help create an environment where the genius of this opportunity-creating technology can truly flourish:

(1) **Guarantee Internet Freedom Now.** The on-ramps to the Internet must be open and accessible to all. If our national conversation is one day going to be broadband-based, we all need to be there. Access denied is opportunity denied. So-called "managed services" and "paid priority" cannot be allowed to supplant the quality of the public Internet service available to us all. "Reasonable network management" practices must never be allowed to cloak competitive one-up-manship. And citizens are entitled to an official venue—the FCC—with access to the arcania of

engineering data so we can determine whether it is reasonable in a given case for anyone being denied the full potential of the Internet and put a stop to it if it is not. Internet Freedom also means guaranteeing openness in the wireless world as well as the wired. As people cut their wired connections, why would we deny them openness, accessibility and consumer protections in the wireless world? The implementation of such rights may need to vary a bit depending upon the technology platform—but the principle must stand. Internet freedom also means protecting consumers by implementing non-discrimination and transparency rules at the FCC. These rules must be put on the most solid possible legal foundation and be quickly and effectively enforceable. If this requires reclassifying advanced telecommunications as Title II telecommunications—and I continue to believe this is the best way to go—we should just do it and get it over with. To expect openness, transparency, non-discrimination and consumer protections to evolve from strictly private management of our nation's critical information infrastructure is to expect what never was or ever will be.

(2) **Encourage Broadband Competition.** Professor Benkler and others have thoroughly documented how other nations have used different pro-competition tools like network- sharing and structural separation rules to avoid dominance by one or two carriers. Recent FCCs were too quick to foreswear such tools. We should be developing contingency plans to curtail network and spectrum monopolies and duopolies.

(3) **Push for Digital Literacy.** One of the best parts of the FCC's National Broadband Plan is its advocacy for Digital and Media Literacy. We all need to know—especially our kids—how to use the liberating new tools of the Digital Age, and we all need to understand how these tools can help—or harm—us. I believe a worthy down-payment toward building this into our educational system is a K-12 online digital-media literacy curriculum, which local schools would be free to use or not. Many private and public entities have developed parts of such a curriculum. What we need now is a private-public partnership to get this up-and-running in the next two years. I am pleased that an inter-agency government team is now focusing on the new literacies, and I urge them to consider this proposal.

That's my plan for action now. The proposals I have made are not something I think it would be nice for us, the FCC, to do. They are things we **must** do if we are serious about making the Commission what it was intended to be and what we should all want it to be—an honest-to-goodness consumer protection agency.

Ensuring that all citizens have access to worthy media, to the news and information our democratic dialogue requires, is not a new challenge for our country. Washington, Jefferson and Madison understood that their fledgling country's future depended upon an informed citizenry, and they found ways—notably a large postal subsidy for the national distribution of newspapers—to ensure the widest possible dissemination of news and information to fuel the nation's conversation with itself. Free broadcaster use of the airwaves was just a later iteration of this same public policy. Today the technologies are new, but our democratic challenge is exactly the same—to build an information infrastructure that serves the needs of the people. I frankly don't know of a greater need.

Meeting this democratic challenge requires democratic participation. Getting our media landscape right is not just the job of agencies, Congresses or Presidents. It's the job of all of us. Steep climb that it undoubtedly is, I, for one, do not despair. Yes, powerful interests spend billions of dollars to make sure the waters of truth don't flow on these issues. But real citizen action can counter that—even in this age when too few people wield inordinate and outlandish influence. It will take dreams, but we've dreamed before. It will take hard work, but we've worked hard before. I have seen citizen action work in my lifetime—even at the FCC! And our nation's long history testifies to generations of reformers, civil rights crusaders, women rights champions, Native Americans, consumer advocates, disabilities activists, unions, media rights defenders, committing to a cause, making a difference, and moving our country forward. It's never easy, that's for sure—just necessary. This is one of those necessary times. My challenge to each of you is to act like your democracy depends upon it. Because it does.

Thank you very much.

*Michael J. Copps is the senior member of the Federal Communications Commission. He began his service in 2001 and was sworn in for his second term in 2005.

Michael J. Copps, "Getting Media Right: A Call to Action" (speech, Columbia University School of Journalism, New York, New York, December 2, 2010).
Used by permission.

Saving the News: Toward a National Journalism Strategy

*by Victor Pickard, Josh Stearns, and Craig Aaron**

[...]

STRATEGIES AND SOLUTIONS FOR SAVING THE NEWS

What stands out from this inventory of potential alternatives for journalism is that the dominant U.S. model of the 20th century—advertising-subsidized commercial journalism—is not the only available option for providing the news that democratic societies require. What is also suggested from surveying the models above is that without government intervention, relatively small, unevenly distributed experiments will likely rise and fall across the country in haphazard fashion. Part of this process is necessary and should be applauded to the extent that it gives rise to quality journalism. But there is much that the government can do to facilitate the transition and help make sure there are reporters on the beat, while also setting aside a space for longer-term efforts to nurture a free and robust press. In other words, as much as the "let a hundred flowers bloom" approach seems warranted, these experiments require nourishment. With targeted government intervention, we can help bring many to fruition. Indeed, with the right policies, we can begin laying the groundwork for a 21st century American press system.

The central task is to manage the transition in a way that permits a soft landing for the key asset for the production of news in a democracy—a large work force of journalists who can make a living writing the news. This transition will have to be agnostic to technology and recognize the disruptive and creative genius of the Internet. It will have to account for the changing norms in journalism and the changing identities of journalists. And it will have to find new business models that can adapt to the loss of print advertising revenues. This situation does not call for a bailout, but a far-reaching national journalism strategy to save the news.

The national journalism strategy must be aggressive but carefully planned, bold but targeted. And it must not be guided by profit-seeking or nostalgia, but rather by the core principles introduced at the start of this discussion:

- Protect the First Amendment. Freedom of speech and freedom of the press are essential to a free society and a functioning democracy.

- Produce Quality Coverage. To self-govern in a democratic society, the public needs in-depth reporting on local issues as well as national and international affairs that is accurate, credible and verifiable. Journalism should be animated by a multitude of voices and viewpoints.

- Provide Adversarial Perspectives. Reporting should hold the powerful accountable by scrutinizing the actions of government and corporations. Journalism should foster genuine debate about important issues.

- Promote Public Accountability. Newsrooms should serve the public interest, not private or government aims, and should be treated as a public service, not a commodity. Journalism should be responsive to the needs of changing communities.

- Prioritize Innovation. Journalists should utilize new tools and technology to report and deliver the news. The public needs journalism that crosses traditional boundaries and is accessible to the broadest range of people across platforms.

In crafting such a strategy, it is important to remember that news has rarely paid for itself. News has always been subsidized. During the 20th century, the model that happened to take root was one in which advertising subsidized news operations. It worked because of the coincidence of printing technologies and a market structure that resulted in monopoly daily newspapers in most American towns and cities. That model is no longer working. But just because advertising no longer supports journalism does not mean that we no longer require news. We still require journalism—perhaps now more than ever. But we must first develop new means for subsidizing the press through new private revenue models or public interventions to restructure or supplement market forces. And it is difficult to imagine how this can occur without government getting involved in some capacity.

The need for policy often seems counterintuitive to many Americans who assume their media system naturally flows from the "free market." Yet policy has always shaped our media system. During his celebrated visit to the United States in the 1830s, Alexis de Tocqueville was impressed to find an array of news and diverse sources of information deep in the American hinterlands. In fact, he was marveling at the direct result of enlightened public policy: postal subsidies for the mail, which was at that time primarily a news delivery system.[156] Today, Americans need to be reminded that there is a legitimate and necessary role for the state in guaranteeing a free and robust press. Government can simultaneously protect press freedom from censorship and promote policies that maximize speech of all kinds.

Our present moment is a critical juncture in American media and a turning point for modern journalism. We have the unique opportunity at this time to re-imagine the structures and policies needed to support the quality news and information we require to hold government and corporations accountable, to understand the world around us, and to participate in our democracy. Our concern is about how to support newsrooms and newsgathering, not a specific platform or method of distribution. We will need new policies that foster innovation and provide ongoing support for emerging news models. This approach avoids rehashing the well-worn debate about the future of journalism that too often devolves into two extreme positions: walling off content versus giving everything away for free; stubbornly clinging to newspapers versus believing blindly in the Internet. It is possible to stake out a middle path, one that embraces new digital technologies while also sustaining vital, professional journalism.

As we shift to a public service model of the press, we must prepare ourselves for a period of trial and error. We need to explore how the federal government can best support the future of investigative journalism, beat reporting, and quality news in America. This is not about newspapers, it is about newsrooms. It is not about protecting old institutions, it is about serving local communities. We understand that the future of this industry will likely be made up of a diverse collection of models and recognize the need for experimentation and innovation now and in the future. The question is, then, what current policies could support greater experimentation with innovative models of journalism?

Saving our vital news media and implementing a national journalism strategy for this transitional moment will require both short- and long-term solutions. Based on our analysis above, we have identified five models with the most promise that should be the top priorities for policymakers:

- **New Ownership Structures.** Encouraging the establishment of nonprofit and low-profit news organizations through tax exempt ("501(c)(3)") and low-profit limited liability company ("L3C") models.

- **Incentives for Divestiture.** Creating tax incentives and revising bankruptcy laws to encourage local, diverse, nonprofit, low-profit and employee ownership.

- **Journalism Jobs Program.** Funding training and retraining for novice and veteran journalists in multimedia and investigative reporting.

- **R&D Fund for Journalistic Innovation.** Investing in innovative projects and experimenting to identify and nurture new models.

- **New Public Media.** Transforming public broadcasting into a world-class noncommercial news operation utilizing new technology and focused on community service.

We make no claims that these models, alone or collectively, will automatically provide a panacea to the crisis in journalism. However, we believe these alternatives are worth further consideration, study and action. All of these models, to varying degrees, attempt to circumvent market failure with structural alternatives that seek to democratize media. Furthermore, they all could be accomplished via specific policy interventions and are politically viable, though formidable challenges are to be expected. Most important, we hope that by highlighting these options, we can begin a truly public conversation about what the future of journalism should look like and point policymakers and regulators toward an agenda that will save the news and serve the public good.

Short-Term Strategies

In the short term, we must decide what is needed to shore up news organizations and keep reporters on the job. Although many newspapers are deeply in debt, average newspaper profits are still 10 to 15 percent.[157] While newspapers are not dead yet and there is still money to be made, we also must realize that given current trends, in a decade—if not sooner—most people will not be reading newspapers in print. With news and advertising decoupled, ad revenue can no longer be relied on to fund bureaus at City Hall or in Baghdad. Thus our efforts should be focused on salvaging and transitioning the essential elements of newspapers—namely, the investigative and local reporting operations—while eliminating the business and commercial pressures that brought about the current crisis. That's not to say new policies should be limited to just helping newspapers. After all, many of the same financial challenges also affect broadcasters and online news outlets. Regardless of medium, we must find ways for trained reporters to make a living doing good journalism.

We believe the best short-term strategies are measures to encourage new ownership structures as well as refinements to the bankruptcy and tax laws that would enable employees, community groups or local investors to take over failing news operations on favorable terms, keep journalists working their beats, and invest in the future of newsgathering. We also endorse the federal funding of a jobs program to train or retrain young and veteran journalists in multimedia and investigative reporting skills. These recommendations would require federal legislation and, in some cases, new IRS regulations. Ideally, policymakers would create a menu of choices that would encourage media companies—whether bankrupt or simply struggling—to sell off properties to local and diverse owners who pledge to operate them in the public interest under a new structure. As new business models emerge, policymakers would also help to provide a bridge that guarantees veteran watchdogs are still on the job and new generations of journalists are building the skills needed for new forms of journalism.

New Ownership Structures

After surveying the options described in the previous chapter, it seems that the most effective means of salvaging struggling newsrooms is to create new owner-ship structures by applying the 501(c)(3) (nonprofit) and L3C (low-profit) models to news organizations. Under either of these models, news organizations could be set up to accept philanthropic donations (which, in the case of tax-exempt newspapers, would be deductible) or investments. And they could be owned, in whole or in part, by a wide range of socially motivated parties, including work-ers, foundations, community organizations and other civil society groups whose primary mission will be to provide a public good that benefits the collective welfare of the local community. As noted above, each of these models afford news organizations a number of benefits and protections not available to their commercial counterparts.

Specifically, the model proposed by Sen. Ben Cardin would offer tax benefits to philanthropic groups and individuals that donate to news organizations, while providing the news organizations themselves with the tax benefits enjoyed by all tax-exempt organizations. To transition to a tax-exempt newspaper will require federal legislation changing current federal tax laws, which could take the form of a revamped version of the Cardin bill. It would revise Sections 501, 513 and 170 of the Internal Revenue Code, which, respectively, would allow newspa-pers to be considered as having an educational purpose and therefore qualify as nonprofits; would exempt qualifying newspapers from paying corporate taxes on their advertising revenue; and would allow donations to these newspapers to be considered tax-deductible charitable contributions.

The precise wording of the Cardin bill, in its current form, could exclude entire classes of newspapers.[158] For example, the fact it mandates that a qualifying newspaper contain "local, national, and international news stories of interest to the general public" seems to preclude smaller community papers and other news organizations. Most important, any bill along these lines should explicitly state that it does not pertain to just newspapers, but also news Web sites and other forms of media dedicated to journalism. However, removing these limitations only would require relatively simple alterations to the text, such as saying "news organizations" instead of "newspapers" and using an "or" instead of "and" before "international news." For either model to become truly viable, nonprofit and low-profit news organizations also likely would need an exemption from provisions in the federal tax laws that prohibit both tax-exempt organizations (like the newspaper model proposed in the Cardin bill) and recipients of program-related investments (like an L3C news organization) from endorsing candidates for political office.

A related initiative is the move toward federal L3C legislation. This initiative could be treated in separate legislation or as part of a larger bill. A federal bill formally recognizing the L3C is probably unnecessary since, as noted earlier, news companies can organize as L3Cs in one of the states where L3Cs are legal. However, a related tax measure at the federal level would make it easier for foundations to make program-related investments in L3Cs. The Program-Related Investment Promotion Act, endorsed by L3C inventor Robert Lang, would accomplish this objective. The Council on Foundations also supports the federal legislation that would facilitate program-related investments in L3Cs.[159]

Other considerations could be written into the newsroom ownership language that would make a 501(c)(3)/L3C initiative an effective bill. For example, news organizations that chose to qualify for one of these ownership structures should also be obligated to demonstrate a five-year strategy for developing a significant Web and digital platform presence. They should also be contractually obligated to hold on to their property for a certain time period before selling, to avoid the establishment of shell companies. Efforts should also be made so these structures benefit ethnic and community media. Finally, news organizations should be required to set up local boards to evaluate how well they are serving the community. The PRI Promotion Act of 2009 would encourage this type of behavior, since it requires an annual report to the IRS specifying how an L3C is fulfilling its social purpose.[160] The first steps in any process to reform the federal tax laws would be hearings held by the tax-writing committees in both the House and the Senate. Ultimately, legislation reforming the IRS code would have to go through these committees.

Incentives for Divestiture

Several major newspapers are already bankrupt, or looking to sell off or shutter properties to escape enormous debt. Absent some intervention in the market, there is a strong chance that these papers will find buyers that are less interested in journalism than they are in maximizing asset value in the short term. Instead of watching them fall into the hands of private equity firms or other consolidated conglomerates, we have an opportunity to build incentives for their transfer to owners more committed to public service and local communities. The idea is to create, via changes to the federal tax and bankruptcy laws, a number of targeted "sweeteners" that could be invoked—alone or in combination—when media properties are being put up for sale that would make new owners or ownership structures, like L3Cs, more attractive than traditional corporate ownership models. As mentioned earlier, federal laws would also have to be changed to protect worker contracts and pensions.

One option clearly worth pursuing here is the utilization of "prepackaged" bankruptcies, which we described above. This approach would allow interested parties to work out future ownership of the assets prior to actually going into court, which dramatically cuts down on costs. These cost-savings, combined with the legislative incentives described below, could make the package more attractive to the bankruptcy judge and ultimately enable public-interest-minded groups to take control of the paper. An advantage of this "soft-landing" approach is that it precludes very few of the options discussed earlier. For example, a failing local newspaper could be bought up by a cooperative of its employees through a pre-packaged bankruptcy; turned into an L3C or 501(c)(3) news organization; accept money from public trusts, foundations and local entrepreneurs; and employ any number of creative online techniques to generate revenue—all while producing journalism and experimenting with new models of sustainability.

Newspaper owners might be more inclined to sell to socially motivated parties if the government offered certain subsidies or other incentives to facilitate the transactions. Perhaps the IRS could be induced to guarantee nonprofits a reduced buyout rate. In addition, government-guaranteed loans and bidding credits could be offered to nonprofits to help them purchase failing news organizations with the promise to convert them into locally owned and controlled multimedia newsrooms. Similarly, if the IRS granted tax relief from a long-term capital gains tax, tweaked the net operating loss rules, and offered other tax advantages to the newspaper seller, legacy owners of failing newsrooms may be incentivized to sell to nonprofits during the bankruptcy process. Substantive debt-relief would help placate creditors and investors to some degree.

These "sweeteners" should be combined with a minority media tax credit that would encourage the sale of news organizations to minorities, women, and other underrepresented groups. Restoring some version of the minority tax certificate will greatly increase minority and female ownership of news media outlets, which currently stand at an appallingly low number.[161] Congress would have to reinstate the policy, and the FCC would enforce it. But this is a policy that is already proven to increase the diversity of media ownership and never should have been dropped from the books.[162]

Journalism Jobs Program

The final proposal for a short-term remedy to the journalism crisis is an attempt to support veteran, qualified reporters and simultaneously to engage young people in journalism. One of the biggest problems with the collapsing business model of print newspapers is the possibility that tens of thousands of highly trained and experienced reporters will dissipate into other sectors of the economy, and tens of thousands of talented young people will be dissuaded from becoming journalists in the first place.[163]

With the recent expansion of AmeriCorps' existing domestic service program, now would be an opportune moment to include journalistic activities as part of its mission. "The Serve America Act," which Congress approved in March, will dramatically increase service and paid volunteer jobs from 75,000 to 250,000 positions. The *New York Times* reports that full-time and part-time service volunteers would work for "new programs focused on special areas like strengthening schools, improving health care for low-income communities, boosting energy efficiency and cleaning up parks." The AmeriCorps expansion—which will cost approximately $6 billion over five years—also provides for a Social Innovation Fund to expand on proven initiatives while supplying seed funding for experimental programs. Volunteers would receive minimal living expenses and a modest educational stipend of $5,350 after their year of service. There are also special fellowships for people 55 and older, as well as summer positions for middle- and high-school students.[164]

Building on Eric Klinenberg's idea, a small percentage of these AmeriCorps jobs could go to journalism positions, fellowships, or even to journalism projects to report on the new initiatives being created through this act. These also could provide a much-needed service if combined with or subsumed under university media literacy programs. A promising model has been implemented recently by a John S. and James L. Knight Foundation-backed initiative at Stony Brook University. The school has hired 50 laid-off journalists to undergo summer training with the goal of joining dozens of universities in the fall to teach "news literacy" to nonjournalism majors.[165] A similar program could be established to hire journalists to teach media literacy and help launch journalistic endeavors at all levels of education. The media literacy program could be expanded to include many more universities through the creation of formal Department of Education grants that might be leveraged using foundation support.

There are other direct avenues for federal government programs to aid in job creation in this industry. The Department of Labor could design a program aimed at keeping reporters employed at existing news organizations or at new outlets. Such a job-creation program would stimulate the economy and offset unemployment payments that might otherwise go to out-of-work reporters. The structure and administration of such a program requires further study, but the basic cost-benefit analysis is promising. If the government were to subsidize 5,000 reporters at $50,000 per year, the cost would be $250 million annually, a relatively modest sum given the billions coming out of Washington. Drawing on Ed Baker's ideas for subsidizing journalists and from the New Deal-era Federal Writers Project, this injection of resources would serve as a bridge to help keep reporters on the beat in local communities as the industry transitions to new business models and new media forms.

LONG-TERM STRATEGIES

Although the short-term strategies outlined above may sustain local newsrooms for the time being, the long-term strategies must provide a safety net for our national media system as a whole. We propose a two-track strategy: The first track is a tech-friendly venture/innovation/experimentation fund, which follows a long tradition of government seeding new projects, from medical breakthroughs to the Internet itself. The second track is building a world-class public media system with a renewed focus on newsgathering and local community service.

R & D Fund for Journalistic Innovation

"The only solution I have to offer is pluralism itself," writes New York University Professor Jay Rosen about the future of news. "Many funders, many paths, many players, and many news systems with different ideas about how to practice journalism for public good (and how to pay for it, along with who participates)."[166] To create the necessary institutional pluralism, and to provide for a future of text-based media read on electronic devices with multiple revenue streams and multiple platforms, we need to think about the new media marketplace as an incubator for innovation. We propose the creation of a government-seeded innovation fund for journalism—a taxpayer-supported venture capital firm that invests in new business models. As a starting point, we are proposing a $50 million per year budget.

Such a fund is not without precedent. The Telecommunications Development Fund (TDF) was created by Section 714 of the 1996 Telecommunications Act to focus investment in small businesses that produce important public goods in the communications sector that were ignored by for-profit venture capital.[167] A private, non-governmental, venture capital firm, TDF was seeded with public funds and authorized to make investments with public service goals. TDF is governed by a board appointed by the FCC chairman. This model could be adopted for a journalism fund with provisions that the board would be made up of representatives from industry, academic institutions, and public interest groups. A firewall would be set up between the board and the journalism initiatives they fund. Clearly, such an initiative would require an act of Congress to establish, though it's crucial that such legislation include provisions to shield the fund from any undue political influence. This new venture capital firm could be set up as a public-private partnership, with federal matching funds for foundation-supported projects.

Whereas many of the other strategies discussed here are aimed at transitioning legacy media into new sustainable forms, the new journalism fund should support forward-thinking endeavors that take advantage of new technologies. Resources should also be used to provide guaranteed loans to startup initiatives, such as Web-based community newsrooms and services, as well as projects that serve communities of color. The idea is to try to catalyze a wave of innovation in journalism 2.0 and to trigger market forces that will help move some of these nascent projects from concept to full-fledged operations.

New Public Media

A true Fourth Estate should be neither dependent on the whims of the market nor subject to shifting political landscapes. Now is the moment to firmly establish a press that is autonomous, yet supported by public money and devoted to the public interest. We need to re-imagine our current public broadcasting system and rebuild it as new public media with an overarching commitment to newsgathering and local community service. This significantly reformed and repurposed national media system should include many already existing pieces: NPR, PBS, community radio, as well as those nonprofit entities not commonly associated with public broadcasting, like PEG television channels, Low Power FM radio stations, noncommercial publications, and community Web sites.

The United States is alone among democracies in how little it devotes to its public media system. Our proposal is based on the vision that these monies would directly support journalistic endeavors by being used to hire local reporters in specific communities. The money would also be used to streamline public media operations: developing new technology and archiving content across the system.

In considering whether state-subsidized media is worth the effort, we should consider the popularity and quality of BBC News or the Canadian Broadcasting Corporation and compare these institutions to our increasingly degraded commercial media system. The BBC is unrivaled in the world as a source for international public service media. Research has shown the BBC demonstrating an independence that compares favorably with U.S. media and calls into question some common fears about government-subsidized media.[168]

The money needed to support this system over the long term could be raised by Congress creating and funding a public trust, or perhaps from a small tax placed on consumer electronics. Alternatively—and immediately—we could increase direct congressional appropriations for public media via the Corporation for Public Broadcasting. By tripling current congressional appropriations, the U.S. public media system could dramatically increase its capacity, reach, diversity and relevance. Given that Congress just passed a nearly *trillion-dollar* economic recovery package, devoting an additional $1 billion to public media annually (which works out to less than 0.2 percent of the stimulus bill) no longer appears so outlandish. Other democracies outspend the United States by wide margins per capita on public media.[169] Nichols and McChesney write: "These investments have produced dramatically more detailed and incisive international reporting, as well as programming to serve young people, women, linguistic and ethnic minorities and regions that might otherwise be neglected by for-profit media." They also note that the government spends several times the paltry $420 million it spends annually on public media on Pentagon public relations.[170]

Challenging commonly held fears about subsidized media, recent academic research shows that news organizations receiving government subsidies are no less critical of government than those that aren't subsidized, and the former tend to present a wider range of voices and viewpoints.[171] Indeed, there is accumulating evidence that, for example, a wide range of Western European publicly owned media and government-subsidized private media consistently produce journalism that is just as critical or more critical of powerful interests as the U.S. press.[172] Suggesting that the Swedish press was liberated to become more adversarial after public subsidies were introduced, Daniel Hallin, a specialist in comparative media systems at the University of California, San Diego, found "very strong evidence that press subsidies don't lead journalists to be timid."[173] A recent comparative analysis shows that public service television devotes more attention than the U.S. market model to public affairs and international news, which fosters greater knowledge in these areas, encourages higher levels of news consumption, and shrinks the knowledge gap between the advantaged and disadvantaged citizens.[174] Nonetheless, for this model to be successful, this public funding toward media should be both guaranteed over the long term and carefully shielded from political pressures.

To be clear, we are not advocating for a direct bailout of the commercial media system—a proposal reportedly being considered in Canada.[175] We are instead calling for the funding of an alternative media infrastructure, one that is insulated from the commercial pressures that brought us to our current crisis. Indeed, our media system has space for both commercial and noncommercial models; what is ideal is a *mixed* media system—one that restores balance between profit-making and democratic imperatives and is better able to withstand dramatic fluctuations in the market. Despite its flaws, we have enjoyed a successful, if grossly underfunded, public broadcasting system for decades. Furthermore, a wholly commercial system focused on advertising revenue optimization and profit maximization will not support the needs of a democratic society.

Our nation's media policy historically has reflected the understanding that the market alone cannot provide for all of our communication needs. However, the window of opportunity to make these kinds of reforms will close quickly. For decades, Congress has tilted media policy to favor the biggest media corporations. Right now, we have a rare chance to encourage legislators instead to "put their thumb on the scale" and create truly public media.

THE CHALLENGE AHEAD

A national journalism strategy is needed precisely because the problems we face necessitate vast resources and long-term planning. The United States will have many crises to confront in the coming years, but the loss of viable journalism must rank high among them. This is a surmountable crisis, but saving journalism and shoring up democracy's very foundations will require the right application of innovative technology, policy reform and public resources. There is not a perfect policy solution to solve this crisis. Rather, it will likely be a menu of policy options that together will help fill the vacuum left by the decline of commercial news. "You never want a serious crisis to go to waste," White House Chief of Staff Rahm Emanuel once said. "It's an opportunity to do things you could not do before."[176] This crisis is a golden opportunity for creating new alternatives. And if true public service journalism emerges from the wreckage, then indeed, there may be a silver lining.

It is becoming increasingly clear that enormous profits can no longer serve as the sole criterion for a healthy media system; focusing on short-term profits at the expense of long-term survival is not sustainable. Indeed, investments in newsgathering can pay off in the long run. Driving this point home, a University of Missouri study based on 10 years of financial data found that, over the long term, investments in newsgathering increase profits more than spending on circulation, advertising and other business operations do.[177] Newsrooms should be liberated from their absentee corporate owners and returned to the communities they purportedly serve. Although local ownership does not always ensure quality journalism, it does encourage local coverage and accountability.

Given recent closures and bankruptcies of major newspapers—and the ongoing struggles in radio and TV journalism—we cannot merely wait to see what organically emerges to replace the news. We must be proactive through public policy and public engagement. The depth of this crisis calls for something more than window dressing or incremental reforms. Unlike in previous eras, when media owners viewed any suggestion of structural reform with knee-jerk hostility, some are now more open-minded toward new models for sustaining local journalism. Media corporations need to recognize that news organizations can no longer serve merely as cash cows. Those that are unwilling to invest in quality journalism over the long term would be doing the public a service as well as protecting their own bottom line if they withdraw from the field in an orderly fashion without leaving a trail of hollowed out newsrooms in their wake.

The rate at which the newspaper industry is collapsing is staggering, even for those who have predicted this crisis for years. Further complicating this challenge is the historical predicament of multiple crises currently facing the United States, including the financial meltdown, the crumbling health care system and of thousands of troops in Iraq and Afghanistan. Journalism simply does not rank as high in the public consciousness. Combined with the traditional antagonism between the Fourth Estate and government, the risk of inaction is great. Nevertheless, given the scale of this problem—one that will only worsen over the coming weeks and months—we must start a national discussion about the nature of the crisis and the need for public policy solutions.

President Obama should use his bully pulpit to place this crisis squarely on the list of national priorities. The White House should convene a commission to revitalize the public media system, modeled on the Hutchins Commission of the 1940s and the Carnegie Commission in the 1960s. Congress needs to foster this debate by holding hearings that bring together the best minds in the country as well as engage the public to address this national crisis. Congress should also commission in-depth reports on the true state of the news business and call for possible solutions.[178] Ideally, the hearings would be followed quickly by legislation in Congress that amends tax and bankruptcy laws, funds innovative journalistic initiatives, and increases support for noncommercial media. The FCC and the Justice Department need to encourage media diversity and not further loosen media ownership limits. The FCC also needs to make sure the public can access quality journalism by developing a national plan for an open, ubiquitous and affordable broadband system.

We need to reframe the debate about journalism as one about an essential public good and a service that is vital for the future of democracy. The government is obligated to provide for a diversity of voices in our nation's media system as well as ensure public access to all media. Among the broader public, journalists and ex-journalists, as well as journalism schools and scholars, have a special role to play in this area. They command a unique perspective on what is at stake and what is possible in terms of creating newsrooms for the 21st century.

Journalism is a critical infrastructure. It is too precious for a democratic society simply to sit back and pray that the market will magically sustain it. The crisis in journalism is undeniably an economic issue, exacerbated by shifting revenue streams, new forms of content creation, and new methods of distribution. But it is also fundamentally a policy problem. While we explore new economic models for journalism, we must also examine what role government can play in supporting this indispensable institution. It is in large part policy decisions —and the political will to make the right ones—that will decide what is next for journalism. Unfortunately, there is no magic bullet. The crisis in journalism will undoubtedly require a menu of responses, not a one-size-fits-all solution. Driven by a growing media reform movement, a period of vigorous experimentation with bold new models is the best hope for the future of journalism, the lifeblood of democracy.

Notes

[…]

156. Alexis de Tocqueville, *Democracy in America*, Anchor Books. Garden City, NY, 1969.

157. Nat Ives, "It's Not Newspapers in Peril; It's Their Owners," *Ad Age*, Feb. 23, 2009.

158. Zachary M. Seward, "Non-profit News Outlets Deserve a Tax Exemption for Ad Revenue," *Nieman Journalism Lab*, March 26, 2009.

159. For information on the L3C federal legislation movement and related topics, see http://www.nonprofitlawblog.com/home/2009/03/l3c-developments-resources.html.

160. According to Robert Lang, GuideStar, the nonprofit database and information clearinghouse, has agreed to publish these reports. Like existing limited liability companies, L3Cs would be governed by an operating agreement among their members, which could easily be drafted to mandate compliance with a community's specific needs.

161. For a report on broadcasting numbers, see Derek Turner and Mark Cooper, "Out of the Picture 2007: Minority and Female TV Station Ownership in the United States," Free Press, October 2007. http://www.freepress.net/files/otp2007.pdf.

162. See, for example, Kofi Asiedu Ofori and Mark Lloyd, "The Value of the Tax Certificate Policy," The Civil Rights Forum, 1998, http://www.vii.org/papers/taxcert.htm.

163. Currently, journalism school enrollment is up. See Brian Stelter, "Digital Defeats Newsroom? J-Schools Boom Despite Crisis," *New York Times*, April 19, 2009.

164. "Expanding National Service," *New York Times*, March 24, 2009; Craig Newmark, "The Serve America Act, a Really Big Deal," *The Huffington Post*, April 23, 2009; "Senate Moves to Expand National Service Programs," *New York Times*, March 27, 2009.

165. "Knight Foundation Backs Plan to Hire 50 Laid-off Journos to Teach 'News Literacy,'" *Editor & Publisher*, March 13, 2009.

166. Jay Rosen, "Rosen's Flying Seminar in the Future of News," *Pressthink*, March 26, 2009. http://journalism.nyu.edu/pubzone/weblogs/pressthink/2009/03/26/flying_seminar.html.

167. S. Jenell Trigg, "Section 714—The Telecommunications Development Fund: Making a Difference?" June 1, 2002. http://www.civilrights.org/publications/reports/1996_telecommunications/section-714.html (this chapter is part of a larger collection by the Civil Rights Forum on Communications Policy titled "The Success and Failure of the 1996 Telecommunications Act.").

168. Jay Blumler and Michael Gurevitch, "'Americanization' Reconsidered: U.K.-U.S. Campaign Communication Comparisons Across Time," in W.L. Bennett and R.M. Entman (eds.), *Mediated Politics*. Cambridge: Cambridge University Press, pp. 380–403, 2001. It should be noted that dramatically increasing support for public media would entail formidable political challenges, yet substantially increased funding for public media is nevertheless more feasible than creating an entirely new entity for supporting national and local journalism. It is often taken as an article of faith that such a model could never flourish in the United States, but it is important to note that a more robust public media system didn't emerge as it did in other nations only as a result of a vicious series of political campaigns led by U.S. broadcasters in the early 1930s and again in the postwar 1940s. See Robert McChesney, *Telecommunications, Mass Media & Democracy: The Battle for the Control of U.S. Broadcasting, 1928–1935*. New York: The Oxford University Press, 1993.

169. Canada 16 times more; Germany 20 times more; Japan 43 times more; Britain 60 times more; Finland and Denmark 75 times more. Nichols & McChesney, *ibid.*

170. *Ibid.*

171. Rodney Benson, "What Makes for a Critical Press: A Case Study of U.S. and French Immigration News Coverage," *The International Journal of Press/Politics* (In Press); Rodney Benson and Daniel Hallin, "How States, Markets and Globalization Shape the News: The French and US National Press, 1965–97," *European Journal of Communication* 22, 27, 2007.

172. Rodney Benson, "Comparative News Media Systems," *The Routledge Companion to News and Journalism Studies*, edited by Stuart Allan, forthcoming 2009; See generally, Daniel Hallin and Paolo Mancini, *Comparing Media Systems: Three Models of Media and Politics*, Cambridge, UK: Cambridge University Press, 2004.

173. Bree Nordenson, "The Uncle Sam Solution: Can the Government Help the Press? Should it?" *Columbia Journalism Review*, September/October 2007.

174. James Curran, Shanto Iyengar, Anker Brink Lund and Inka Salovaara-Moring, "Media System, Public Knowledge and Democracy," *European Journal of Communication*, Vol. 24, No. 1, 5–26 (2009).

175. *The Canadian Press*, "Feds Consider TV News Bailout," April 8, 2009.

176. David Leonhardt, "The Big Fix," *New York Times Magazine*, Jan. 27, 2009.

177. Shrihari Sridhar, Murali K. Mantrala, Prasad A. Naik, and Esther Thorson, "Uphill and Downhill: Locating Your Firm on a Profit Function," *Journal of Marketing*, Vol 71 (April), 2007, 26–44; Robert MacMillan, "Study Shows Newsroom Spending Raises Newspaper Profits," *Reuters*, February 15, 2007. See also Tom Rosenstiel and Amy Mitchell, "The Impact of Investing in Newsroom Resources," *Newspaper Research Journal*, Vol. 25, No. 1, Winter 2004.

178. Similar hearings and reports were conducted in the 1940s around concerns about the rise of one-newspaper towns. For example, see Special Committee to Study the Problems of American

Small Business, "Survival of a Free Competitive Press: The Small Newspaper, Democracy's Grass Roots," Senate Committee Print 17, Eightieth Congress, First session, 1947. See also, Pickard, *ibid*.

*Victor Pickard is an assistant professor at the Annenberg School for Communication of the University of Pennsylvania.

Josh Stearns manages Free Press's journalism, public media, and media consolidation campaigns.

Craig Aaron is president and CEO of Free Press and the Free Press Action Fund.

Victor Pickard, Josh Stearns, and Craig Aaron, "Toward a National Journalism Strategy," in *Saving the News: Toward a National Journalism Strategy* (Washington, D.C.: Free Press, 2009), 39–48, http://www.freepress.net/files/saving_the_news.pdf.

Used by permission.

The Carnegie-Knight Initiative on the Future of Journalism Education: Improving How Journalists Are Educated & How Their Audiences Are Informed

by Susan King*

I'm reminded of an old newsroom saying—"Better to be lucky than good"—when I look back at the almost seven years of the Carnegie Corporation of New York Journalism Initiative. It began as a somewhat unfocused reaction to the wholesale worry about the state of journalism at the end of the 1990s. The Board of the Corporation and the then newly appointed president of the foundation, Vartan Gregorian, wanted to respond to what was seen as an increasingly entertainment-focused news business shedding its values and foreign news bureaus faster than it could stop the red ink.

The need for a democracy to be strengthened by a vital news business was the impetus for the Corporation's initiative. After all, positive change cannot happen in school reform, the immigration system, in international affairs, nuclear non-proliferation, or the understanding of Islam—indeed, in almost any area of our national life or international relationships that lies within or beyond the scope of the Corporation's work—unless vibrant news media engage the American public about the issues of this still-emerging century.

Since education is a foundational value and tradition at Carnegie Corporation, we decided to focus our initiative not on what was happening in U.S. newsrooms, but instead on what was happening within journalism schools at some of America's most prestigious research universities. That was the lucky part of our decision-making: our focus on a "pipeline" strategy that would affect the next generation of journalists. By 2009, the upcoming generation of newsmen and newswomen was clearly more critical to the debate about the news business than the middle-aged "leaders." The revolution in news via the Web was challenging the financial model of even America's most secure newspapers, as well as transforming the entire way that the news is delivered, consumed, and produced.

There is an irony for me in the fact that Carnegie Corporation's journalism work began in Silicon Valley, where the Internet transformation was born, and that it took place at the home of Walter Shorenstein, who, already close to ninety at that time, represented the world of news as it was practiced in the last century.

A successful businessman, Shorenstein has always been predisposed to the need for change. As a tribute to his daughter, a well-respected CBS newswoman who died prematurely, he began the Joan Shorenstein Center on the Press, Politics and Public Policy at Harvard University. It is both a teaching and research center and a think tank, and is led by Alex Jones, a Pulitzer Prize-winning reporter. The Shorenstein Center could be described as an institution at the pivot point of assessing the changing landscape of news.

In 2002, at Shorenstein's California home, Alex Jones and Orville Schell, dean of the Graduate School of Journalism at the University of California, Berkeley, assembled a few dozen deans to assess the state of the news business and to consider where it was heading as the digital challenge emerged. The deans felt they were attracting some of the smartest and most experienced students ever. But they feared that the "dumbing down" of the news business—particularly in local television news, but also network television—and the abandonment of basic beats by newspapers threatened their students' careers. They saw a crisis brewing in the opportunities available for their students and toyed with the idea of creating some university-based news business that could fill this serious-news lacuna with student-produced news and analysis.

Many times during the three years after the Shorenstein gathering, a handful of deans strategized with Gregorian and me to think about the future of news and the role that a journalism dean at a great university might play in the national conversation about changes in the news business. Gregorian, a former university president, believes that deans and other members of the academy must take on leadership roles in society. He challenged five of America's top journalism deans to become the nucleus for change in journalism education. This is the story of how a lucky strategy for changing journalism education has helped transform America's journalism schools and create an incubator for new forms of serious journalism.

Our conversations with deans began to frame a view of a journalism degree that demanded a higher quotient of intellectual pursuit along with the practical experience of producing news. In 2002, a dust-up at Columbia University, precipitated by Lee Bollinger, the University's new president, over selecting a new journalism dean, helped spotlight the need for subject depth in a journalism curriculum in addition to traditional skill-building. Too many schools of journalism continued to attract undergraduates who primarily wanted to take how-to classes to develop newspaper clips as well as radio and TV reels they could use to get a job. The emphasis on producing graduates ready to go out and get first jobs, rather than developing industry leadership, prevailed.

When Bollinger, a noted First Amendment scholar and lawyer, closed down the search for a new dean at the fabled Columbia Graduate School of Journalism, demanding that a dean must have the intellectual stature to lead a graduate program at one of America's most prestigious universities, he created headlines. There were guffaws and snickers that the academy was being pretentious about a business that had been built on the image of the hard-driving, hard-drinking, smart-but-maybe-not-schooled, "get me rewrite" reporter.

Carnegie Corporation did not want to enter into the age-old debate about whether journalism education demands intellectual rigor or is basically a skill building experience. So Gregorian convinced McKinsey & Company to undertake a pro bono study of journalism industry leaders to assess their need for journalism school graduates. The industry was in the early throes of a changing business model. Journalism jobs in the twenty-first century were bound to be different than in the last century—*how much* different was not yet clear. But the survey emphasized three clear needs in the industry:

1. A need for analytical thinkers with a strong ethical sense, as well as journalism skills;

2. A need for specialized expertise: insights into medicine, economics, and other complex topics, and firsthand knowledge of societies, languages, religions, and cultures; and

3. A need for the best writers, the most curious reporters.

If executives still harped on the same old saw that journalism education was not critical to the business, there was also a growing realization that the majority of the recruits entering newsrooms were graduates of journalism schools. Also, the dismantling of newsrooms, which had gained steam by 2005, meant that new recruits were not getting shaped by the culture of major news organizations, but had to arrive with a sophisticated view of their profession and their work.

Training of new recruits and editorial redundancy were two items that did not survive tough economic times. Bill Keller, executive editor of *The New York Times,* had been skeptical that journalism education was the cure-all for producing better-educated journalists. However, during a panel discussion in New York in January 2008, and before an audience of two hundred journalism faculty and students, he described himself as a "convert to the cause of journalism schools." Keller confessed that if asked if he believed journalism schools were necessary a dozen years ago:

> I would have said, "Journalism schools—ehh." I didn't go to a journalism school and we at the *Times* don't hire people straight out of journalism school. We hire them from major newspapers where they've already had experience. [My advice would have been]... follow the traditional route: go find a decent local or regional newspaper, apprentice yourself

to that mythical grizzled editor who will teach you the skills and the values of journalism, build a body of work and learn by doing. . . . [B]ut a lot of those local and regional newspapers no longer exist. Many of those grizzled editors have been bought out. . . . Nobody has the time to take you under their wing and teach you basic stuff.

Keller admitted he now realizes that since so many people at his paper and others do spend time in journalism schools, "it matters that that time be useful."

The report that McKinsey produced for the Corporation in 2005, *Improving the Education of Tomorrow's Journalists,* supported Gregorian's view that journalism as a profession is too important to leave to the vagaries of experiential learning. The report also surfaced the belief of editors and news leaders that students need an array of skills as well as intellectual opportunities to investigate the world. It reinforced the vision emerging from the Corporation that university-based journalism programs need to offer students multidisciplinary opportunities such as those that integrate the role of religion in geopolitics, examine the place of medical advances in influencing policy options, and look to history for context in international coverage. The world is changing at breakneck speed, and students need to know more.

Indeed, with every change in the news business, experienced, focused, specialized reporters are increasingly becoming the coin of the realm. Emerging as the news powerhouses are websites with deep coverage of specific topics like politics, health policy, business, arts, and international issues rather than "everyman" publications focused on broad topics. Along with innovation that requires Web skills, journalism schools have to be innovative in the kinds of subject courses they offer.

By the time the McKinsey study was complete, the Carnegie Corporation sponsored conversations featured five prestigious universities and five leading journalism educators: Geoff Cowan, dean of the Annenberg School for Communication and Journalism at the University of Southern California (USC); Orville Schell, dean of the Graduate School of Journalism at the University of California, Berkeley; Loren Ghiglione, dean of the Medill School of Journalism at Northwestern University; Nick Lemann, dean of the Graduate School of Journalism at Columbia University (Lemann was the dean chosen by Lee Bollinger following a task force report the University created to examine what was needed in a leader of a major research university's journalism school); and Alex Jones, director of the Shorenstein Center on the Press, Politics and Public Policy at the Harvard Kennedy School. These five crafted the three-pronged initiative that would win the backing of Carnegie Corporation and, just as importantly, the Knight Foundation.[1] Eric Newton, vice president for the journalism program at the Knight Foundation, participated in the intense meetings during which the initiative was shaped. The deans put together a proposal for grant funding that emphasized:

1. The Corporation's priority of curriculum enrichment;

2. An experimental learning lab —the News21 Incubators—that would, under the leadership of professors, dig deep into content learning while producing new forms of storytelling; this focus on innovation is a Knight Foundation priority;

3. Creation of the Carnegie-Knight Task Force, which would give the deans a leadership platform for research and for making policy-focused recommendations and statements about the news media.

Knight's president, Hodding Carter, joined Vartan Gregorian in New York for the launch of the multimillion-dollar program in 2005. By 2008, with the involvement of Carter's successor, Alberto Ibargüen, the initiative grew from the five original deans[2] who helped create it to include representatives of twelve universities. Along with USC, Berkeley, Northwestern, Columbia, and Harvard's Shorenstein Center, the other institutions that joined the initiative as full players are the College of Communication, University of Texas at Austin; the School of Journalism and Mass Communication, University of North Carolina at Chapel Hill; the College of Journalism and Mass Communications, University of Nebraska–Lincoln; the Philip Merrill College of Journalism, University of Maryland; the Missouri School of Journalism, University of Missouri; the S.I. Newhouse School of Public Communications, Syracuse University; and the Walter Cronkite School of Journalism and Mass Communication, Arizona State University. A strategy, initially conceived by the Corporation to change journalism education with a few select, well-respected schools, became a strategy encompassing geographic diversity, private and public universities, and the strong, collaborative voices of top journalism school deans.

When the Carnegie Corporation challenge to journalism deans began, it was not envisioned as a long-term grant-making strategy. It was a call to action by prominent deans to take leadership in this moment of change in journalism and to make a difference. Once the discussions became serious and the deans outlined an action plan, Gregorian promised two years of funding but insisted that the president of each university underwrite the third year of the proposal from their own discretionary funds.

This grant condition was not intended to be a simple "matching funds" component, but rather a way to involve the university presidents—and involve them deeply, since it demanded a financial commitment on their part. Gregorian made trips to each of the first five campuses and won the presidents' endorsements, which were followed up by a commitment in writing from each president. Gregorian believed strongly that university presidents often saw the journalism schools—no matter how excellent their reputations—as cash cows that did not need their attention and support. Gregorian wanted to change that perception, and when the next seven schools were invited into the Carnegie–Knight Initiative on the Future of Journalism Education, the presidents eagerly agreed to participate and cover the entire costs of the third year. By then the initiative had become prestigious and the presidents wanted their journalism schools to be members of this major change effort. That the dozen deans now involved in the initiative continue to meet twice a year on one another's campuses, and that the president of the university serving as the venue for the gathering always speaks to the assembled group at a dinner, is clear indication that these presidents are involved in the success of the venture.

But assessing other elements of the initiative is not so easy. The fall of 2009 marked the fifth year that journalism students were able to benefit from the change their deans have nurtured. However, it must be noted that some schools have benefited more than others. Some interdisciplinary, integrative courses have made a major impact on campuses, others not. News21, a summer powerhouse for students and professors alike, has yet to change the culture of experimentation across the entire curriculum. The revolving door of deans—the turnover is more rapid than we expected when we began—has meant many restarts and the need to get new leaders invested in a strategy they did not create or a grant for which they cannot take credit.

The University of Texas won a renewal for its curriculum work around covering the Latino community, an effort enriched by a strong partnership with three well-respected centers at the University: the Center for Mexican American Studies, the Brazil Center, and the Lozano Long Institute of Latin American Studies. The additional funding led to expansion of this work. Seeing the power of these "bridges" across the campus, Roderick Hart, dean of the College of Communication, and Tracy Dahlby, the new director of the School of Journalism, decided to create deeper relationships and new courses with other leading centers at the University. They call their renewal strategy The 21st Century Journalism Challenge: Bridging Campus, Community, and the Digital Media Divide.

The University added courses that take advantage of the resources of many of its most significant campus centers and departments. One new course, Practicing Investigative Reporting in a Globalizing World, involves the faculty of the Lyndon B. Johnson School of Public Affairs, with its emphasis on both state politics and geopolitics. All new courses will involve challenging, rigorous curricular changes and will encourage students to produce reporting projects that will feature the University's newly upgraded news service, CapTex, a service offered to news organizations across the state.

With a new head of the University's journalism school, there was new energy and a willingness to lay out markers for metrics that could try to measure the power of these curricular changes—not an easy thing to evaluate and not a well-defined goal when we began in 2004–2005. Nonetheless, Dahlby outlined metrics that included measuring student demand, campus-wide involvement of UT Austin faculty and departments, industry involvement, and reader/viewer/listener comments on the CapTex website.

Those metrics were welcomed, but further tweaked by Lorraine Branham, the new dean at Syracuse's S.I. Newhouse School. Branham was well versed in the opportunities presented by curriculum enrichment grants; she had joined Syracuse University after leading the first phase of UT Austin's curriculum enrichment work as director of the School of Journalism. Reviewing the curricular experiments at the Newhouse School, Branham put her leadership behind one of the two experiments. Although legal reporting is a staple in many schools and such a program, with Carnegie Corporation funding, had been initiated as a new minor in 2006, it had not attracted enough students. Branham therefore decided to replace that minor with a science partnership that emphasized climate change and the environmental sciences. A second minor, also instituted with Carnegie Corporation support, focused on journalism and religion, featuring challenging courses in the geopolitical dimensions of religious thought; it, too, did not attract as many students as hoped. Nevertheless, Syracuse continued to develop the minor, believing it was a strong offering that could set the school apart.

The University of Missouri also received a renewal of its curriculum enrichment grant in June 2009 and decided to continue its emphasis on arts reporting, one strand of specialization that the journalism school had not been able to offer students before the Corporation provided support. Student involvement and faculty participation throughout the campus fine arts and performing arts schools were high, and Missouri was already certain that this incubated curriculum specialization would continue after Corporation funding ended.

When Ernie Wilson joined USC's Annenberg School as dean in 2007, he found that the initiative's support offered him the opportunity to encourage deans at other USC schools to collaborate. Following the University of Missouri's lead, Wilson wanted to strengthen USC's arts offerings since the University is known for its creative schools, like the USC School for Cinematic Arts. A new master's program was already under way as a result of the first round of funding, but Wilson wanted a sweeping campus-wide relationship with other schools. With the ability to offer Carnegie professorships to collaborating professors and formal cross-school courses, Wilson was able to negotiate an important interdisciplinary strategy early in his deanship.

The master's degree program in specialized journalism (the arts) is a partnership with the five art schools at USC: the Roski School of Fine Arts, Thornton School of Music, and the Schools of Theatre, Architecture, and Cinematic Arts. Tim Page, a Pulitzer Prize-winning music critic, was recruited to teach two courses in the new program: Arts Writing Practicum and Arts Criticism and Commentary. After the first year, the number of students who enrolled in the M.A. program has almost quadrupled. As Sasha Anawalt, director of arts journalism programs at the USC Annenberg School, puts it: "[Students] are learning to write well from Tim Page.... Good writing that contains original thinking and is inspired by exciting, solid ideas is—and will mostly remain—the program's bedrock."

Two schools turned to a less integrated strategy for offering their students exposure to the great minds at the university. At Berkeley, a course called Key Issues focused on a series of three big ideas each semester and was taught by major professors on campus who each lecture for a month. Each semester, the subject matter was chosen in light of major news events in the political or policy world. It was deemed so successful a way to expose their students to big ideas that Key Issues is now a required course at Berkeley's two-year graduate program.

Neil Henry, the new dean at Berkeley, was a professor who taught a course the first year of the Carnegie-Knight Initiative on African reporting that emphasized interdisciplinary collaboration. His interests allowed him to recruit a professor from the Center for African Studies at Berkeley. He became a total convert to the idea of team teaching and what it offered students and journalism professors in terms of depth and insight. Henry's leadership as dean reflects that commitment to deeper content learning.

The Merrill College of Journalism at Maryland created a similar course, called the Carnegie Seminar, that also changes topics each semester. The students have taken on serious material, from Islam to nuclear proliferation. Some students, though they speak highly of the quality of the lectures, complained that the complexity of the subject matter made the course tough going. The professors confessed that they learned much about the need to communicate difficult ideas more clearly, especially because it is journalists who frame these issues for policy discussions.

Deb Nelson, who runs the seminar and the one-credit journalistic practicum connected with it at Maryland, has continued to choose topics that resonate with major news events. The course for 2009 focused on economics, and was so popular it was oversubscribed. Nelson, determined to keep the seminar culture of the course, and in order to offer the journalism students an intimate opportunity to interact with some of the University's star professors, found a "very large table" to maintain the seminar format.

Jean Folkerts, a new dean at the University of North Carolina, Chapel Hill, came to her position predisposed toward interdisciplinary curriculum. She believes journalism schools sometimes create rigid boundaries around the forms of journalism: documentaries, dailies, magazine writing, and multimedia, among others. She wants to keep the skill building as a critical component in assignments students produce while also promoting deeper learning in specialized subjects. She plans to do so by exposing students to the richness and culture of other schools and other departments, including business, public health, and law.

Within a relatively short time, Folkerts feels the University has already broken down walls in this respect. Professors in the department of energy frontier research who saw this past summer's News21 student reporting projects—which had emerged from the new interdisciplinary coursework—asked to partner with the journalism school on solar power experiments not only on campus, but also within the Research Triangle area. "This is a connection to an important initiative on the UNC campus and in the region and I think fulfills expectations of introducing a higher level of intellectual capacity into the journalism curriculum," Folkerts reports.

Two interdisciplinary courses developed in the last year with the Kenan-Flagler Business School at North Carolina drew strong student attention in both the journalism and business school. Both courses focused on "of the moment" issues, Digital Media Economics and Behavior and Leadership in a Time of Change. The linking of business majors with journalism majors created unintended outcomes beyond the dynamic discussion from different perspectives. Extracurricular collaboration meant that when the Kenan-Flagler Business School mounted its annual Leadership Day, which features successful entrepreneurs and senior Fortune 500 executives, the journalism students were invited as well. The emphasis on entrepreneurship was also recognized by the University's vice chancellor for research and economic development, who committed supplementary funding to support a research study of the media's handling of entrepreneurship over the past ten years.

Convinced that the intellectual capacity of journalism education will make the difference in the future, Folkerts has partnered with Nick Lemann, dean at Columbia, to produce a strategy for change in graduate journalism education.

It will create clear standards for what is taught and what is learned by a student earning a master's degree in journalism, building on the boldest experiment under way in journalism education. At Columbia, a new M.A. in journalism requiring a mastery of politics, business, science, or culture and the arts is being offered along with the usual M.S. in journalism, which focuses on journalistic techniques.

This attempt to define graduate journalism education echoes the work a century ago of Abraham Flexner, who, with support from another Andrew Carnegie-founded institution (The Carnegie Foundation for the Advancement of Teaching) investigated medical schools in the United States and Canada. He called for an overhaul that set medical education in a new direction. As a result, many medical schools that did not have the intellectual capacity closed, but the standards developed during that time, and the focus on clinical practice, led to the superior reputation of American medical training. Flexner's success presents itself as a challenge to this current journalism reform movement, although it is not a perfect analogy. Unlike doctors, journalists do not need a certificate to practice their craft; but like doctors, they need theory and practice.

Folkerts and Lemann know that the marketplace will determine the real success of the change that is under way. Lemann tracks his new M.A. journalism students each year to document the opportunities they are finding in journalism. The results have been encouraging, with more than 80 percent of each new graduating class securing important, rather than simply entry-level jobs. Many have entered the brave new world of the Web, where their focus on deeper learning gives them an edge. Both Folkerts and Lemann also believe that a clear declaration of what it means to obtain a master's degree in journalism will signal to students and the industry that not all degrees are equal.

Since 2005, when this $16 million experiment in journalism education reform began, the criticism has been that it is an elite strategy, housed more at centers of graduate work and not where most new journalists emerge. If the strategy of change works, the ideas that emerge from the dozen members will spread wider and influence how journalism is taught across the country, particularly to undergraduates.

Tom Fiedler, the new dean of the College of Communication at Boston University, knows intimately the curricular experiments that are under way across the country. After a thirty-year career at *The Miami Herald*, from reporter to executive editor, with a Pulitzer Prize on his resume, Fiedler spent a year at the Shorenstein Center. While there, he, along with Wolfgang Donsbach of Dresden University, produced a midterm report on curricular change under way since 2005 at the Carnegie-Knight universities.

As a new dean, Fiedler brought a determination to create a department that was an incubator for change and that echoed what he learned in his report for the Shorenstein Center. Fiedler was so influenced by learning about Flexner's strategy in changing medical schools that he borrowed the idea of that "clinical practitioner," who had transformed medical education from one of theory to one that was both theory and practice. Fiedler established a position of clinical professor of journalism and hired a former Boston investigative reporter who could take advantage of the assets of the University and produce serious news for the Massachusetts community with the help of student research and know-how.

Fiedler, recently out of the news business himself, believes that it is crucial for universities to experiment with both interdisciplinary learning and new journalistic forms. It is this experimentation that he thinks will sow the seeds of success for both journalism education and the news industry.

Rich Gordon, associate professor at the Medill School of Journalism, has been experimenting since 2005 with the idea of interdisciplinary education at Northwestern University. Although he found the News21 incubators to be exciting opportunities for students, he does not believe the real innovation in journalism education resides there. He believes the innovation can be found in the way professors think and teach ideas to a new generation of students.

Gordon may be an apt spokesperson for what it means to change the way journalism is taught at a respected research university, having been involved in three different educational experiments at Northwestern. As a result, he has a good sense of what works and what does not. He acknowledges that all three experiments "jump-started" the kind of curricular changes needed to get students ready for a different profession.

His first foray into curricular change came in 2005, when he created an interdisciplinary, team-taught course that was a prelude to the summer News21 incubator. The seminar focused on the idea of "privacy, liberty, and homeland security—not a simple narrative thread that the mainstream media would naturally cover, or do well, and therefore a topic that needed experimentation," says Gordon. By crossing disciplines, students learned the issues from different perspectives, paying attention to the areas where they intersected.

Gordon argues that this combination led students to ask better questions and follow story lines that were not clearly evident in the post-9/11 world—in other words, story lines that were innovative. That summer, one Northwestern student's discovery that the Department of Education in the Bush administration was mining student loan databases for terrorist suspects made national headlines. The seminar also morphed into something broader. Northwestern has won a grant to create an entire track focused on national security issues. A minor is now being offered to graduate and undergraduate students around the issue of national security and liberty, and scholars are examining how audiences respond to this important but sometimes difficult-to-understand news subject.

Next, Gordon co-taught a course on statistics that he wanted to be "relevant, not watered down" for journalists, and that attempted to give them a foundation in the quantitative method. "It wasn't successful," Gordon says flatly. He gave up on the course, although Medill is still trying to craft one that will ground students in the important questions around statistics.

This past spring, Gordon created a new course on network theory with Northwestern professor Noshir Contractor, who holds a joint position in the Schools of Engineering, Business, and Communication. "It's a hot area of academic research in almost every discipline but not in communication and journalism," says Gordon. But it is a course, he insists, that makes "a strong case for curricular innovation." He believes this kind of interdisciplinary thinking offers students windows into the new world they will navigate, and therefore is even more valuable than the hands-on experience of the News21 incubators.

For Gordon, these three curricular experiments show the power of interdisciplinarity as well as its shortcomings. As he put it, the initial seminar on privacy, liberty, and homeland security "is living on"; the statistics course taught us "what not to do"; and the network theory course, in its first iteration, "will have an impact on our curriculum beyond the grant."

What all these experiments in curriculum across campuses have in common is that they stretched the faculty, borrowed talent outside the journalism school, and, in an interdisciplinary fashion, approached subjects in new and experimental ways.

From the very beginning, Carnegie Corporation's call for journalism education reform has been focused on a vision: a vision of journalism that exists to serve the public, a vision that is about deep thinking, and a vision dedicated to telling the unfolding drama of today's history in a context that will keep the nation's electorate informed and prevent it from being manipulated. That vision is also based squarely on the idea that the university should serve as the centerpiece in the process of developing reporters, editors, and producers who want to tell the stories of their times; who want to help ensure the freedom of the American public; and who expect to become members of a profession worthy of its First Amendment privileges. It demands leadership from two university players: the president and the journalism dean.

That vision has driven our initiative, and it will be the key factor for judging the initiative in the future. We do not expect each and every grant to reveal a picture of a renewed world of journalism education. We *do* expect that the twelve deans, and the twelve university journalism institutions that have accepted the mantle of leadership in the Carnegie-Knight Initiative, will rise to the challenge by demanding more of their students, more of their faculty, and more of the industry. We ask ourselves each year, and we continuously ask the deans: a dozen years from now, what difference will this initiative mean to those who follow?

Over the next few years, we will not be supporting the deans with further grant funding. To continue its push for change, the Corporation has instead decided that it will use the convening power a foundation possesses to bring deans and their faculty together to examine the experiments under way on their campuses, to evaluate the News21 incubators to see if they are producing new ideas for storytelling that can serve the business, and to assess changes in the industry. Recently, the Corporation supported a few targeted research projects that are looking into the critical changes under way in the business models of news. Foundations do not make things happen, the people and institutions that they support do.

The Corporation will also rely on a few of the deans to take leadership roles in thinking about the future. Christopher Callahan, the dean of the Walter Cronkite School at Arizona State, has agreed to lead the three-year expansion of News21. (At the time of the renewal of the Corporation grant, in order to better serve all twelve members of the initiative, eight campus incubators were created that drew students from all twelve campuses, and Callahan assumed leadership of the experiment now involving more than ninety students each year.) Callahan has also begun searching for a sustainable model to cover costs after 2011.

As mentioned above, Columbia's Lemann is leading a small group with North Carolina's Folkerts to set standards for what a graduate degree in journalism should mean. Alex Jones has already stated that the work on journalism education is important enough that it will become a permanent part of the Shorenstein Center's work, which, until this point, has focused more on professional journalists than the "pipeline": a Web-based journalistic resource focused on issues will be open to all journalism professors and students.

We believe that the dozen deans now in the leadership seat at the twelve universities participating in the journalism initiative have an opportunity that few before them have had. They have a spotlight, they have standing, they have a community of like-minded deans who are not sleepwalking through accreditations and boring debates over how to teach on the "new" digital platforms. These deans have the chance to respond to the findings of the McKinsey report that began our initiative and to justify their role in building the news business of the future. They know that new journalists have to be smarter, better educated, more nimble and entrepreneurial than their predecessors if they are going to make it in a business in which the future is just being written.

We believe deans at journalism schools should have the same clout with the industry as deans from business schools and medical schools have with their professions. Clearly, articles like this that focus on the changes under way erase what was perhaps an unfair reputation about most journalism programs: that they are bastions of old-timers who tell stories about the way it used to be in the golden age of journalism. I have found an energy in these twelve schools that are led by men and women who care deeply about the business and who, unlike many of their colleagues working today in the news business, have the luxury of being able to take risks. They are preparing their students for a new world of news, and although no one can say what that world will look like, most of the faculty are anxious to experiment with new forms as long as the journalistic values of information, evidence, analysis, and ethics are not compromised.

Market forces are eroding, reshaping, and changing the news business at a frantic pace, and the thoughtful, long-term thinking that exists in foundations often does not match the heartbeat of change under way in the commercial media. But degree-granting institutions like journalism schools do not turn on a dime to embrace change, and for that reason, they are good partners with foundations. By definition, universities must constantly renew themselves, and although they are in constant motion preparing for the next semester, they also always have their eye on the next decade.

The real results of the Corporation's work in journalism will be seen a decade from now, when the graduates of these institutions (and graduates of other institutions challenged by our vision) are making the decisions about news. I do not know if these graduates will be making the decisions in great newspaper newsrooms, at small international documentary start-ups, in daily, city-focused Internet websites, or at their personal laptops connected to some virtual news "way station." But I do expect them to be defining the news that I read, watch, and hear. And I expect that news to be more informative, more multilayered, and more interactive than it is today.

NOTES

1. Three reports have been produced by the Corporation to capture the evolution of the industry at a time of change: *The Business of News: A Challenge for Journalism's Next Generation* (2002), *Journalism's Crisis of Confidence: A Challenge for the Next Generation* (2006), and *Journalism in the Service of Democracy: A Summit of Deans, Faculty, Students and Journalists* (2008).

2. Throughout this article, in referring to the five deans who helped to create the Carnegie-Knight Initiative on the Future of Journalism Education, I am including Alex Jones, whose title, as noted earlier in the text, is actually director of the Joan Shorenstein Center at Harvard. Jones's pivotal role in the early conversations about journalism education and his leadership of an important journalism-focused Center made him a valuable addition to this leadership team of deans.

*Susan King is vice president, external affairs and director of Journalism Initiative, Special Initiatives and Strategy at the Carnegie Corporation of New York. She is responsible for the corporation's relations with outside groups and for devising strategies to ensure the corporation's work has an impact on society.

Susan King, "The Carnegie-Knight Initiative on the Future of Journalism Education: Improving How Journalists Are Educated & How Their Audiences Are Informed," *Daedalus, Journal of the American Academy of Arts & Sciences* 139, no. 2. (Spring 2010): 126–137, copyright © 2010 by the American Academy of Arts and Sciences, http://www.amacad.org/publications/daedalus/fall2009/king.pdf.

DISCUSSION QUESTIONS

1. Can traditional media win back their readership? If so, how?

2. Some of the articles in this section suggest that readers will pay for good journalism online and that they will donate to keep traditional newspapers going. Do you agree? What are the civic implications of a two-tiered system of paid and free journalism?

3. Michael Copps asserts that "The news and information journalism we depended upon is fast disappearing from old media and has not found the sustaining resources it requires in the new." Do you agree with this assessment? Why or why not?

4. Does government have a role to play in helping traditional journalism and guiding the transition to new media? Should the United States develop a national journalism strategy?

5. How can we ensure that all citizens have access to creditable media that our democratic dialogue requires?